DATE DUE			

A MOST EXTRAORDINARY PAIR:

Mary Wollstonecraft and William Godwin

Also by Jean Detre

A HAPPY ENDING

IN MY FATHER'S HOUSE

A MOST EXTRAORDINARY PAIR

Mary Wollstonecraft and William Godwin

BY JEAN DETRE

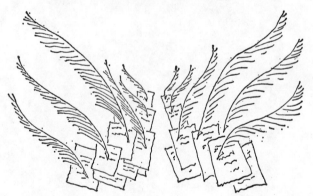

1975

Doubleday & Company, Inc., Garden City, New York

ISBN 0-385-07334-8
Library of Congress Catalog Card Number 74-25101
Copyright © 1975 by Jean Detre
All Rights Reserved
Printed in the United States of America
First Edition

The business of a biographer is often to pass slightly over those performances and incidents, which produce vulgar greatness, to lead the thoughts into domestic privacies, and display the minute details of daily life. . . .

—Samuel Johnson

To live over people's lives is nothing, unless we live over their perceptions, live over the growth, and change and varying intensity of the same—since it was by these things they themselves lived.

—Henry James

In the National Portrait Gallery hangs a picture of Mary Wollstonecraft, a picture of her as she was a few scant months before her death. I remember the child I was when I saw it first, haunted by the terror of youth before experience. I wanted so desperately to know how other women had saved their souls alive. And the woman in the little frame arrested me, this woman with the auburn hair, and the sad, steady, light-brown eyes, and the gallant poise of the head. She *had* saved her soul alive; it looked out from her steady eyes unafraid. The price, too, that life had demanded of her was written ineradicably there. But to me, then, standing before her picture, even that costly payment was a guarantee, a promise. For I knew that in those days when she sat for that picture, she was content. And in the light of that content, I still spell out her life.

—Ruth Benedict, *An Anthropologist at Work*

AUTHOR'S NOTE

I have taken one liberty: I have imagined that Mary Wollstonecraft, in the last year and some months of her life, had been keeping a journal in the style of her frequent letters to Godwin, in the colloquial, vivid, self-assured style perfected in the "Letters Written in Sweden," which had appeared earlier in the year. The journal is an invention. The letters are, however, all *actual letters*.

For his generous permission to transcribe and publish the complete correspondence between Mary Wollstonecraft and William Godwin, I wish to express my indebtedness and appreciation to Lord Abinger. I would also like to acknowledge the friendly assistance of the New York Society Library; the services of the New York Public Library and their Newspaper Annex; the facilities of the Reading Room at The British Museum; the courtesy in making available the Abinger material on microfilm of the Bodleian Library, Oxford, and The Carl H. Pforzheimer Library. For her confidence and encouragement I wish to express my gratitude to Betty Prashker of Doubleday, as well as to my agent, Wendy Weil.

July 1, 1796

This morning, awakened before seven o'clock by a heavy hammering on the door, I peered out through leafy branches of the chestnut trees before my house to see a sofa which, though never to my liking, I *still* cannot afford to replace. Two men, supporting it between them, staggered under its weight. Fanny had run out in night-clothes, without any slippers on, to watch the performance, and was crowing with delight, as though the work of easing the sofa through the door were some clowning all for her. Looking down, I could see it being prodded through the entrance, disappear, then a hand reach out to whisk Fanny back into the house. I had to laugh at the sight. So into No. 16 Judd Place West, Somers Town, of which I have leased the first two floors for my child and me, the furniture brokers bring all my stuff from Store Street.

Three years ago I last laid eyes on my things in their familiar surroundings when, closing the door behind me, I intended to return within six weeks. I do not remember a backward glance, so eager was I to be off. Yet at Dover, when the packet was detained, I nearly rushed into the first coach back to London, knowing that, once across the Channel, I would be helpless to support those of my friends who might suffer imprisonment; I would rather myself have been shut into Newgate than to endure even the thought of Mr. Johnson standing trial for having published our several supposedly *treasonable* works. I shuddered in indecision, but did not turn back. To France!—where Destiny led me, and where, shortly afterwards, declaration of war bound me, should I have wished to return.

Now new rooms, fresh starts, re-arrangement of old things breathe such sweet zephyrs of hope for the future, blowing clear away the gloom perpetually overhanging aspects of my past, that I seem to stand on a threshold of happiness and, looking about, feel almost lightsome.

At my chimney-piece the fire-screen recalls those rooms, when first I came to London, where my sister stitched those fugitive hares in a tapestry of field-flowers with a puckered expression of disappointment she has on her face whenever she sinks into a train of thought. Poor Everina! How I dread her visit. With her odd notion of dignity, she will have to find fault with some thing, I am sure. My two sisters have been less fortunate than I. But be that as it may, the fire-screen is in its place; the high-backed chair that preserves one's back from winter draughts; the sofa between the two windows; the tripod table I am so fond of; the long deal table on which I write. I even locate, in a box of oddments, my old green blind which, to Fanny's mirth, I put on to see whether it still fits . . . as though years of living through the Terror could be thought to have so transformed me that, by now, my head should be all bulges and bumps above the brow like one of Dr. Lavater's physiognomic specimens, signifying a brain ponderously swollen—by imbecility or genius, the Lord only knows.

Marguerite has been flogging a rolled-out rug with the face of a Jacobin giving vengeance to an aristocrat, while my little darling follows my every movement with her large dark eyes. I have only to walk to the window to look out at what I take for the sound of the mail-horn, and Fanny's glance moves with me above her crust of bread, her cheeks still wet from an outburst that, fortunately, passes like a summer storm. Strange is it to see Imlay's expressions in that small, round, innocent face.

I regret being obliged to use his name, and would not continue with such usage, except for Fanny. A woman alone—but, no, I will not expatiate on this sad subject. It is odd how *Miss* has become a term of reproach, denoting childishness, flippancy, or some other contemptible quality; in the strictest society a fourteen-year-old girl will be addressed as *Mrs.* though she still romp and lisp. It was *Mrs.* Wollstonecraft who became Mr. Johnson's assistant. Yet I recall that in my answer to Burke, I published *with no name on it at all*, as an expression of hope, it appears to me now, that the work might be judged on merit alone, rather than suffer the stigma of questionable authority. Wondering who had written such a bold reply to Mr. Burke, critics assumed it to have been a man, so that, wishing then to prove a point about their prejudice, I let Mr. Johnson in subsequent printings use my name. As a writer, then, I remain Mrs. Wollstonecraft; as a mother Mrs. Imlay, in both cases the *Mrs.* a mere courtesy title.

The books have not been got to, the boxes and boxes of them. At my request Marguerite cuts the cord from one of them and—prophetically?—what pops up to greet me is a volume of "La Nouvelle Héloïse." I stand turning its pages, coming to myself as one truly does in the company of an understanding friend. And then, my thoughts turning to my new and best friend Godwin, I decide on impulse to send the volume around to him by Marguerite, to his house but a step away from my door.

To Mr. Godwin   25 Chalton Street   Somers Town

I send you the last volume of "Héloïse," because if you have it not, you may chance to wish for it. You may perceive by this remark that I do not give you credit for as much philosophy as our friend, and I want besides to remind you, when you write me in *verse*, not to choose the easiest task, my perfections, but to dwell on your own feelings—that is to say, give me a bird's-eye view of your heart. Do not make me a desk 'to write upon,' I humbly pray—unless you honestly acknowledge yourself *bewitched*.

Of that I shall judge by the style in which the eulogiums flow, for I think I have observed that you compliment without rhyme or reason, when you are almost at a loss what to say.

Mary Imlay

It was Godwin who was able to help me find quarters, once I had decided against going to Switzerland or to Italy to live. The nearness of his lodgings seemed an advantage that pleased him, so that, wishing to please him, as I wish also to please myself, I hastened to determine upon the place. Some chance remark of his made me wonder then if my closeness had not made his heart heave with trepidation, yet when I had decided that our neighbourliness would make him try for a footing of greater formality, he undoes all expectations by sending me a poem praising—I blush to think!—my beauty, my quickness of feeling, my sincerity, my

reason and imagination, none of which intrudes upon the other
. . . Reading through the list, I wonder if a virtue isn't thrown in,
simply to make a line rhyme with the one that went before, as
casually as you'd toss a bone into the soup. I begged him simply to
express his *feelings*—his diffidence leaving me, virtually, to guess
at them. I take it he is pleased to have me near . . . but my difficulty is that I *must take it*, that is, divine the feelings of his heart,
locked tight, by habit. Philosophy—perhaps the English brand
alone, for Rousseau can be said to be thoroughly otherwise—has
hardened his heart. Yet I have seen in his eyes, which are said to
be the windows of the soul, such a shine of warmth, when he least
suspects that he is being examined. Still, *how* am I to know what
lies in his heart, unless he choose to tell me? And now he goes to
Norfolk for a fortnight. Well, Godwin, you are a *little* in love
with me, whether you know it or not.

July 4, 1796—Monday

I have been all the way to St. Paul's Church-yard to give Johnson
some trash. Will my debts never let me leave off reviewing? I was
low-spirited, in the end, vext by Johnson's coldness of manner. I
did not choose to stay to dine with him. Instead, I trudged home,
dining alone on cold boiled mutton, and, afterwards, ready to
weep from nerves, mournfully fell into a chair, only thinking of
the means of getting money enough to extricate myself out of my
difficulties. Johnson I can make no sense of. Either he is half
ruined by the present public circumstances, or grown strangely
mean—at any rate, he torments me. He says he *will* stop publishing
the *Analytical*; yet goes right on, month after month. He com-
plains that it is impossible to know any longer what to print, since
a pamphlet when published is *not* a libel, but afterwards is proved
to be so in court. The heart has been torn out of him for those who
are outlawed, impoverished, disgraced—and for those poor
wretches given sentence of transportation to Botany Bay. He
says he hardly ceases, even in sleep, thinking of all the needlessly
wrecked lives, such as Rowan's, ruined on the testimony of two
police informers for having printed a leaflet announcing a meeting. At Hardy's trial they read as evidence, I hear, Johnson's pub-

lished pamphlet of the letter of the London Corresponding Society that Joel Barlow carried to the Convention in France. It is said of Johnson that he sat in the witness-box like a ram-rod, replying to the prosecutor's questions by no more than *I am, I do, I did, I had.* Godwin watched from the gallery throughout the trial, but he has such an oblique way of presenting affairs, mostly by their philosophical principle, that one misses a certain lively rendition. His good friend Thomas Holcroft did better, one afternoon, energetically dancing from one role to another to act out all the parts. I have to trust others to tell me what I missed during an absence of three years. I regret . . . no, it is not fair to say: I do not regret any thing other than England's aberration in charging righteous men with seditious libel and high treason, when patriotic duty clearly demanded their voices be raised in calling for a redress of grievances. We were so secure in the justice of our principles of action that we could not foresee being so cruelly condemned. This morning I saw how much a friend of mine has been wearied and altered by this state of public affairs. He suffers acutely from shortness of breath, a malady which dates from the trials, but shrugs off sympathy. His aloof expression does not vary, even when I attempt to re-assert our old intimacy—with him who was once father, brother, and benefactor to me. I pray God I do not forget my indebtedness to him, nor my love.

I remember him—mild-mannered, infinitely kind—saying so little, when I came to speak to him at St. Paul's Church-yard, that I almost fainted during one of his judicious pauses. He must have been then nearly fifty years of age, very much the Baptist farmer's son in his integrity and spareness of speech, a speech still flavoured by a word or two from Liverpool, as, when impassioned, there creeps into my language some thing of Yorkshire. We sat together in a little corner of his office. I was affected by his formality and had trouble, at first, speaking. The harassments of life had made me so thin that I looked lately bastilled. The mind preying on the body, in painful warfare, had made Ireland, where I had been confined as governess almost entirely to the society of children, a solitary and almost unendurable misery relieved only by a firm determination to change my life. I treasured my resolution in secret, never breathing a word of it, even in letters to my sisters, for fear of being prevailed upon by exhortations of caution. I determined to follow Mr. Johnson's advice, when he paid me ten guineas for "The Education of Daughters." Even had his advice been spoken heedlessly, without serious reflexion, it was my straw in the flood. I would learn French, Italian, German (*Hindoo*, if need be), if by such knowledge I could render myself useful. Years of desperate attempts at independence made me catch at such a means and keep resolutely to my plan of action. Nights, in bed, once free of my duties, the bed-clothes dragged as high as they would reach, in the cold and damp of my room at the top of the castle, I would start again where I had stopped the previous night in the pages of Rousseau's "Émile," both nose and ears pink with cold. I might equally have been glowing from fever . . . but it was, in truth, rage that reddened my cheeks. Are we always to be judged by men? Are we women always to remain unknown to them—told what is natural to us, what is feminine, determined only by *what they wish us to be*—are we always to conform to their orders? Through "Émile," I admit, I learned French. But some thing equally valuable infused me, though remaining for a time inactive, in the form of a profound resentment that would have to be expressed. By the time I sat, knee to knee, with Mr. Johnson in his office, I was, although trembling, absolutely committed to his proposal that I work for him. Was I prepared to translate the political pamphlets coming in, at a great rate, from France? Could I be trusted to do a little Italian, from time to time some German? He was expecting a M.S. in Dutch that needed alteration, if not rewriting, for the English market. *Yes, yes, yes* . . . far better to fail in the attempt, than to be deterred by diffidence. I started to give an account of my preparations over the last year in Mitchelstown. Johnson seemed to edge a little out of his chair at such passionate avowals. I needn't have bothered; he had already decided on me. Undoubtedly the Reverend Hewlett had said many kind things. Fuseli seems to have sworn I knew Dutch; never mind, was what he said, when I challenged him for his falsehood, it can be learned in a week.

So it was I was to become a new genus—writing, writing, *writing* for independence!

Tuesday, July 5th

What a bright sunny day! Strollers enjoy the fragrant fields before my windows. The grass is thick and springy, half hiding the wild sweet pea and the clover. I stay in, after a wearisome sleepless night, having worked late on some corrections for Johnson. Marguerite has taken them to him. Since she is gone, I delight Fanny by entrusting her to run to the corner for the news paper. I stand on the look out for any harm that might befall her during her adventure. She holds up sixpence to the paper-seller and stiffly sticks out both her arms, as though for freshly laundered linen. Her expression, only slowly melting away over the past hour, is fierce with pride in her courage. How early is our need for independence! How much self-esteem comes from doing a task on our own, before even we are able to say so, at the tender age of two.

On reading the paper I recall that yesterday was an anniversary of the American Declaration of Independence. Letting the paper slide to my lap, I searched mid-air for the visionary ghost of myself as a young girl when, thrilled by living through such fateful days, I pricked up my ears at any discussion of those traitors who would certainly be brought to their knees in a mere month's time. I recall whispering mutinous prayers for them. I hoped the rebels would resist to their death. Their heroism then could not fail to move hard hearts. The principle of action behind their struggle struck a chord of understanding in my soul. I was at the time seventeen. Not till a year or two later did I take to reading a paper, having decided, that winter at Bath, to improve myself by any means within my power: to listen diligently to conversation, to keep a journal and to read either the London *Times* or the Bath *Journal*, whichever I might take to my room. I worshipped Edmund Burke, who, with the corruption of time, has so much disappointed me; but then, reading the debates in the House of Commons, wherever *he* stood, there I would silently take my stand . . . silently, I say with shame, remembering how I felt obliged to nod assent, whenever Mrs. Dawson railed against the insubordinate rabble who had dared to threaten the Crown.

I would accompany Mrs. Dawson daily to the Abbey and sit

beside her—for my spiritual guidance was of concern to her. I also accompanied her to the baths—but here was made to wait, while she drank the waters, either waiting at the door, like a dog, or on one of the benches around the pump-room in a section reserved for those of inferior status. There was no ambiguity there. *The New Bath Guide* which Mrs. Dawson had sent me to buy, with a shilling handed me, made no bones about such as *me* in its list of regulations. The premises were only for ladies of quality. One may ask to day, when fashion in dress has so changed, all in the spirit of egalitarianism, how one could tell at a glance a gentlewoman from a paid companion. To day I generally wear simple light-coloured muslin, during the day, unadorned, without stays beneath, so that the contour of bosom and hip are revealed; from the high waisted gathering fall long folds, much like the ancient *chitons* of Greece. The Revolution blew away in one violent gust the immoderate artifice that so severely separated the classes and hampered the female body. But in Bath in '78 I was a little grey mouse creeping after Mrs. Dawson, who walked so grandly and rustled as she walked, unapproachable both before and behind by virtue of bustle and bosom. She habitually carried a parasol, an indispensable for her money and a snuff-box—all of which she would impetuously thrust at me whenever she was about to pounce on some desirable article in the shops. I wonder now if it was not immoderate greed that had made her ill. I attributed her illness then, I remember, to a lifetime of living within rigidly boned corsets, and of never taking exercise, which may have caused from poor circulation the pain that so often left her groaning upon her bed. A widow in her forties, she travelled up and down England's spas in search of a cure. Poor creature, whom not one single member of her family could tolerate for more than the time it took to drink a dish of tea. It has been a long time since I wondered at her fate—she is, I suppose, still tyrannising some small sickly mouse, such as I once was, her severity of expression relieved only by the sight of some frippery she might hang about her neck. What on earth made me think of her . . . ? Ah, yes, Mrs. Dawson's speeches on the irregularity of the American rebels whom, by God, she would have punished for their disobedience. Where she was without reason for a custom—and as there never has been reason for the rich to rule the poor—she would invoke God, looking upwards with her long dour pinched expression and, at such times, often dragged me to my knees to pray with her for God's justice—that justice which I could only hope He would send, in terms such as He and I, though certainly *not* Mrs. Dawson, had previously agreed upon.

July 8, 1796

Fanny has the fever. I sit in—unable to decide whether to send around to ask some one such as Mr. Twiss, with his inevitable endless recitations from Shakespear, to keep me company, this evening, or to resign myself to melancholy. In my thoughts there seems to be nothing but reminders of cruel disappointment. Fanny sleeps. How I wish, while fulfilling the duty of a mother, to have some one similarly bound beside me. To be too long alone with children, even one's own, is a deprivation—I allude to a need for rational conversation. In the castle at Mitchelstown the prattle of my girls was useful as a basis of an exercise which would become the "Original Stories"; yet, at the time, I remember sorrowfully writing to Mr. Johnson on the subject of the enforced isolation of my sex—however, we receive but little understanding there. If Fanny were well, I might go out. I know I must rouse myself from the torpor and listlessness of too much solitude; for when I do, I often find myself amused. I have made a few new acquaintances by my efforts. It was I who sought Godwin out— I seeking *him*, rather than he me. Will that turn out to be a good thing or a bad thing, I wonder.

It was in January last that Mary Hays arranged her small gathering. I went, stony-faced with habitual misery. But in the easy warmth of her little parlour I listened and loosened, and finally joined in some argument or other, speaking at length to Holcroft, I don't remember of what. There were only the four of us. I noticed Godwin looking my way, averting his eyes when I attempted to meet his glance. I found the manner teasing and wondered at it. When Mary Hays had sent him a note to ask him to come to meet me, he had written back, she told me, that Mrs. Wollstonecraft had in the past amused herself by depreciating him, but that, all the same, *he* had never said a word of harm against her. What could he have meant by that? I do some times raise a laugh at another's expense without being fully conscious of it. The comment made me ransack my memory of our first meeting—at Johnson's it had been. Godwin said, when we recently spoke of it, that he had come that evening to hear Tom Paine, but that I did all the talking. Paine doesn't talk!—he's famous for taciturnity, when there is more than one other person in the room. But Godwin, ignoring Paine's habits, was peeved at my not sitting back with all the due modesty of my sex. Well, it is simply not my style! Godwin's journal recalled to him that our discussion was on the subjects of monarchy, Horne Tooke's trial, Voltaire and religion—which would have been fairly routine, at the time, around Johnson's table. I have hardly any recollection of the occasion, except for having perceived, that first meeting with Godwin, a certain slowness of speech, nearly a sermonizing, that ran the risk of droning on into a full-bodied snore. I wonder if, perhaps, just such observations, on my part, are what made Godwin brace himself on entering Miss Hays' parlour, the evening she gave herself so much trouble to bring together "Political Justice" and "The Rights of Woman."

It was not, I think, immediately after that evening that I chose to seek him out, having then in mind to take Fanny to France, where I wished her to be raised. I had been writing a theatrical piece. Having learned from Molière that a tragic situation, seen remotely, may be *made to seem* comic, I chose to make my despair farcical to try to have done with it. After finishing a draught of the play, I was away most of the month of March in Berkshire. Spring came, as it is wont to do. Ever my antidote for ill health, I went walking, for hours on end, under the trees which grow so sturdily in those parts, seeing the first verdure push through the earth, feeling gently sustained and restored by nature; my head growing more free of musings on the past.

Once back in London, I longed for rational conversation and only then thought of Godwin. I knew he lived in Somers Town and, by chance, on one of my errands, passed his house. It was with a childish feeling of wrong-doing that, as I walked by, I lifted my glance to what I supposed to be his front door and saw through it to a clothes-peg in the hall.

It seemed, as I reflected later, foolish that I had not carried out my intention to ring his bell. After all, why not? It is time to effect a revolution in female manners! It is time to separate morals from mere local manners! I am the only judge of my own right conduct. I feared, however, that Godwin, no matter how politically radical, might conventionally disapprove of a woman calling upon him alone, condemning such action as unbecoming to the female sex. Whether it was *his* condemnation I feared or my own, I do not honestly know. I reasoned with myself that, if he spoke out on the subject, I could argue and win the point. But if some inner restraint *of mine* held me back—some animal stupidity within—it would be harder to beat it forward by reason, so brutish and sluggish these held convictions seem to be. What did I fear? After all, the author of "Political Justice" is hardly a Portuguese— the custom of that country being that a man considers a lady to be insulted if, at the least opportunity, he does not attempt some gross familiarity. I had a taste of such rude experience, when in Lisbon. All that night I tried to arm myself against my fears—I who have conversed, man to man, with medical men on anatomical subjects, and compared the proportions of the human body with artists, oblivious of the *absurd* rules of mock modesty. I know that no sensible woman can be insulted. I thoroughly believe that. Clarissa, accusing Lovelace, saying he has robbed her of her honour, has a false notion of what honour is. I do not believe a woman can be degraded without giving her moral consent. And I refuse to allow that the sexes are obliged to live in a state of warfare, rather than in mutual understanding.

The day following my peek through the fan-light of Godwin's door, I sallied forth once again in the same direction. Poor Godwin, lurking all unsuspecting in his lodgings, would have to make out my unexpected visit on whatever terms he could. Perhaps, by reasoning that Necessity rules, he shall tell himself that I could not have acted otherwise. My heart beat hard, ungoverned by reason. We *are* odd beasts, divided and perturbed, as we always seem to be. I raised my hand to ring his bell. My one fervent hope was that it might not be answered—that I still might silently, unseen, steal down the street and steady my breathing as I walked the way home. The bell gave an unnaturally loud clamour. I listened. All I could hear were my own heart-beats. Then there came a light tread of a servant girl who would certainly tell me he was not at home. The door opened—there stood Godwin, his eyes hooded, whether from sleep or the strain of concentration, I dared not ask, as he stood before me in his Calvinist clothes and, with instinctive good manners, opened wider the door, bidding me enter.

I was led into a room that had in it, to one side, a desk and a chair and, on the other, two hard chairs with a small table between them, all of a spareness and symmetry that immediately identified the straitened circumstance of a scholarly man. I began to babble how Talleyrand, once paying me a call in my lodgings, had had to drink tea one hour and wine the next *from the same cup*, so bare had I been of accoutrement. I risked a sweeping glance in Godwin's direction, fearful that he might have followed my association of ideas and taken offence. But he seemed only to listen tranquilly and, when he had determined that my anecdote had reached its desired point, he offered that he was now much less principled than he had been several years before, when determined not to spend a penny on himself, which he did not imagine calculated to render him a more capable servant of the public good. Any one else might have then smiled, if only to insinuate that the very firmness of his character might be considered a weakness, or to seem to say that such an ideal was often difficult to uphold. Not Godwin.

But finally I made him smile! It was by a remark that all of us seem to give to others what we ourselves need: that my own longing for conversation is what I brought him now—I then looked about for some apt comparison, raising my eyes to his to add that it was somewhat in the spirit of the way Hardy had showed his own personal bias when, as a shoemaker, he had thought to have Barlow take to France for the troops, along with the Letter to the Convention, five hundred pairs of boots. He smiled, noticeably relaxing at my stated purpose. We had, he recalled, met at Barlow's. He had refreshed his memory in the pages of his journal, where he'd noted that we had spoken of Montesquieu's concept of self-love and the idea of perfectibility—topics which may well have excused me for bringing to them some leavening lightness.

I think that he reasoned that it was on impulse that I had chosen to pay a call. For courage, I had provided myself with a pretext for the visit, but it was now unnecessary to produce it. Yet, when the first extended silence fell upon that deserted room, I felt that, were Godwin afterwards to wonder at my motives, it would serve to quiet any suspicion of his that I might have come *for some thing,* but had gone away without giving any account of it. I told him, therefore, as I had thought to do beforehand, that I was once again Johnson's assistant for the *Analytical,* reviewing and giving out books for review; and that I was, as it happened, reading, at the moment, Mrs. Inchbald's second novel, "Nature and Art." I couldn't say what it might serve, except perhaps to enhance my admiration for her, but I would like to know her. He said he was going with her to theatre the following evening, and would speak to her. With that I rose, gave him my hand, and departed—the slightest bit discountenanced that, in the end, I had used a woman's wile that I pretend to despise.

What next? I keep no journal—or kept none till now, and for some months in Bath—so that I have to resort to memory to rec- ollect that it was late April that, accustomed to his solitary mutton- chop, Godwin broke all laws by asking me, Mrs. Inchbald, Dr. Parr with his two daughters, the MacKintoshes, Thomas Holcroft and some others to come to dine in his lodgings. It made twelve of us—and three chairs. When a neighbouring coffee-house sent two boys carrying all they could carry in the way of straight chairs, others following with provisions, Holcroft, whom I find witty and kind, set the stage as if for one of his plays. He bawled directions for the chairs to be placed where he thought best, and then put us in them like so many actors, for what he designated a yet- unwritten play, to be called "Things as They Are: or, The Phi- losopher's Entertainment." His gay spirit made us fall into the easiest conversation with one another. Rarely intimidated as I am by men, since I seem to have the means to dispel their impassivity, some ladies, on the contrary—shades, perhaps, of Mrs. Dawson or Lady Kingsborough in Mitchelstown, to whom a position of servi- tude made me once mute and miserable—seem to assume superi- ority over me by a mere swift killing glance. I had hoped for Mrs. Inchbald's friendship; I had even imagined her comfortably reclin- ing in my blue chair, listening to me read my play aloud, chiding me gently where my first impetuous theatrical steps seemed to stumble. But the chill of her greeting was sufficient to discourage such hope. Yet, I hear, she is a tender friend to Godwin, who could not do without her literary counsel, and of Holcroft as well.

Godwin was gallant to all the ladies. When my turn came he asked, with barely preamble, if I knew that my book of travels, which he had lately read, was calculated to make a man in love with its author. He did not say *he* was that man. And he did not leave his praise unqualified. He said that the tone of voice recounting my perilous adventures was all gentleness and delicacy, whereas he had remembered, from the past, some thing harsh and rugged in my writing. His remark brought all sorts of replies to mind. Indeed, I was on the verge of saying some thing sharp, when I turned and saw marked on his face an intense struggle to say exactly what he was feeling. It is not at such times one cuts another short. In a state of obstinate sincerity, he seemed sincerely to be searching for words to express compassion.

The "Letters" had appeared in January. By the end of February the book had generally been so well praised that I departed for the country with a sense of real liberation from the past. The publication had served to characterise, for myself, quite as much as for others, my curious present position in life, to have turned me from feeling lost in the maze of a most agonising obsession to being sound in heart and mind again. To have sufficiently regained the power of reason to have been able to arrange the "Letters" into some kind of order already indicated a certain degree of recovery. To then have won the attention and affection of my readers revived my wounded self-esteem. It was thus that the month of March in the country had given a more optimistic turn to my thoughts.

In April, back in Town, as I was walking along the New Road, a horseman came along behind me, passed swiftly by and reined up hard. My train of thought, as I walked in the soft air of early spring, had captivated me to such a degree that I was only dimly aware of a rider dismounting. I then saw that it was Imlay. He was standing rather awkwardly, long-legged and in high spirits, in a new riding habit, the reins of his mare sliding loosely through the fingers of his yellow gloves. My pace had brought me on a level with him on the path. Walking beside me, he excused himself for having failed to inquire after my health and Fanny's, since his arrival from Paris some weeks before, explaining as extenuating circumstances the rigours of his many commercial commitments. I interrupted him with a gesture he must sufficiently have recognised to break off what he had been saying. We walked for a moment in silence. He had begun gnawing the end of his moustaches in a way he has when contradicted. So many subjects useless to discuss came to mind; but there was one I felt impelled to broach. Had he heard of my published "Letters"? He replied that he had and, with a wry look, protested the role I had given him in my narration. He said he hoped some satisfaction had come to me from such a false rendition of his character. I felt, at once, the old anger. I stifled it as best I could. Our steps were matched, our feelings scarcely companionable. At the moment, we were approaching a cross-road where a cluster of aspens in new leaf were agitated by the breeze, a late afternoon sun, low on the horizon, faintly tingeing them red. I pointed, somewhat languidly, behind the trees, saying I had an appointment. Imlay, his eyes widening, seemed to acknowledge, with some surprise, that there was to be no argument between us. I saw him mentally gather himself together to go. But first he had to turn his suddenly shining gaze on me, in a way that—I could see now—was all mechanical illumination, meaningless, unfeeling, practised for its impact, and as precisely cold as some similar reflexion from ice or snow. Under the dark bristles of his moustaches, his lips, slightly pouting, parted in a slow half-smile, as if to remind me of their soft intensity. The mare snorted behind his shoulder. I gave a nod. And that is the last I have seen of him.

It is a year since I went to Tønsberg in Norway to take care of some of his business. It is almost exactly one year, for I remember wondering if only I, for miles around, might be the sole observer of the anniversary of those monumental events that had been precipitated by the storming of the Bastille. I was alone in Tønsberg. I had thought it necessary to spare Fanny that part of the trip, since she was cutting teeth, the journey requiring six days by boisterous seas and rude makeshift roads. Besides, I had little idea what comfort to expect in Norway. It was with a sinking heart that I had left Fanny in Gothenburg in the care of Marguerite, who wept both from fear at being abandoned, and at my going on alone. Her alarm that I might again faint, injuring myself, had made her beg to accompany me, and my poor lamb had woken to join in with her own lusty cries, so that the memory of parting, imprinted indelibly on my mind, drew tears to my eyes when, wrapped in my great-coat, I lay down on a heap of dropped sails on the deck of the ferry to watch the receding shore.

At Tønsberg I learned that the transaction I had come for would require my remaining for some three weeks, which made me lament all the more my separation from Fanny. But since I was obliged to wait and there was little to do about it, I decided against spending the time in useless melancholy, and settled myself within a quiet inn that commanded a view of the sea. An arrangement was made through the Mayor of the town, with whom I had my business, to have a young woman who spoke some English call on me twice a day to translate my wishes. I determined to regulate my time in such a manner that I might enjoy as much sweet summer as I possibly could. As it was not possible to bathe in the sea near town, the young woman proposed rowing me to a nearby pebbled cove. Since she was pregnant, I insisted on taking one of the oars, learning to row. I do not know a pleasanter exercise. I soon became expert. Out on the water, with an eye vaguely curious, I watched white sails turn the headland or seek shelter under the pines of the little islands. I would watch fishermen calmly casting nets, while the sea-gulls hovered overhead. Every thing seemed in perfect tranquility, as we rowed beneath cliffs scented with juniper, and heard the mournful call of the bittern and tinkling bells from the cows, slowly pacing one after another along an inviting path. I gazed and gazed—my soul diffused in the scene.

One day, by chance, walking on a pathway along the shore, I found a little stream that flowed into a rock basin where the cattle drank. I cupped my hands to the fresh water spouting from a cleft in the rocks and, as I drank, prayed to the fountain nymph for restoration. Nearby, higher along the stream, on a flat mossy rock, I happened a while later to stop to rest. Some thing about the place immediately reminded me of Dr. Johnson's "*I sat down on a bank* . . ." It had been on his journey to the western islands of Scotland in as rude a nature, I imagined, as the one I found myself enjoying. I felt the spirit of that powerful man, who once had clasped me by the hand and searched my eyes, that man so distressed within his soul that he had deliberated writing the history of his own Melancholy, its life as long as his own, only fear that such a labour would prove, in the end, too disturbing, deterring him. The strength of this compassionate man infused me with renewed capacity. I sat—oh, longer than an hour!

To continue wasting my life waiting for letters from Imlay that, when I tore them from their envelopes, left me as impoverished as before—was it for this the Creator had blown the spark of life into me? It was a period of particular anguish. It was not clear if, for Fanny's sake, we might again live together—I hung on his decision. Yet, at that moment, so far from any living soul, in a timeless sphere of savage forests, the importance of the outcome of our domestic situation suddenly dwindled. In that immense countryside, I might, like dryads of old, become transformed, spreading wide branches to the sky, or might plummet like a feeding gull upon the soft breast of the ocean, to feed and float on some easy current that would sustain me, as it carried me far away from human cares. The wild woods, embracing the sea, had given me back a composure that, I suspect, was equally the consequence of long walks, riding, rowing, sea-bathing and good nourishing food. Detachment from my cares had aroused me to conceive—as Dr. Johnson had similarly conceived in such a setting—the notion of finding out all I could of the habits and history of the Norwegians to write a small book, in epistolary form, for publication on my return to London. Only afterwards did I enlarge my plan to include Sweden and Denmark as well, and what I saw of Hamburg. Little did I know that my letters to you—pugh! the habit is again upon me of saying all that is in my heart to him whom I loved—little did I know that, since any re-arrangement of my material, in trying to delete our persons, his and mine, from the narration would make it stiff and flat, I would, at last, simply relate the effect of the total experience of the journey.

Thus was the book born—a book praised over all my others— the one that Godwin says would make any man fall in love with its author.

Friday, July 15, 1796

At last a letter from Norfolk! Godwin asks me to have Marguerite —he anglicizes her to plain *Margaret*—drop word in his letter-box

for his friend Mr. Marshal to expect him at seven in the morning
on the 20th. The intimacy of the gesture of having *me* announce
his coming thrills my heart—a heart, I'll admit, that had thought
itself abandoned, as it waited to hear whether *his* had grown cold.

Shall I write a love letter? he asks. And indeed he proceeds saying my company infinitely delights him, that he loves my imagination, my delicate epicurism, and loves the malicious leer of my
eye, which is the first time any one has chosen to take as a virtue
the slight dragging down of the lid of my eye, a result of the
stroke I suffered in France, a defect devoid, I can vouch, of any
calculated meaning. In short, he ends, he is devoted to the bewitching *tout ensemble*.

He draws a charming portrait of himself as reticent lover, saying
such things as lovers say, "with speaking glances (through the glass
of my spectacles)." Oh, Godwin, you please me very much to day.
When you make love, you say in mock epic style, it shall be in a
storm, as Jupiter to Semele, whom he turned to a cinder. Do these
menaces terrify me?

Yes, Godwin, they do. I, who resolved to put away any impulse
of the heart, since every tie becomes a shackle, find, on examining
myself more closely, that I am so constituted that I cannot live
without some particular affection—nor without the passion which
quickens to rapture when summoned. For can any thing extin-
guish for long emotions that lead to the delights we were formed
to enjoy? Even when deadening one's feelings to aim at tranquility, as I was forced finally to do with my feelings for Imlay, imagination will animate the coldest clay.

So 'tis Friday. Wednesday next my admirer, which Godwin
swears himself to be, returns—he *says* to depart no more.

MW TO WG

July 21, 1796

I send you, as requested, the altered M.S. Had you
called upon me yesterday I should have thanked you for
your letter—and—perhaps, have told you that the sentence I *liked* best was the concluding one, where you tell
me that you were coming home, to depart *no more*. But
now I am out of humour I mean to bottle up my kindness, unless some thing in your countenance, when I do

see you, should make the cork fly out—whether I will or not.—

July 22, 1796

I had been, yesterday, just the slightest bit annoyed that my friend Godwin should appear more interested in the state of the essays he had left with me, for comment, before departing, than for a sight of me. I sent his pages to him and the little I had written by way of commentary—having more practical experience in the raising of children and the needs of their education than he. Receiving my note, he bade Marguerite say he would come to see me at tea time, unless I somehow stopped him by putting into his way the obstacle of another appointment, which might take me out. I was, as it happened, free. Awaiting Godwin, full of private things to say to him, who should unexpectedly appear but Opie! I had no reason, or could think of none, at the moment, for sending him away. I had not planned it thus, though I worried Godwin might read in Opie's presence an obstacle purposely set on his path, or worse, as some insidious female tactic to incite jealousy. How little I seem to know him! He entered with the most disingenuously happy expression on his face, greeted Opie with sincere pleasure at seeing him and sat down ready to bubble over about his visit to his mother's and the state of things in Norfolk. So there we sat, all three, Godwin, Opie and I, over tea and biscuits, and not a pleasanter hour have I spent in the longest time. Godwin, shortly having to leave, asked if he might partake of my habit of drinking tea tomorrow, since . . . but he left unfinished the sentence he had begun. I am plagued with imagining possible endings —because he had to rush to an appointment with his publisher? Because he wished to have me all to himself? Because he cannot henceforth do without seeing me daily? What was on the tip of his tongue? Am I never to know?

July 23, 1796

Godwin has been here to day. He has finished reading "Mary." I find it strange that he, whose good opinion of me I wish to have, prefers aspects of me which I often presume to be the weaker, less favourable sides of my nature. I brought "Mary" to Johnson, when I went to work for him some eight years ago. Now I am inclined to think the narrative, which adheres closely to the truth of my earliest experience, a very crude production, indeed. Yet, while Godwin disdains what he considers my forwardness of manner and masculine style in the other works, the disquisition of Mary's tribulations moved him, he says, to tears. Yet if he did not want better to know this *Mary*, would he have found that "Mary" quite as compelling as he says?

In my long postponed notion to write a sequel to "The Vindication of the Rights of Woman," I meet only resistance in Godwin, who hurts me by reference to its offences against grammar. It is all I have managed to get him to say of it. I wrote it in six weeks. When I told him so, he was fairly impressed. Our habits are so different—he regularly keeping to his schedule of three hours each morning, whereas I often imprison myself in prolonged periods of solitude, during which pleasure and friendship are banished. Godwin says I am weakest when I try to write a work of reason rather than of imagination. I did not wish to argue the point, but it is certainly masculine egotism which makes so little of the fact that—on a subject as important as the education of the young—I have experience not only from having been a governess, but from having run a school, with every practical problem arising from such a circumstance, whereas Godwin, in writing on education, is never brought to earth by any practical or human limitations. My theories are *all* practical—theories, I might add, which Condorcet was arranging to have me present to the Convention, with the end in view of reforming the educational system of France, plans which came to violent termination when the Twenty-two were put to death. I said none of this to Godwin, for he was in such friendly humour, sitting here to day, that I could not take him to task for preferring my feminine sensibility to the forwardness in my character. We women are not loved when we are forthright with men. We are asked to use the wiles of our enslavement: our prettiness, our softness, above all our cunning. I failed to point out his error to Godwin, only so that he should not think me as argumentative as, apparently, he thought me once at Johnson's table. It is true that suffering has broken off the sharpness I once had. But I am no more proud of that time-telling softness than would be a race-horse that has outlived both vitality and strength. Yes, I am softer—having ruled my sarcasm which so often wounded others. But must I, by virtue of being female, choose to be toothless? And if I were what Godwin *says* he wants me to be, would he come around to read me his essays?

A nostalgic note crept into our conversation. I had said some thing about the time I had lived at Hoxton . . . I stopped at a curious look that overspread Godwin's face. I could hear the ir-regularity of his breathing in the stillness of my room. We might have met *then*, he said. He had been a young dissenting student at the Academy at Hoxton, remaining some five years. My family spent little more than a year, in Queen's Row, there. I was fifteen. Godwin, slightly older, was reading metaphysics, he says, sixteen hours a day. Could we have met? Could we have passed on the street? Might we have exchanged the friendship of our young un-tried hearts? It is idle speculation to say that we *might have* met in 1776 and have been impressed with one another as greatly then as we appear now to be, but . . . no, it is too difficult to make the effort of imagination that would exclude so many actual pursuits of so many years. With sad smiles, we admit that, so concentrated were we both on plotting a personal course in life, at the time, that we should not have recognised each other, except by the most remote acknowledgement. Still, it is a thing of wonder that, un-knowingly, we may have brushed by, like two angels in heaven before being borne to earth.

We seem—perhaps Hoxton gives us the predilection—ever to hover at the northern boundary of London. The New Road from Paddington runs right past us here in Somers Town, continuing to Pentonville—where I took temporary quarters on coming back from Berkshire—and on straight as a die to Hoxton, where some day Godwin and I have promised ourselves we shall walk. I want him also to come with me to Newington-Green, some few miles north of here, to see where I had the school near Price's meeting-house and so much there that causes painful recollection. We speak of such possible future events with the sweet assumption of continuing affection. He was to day reluctant to leave; yet only his eyes told me so.

July 24, 1796

Godwin visited me to day, as he had promised. He sat on my small ladder-back chair and gulped down his tea. I'd been recounting how a boy educated apart from other boys, as the Irish gentry raise their sons, will become as gloomy as a hermit, later good for nothing but to spend time in company, drinking while telling ribald stories. I got not the slightest response from my friend. He sat stolidly on the little chair, in silence, reflecting, then asked if I would take offence at a criticism whose sole intent was my betterment. I blushingly said that I wouldn't in the least take offence —but it popped to mind, with horror, that the lemon-yellow cambric gown I was wearing for the first time might be too revealing, and that he was about to tell me so. Reclining at one end of the sofa, I looked around as if thinking to throw myself beneath some thing, or to pull some thing, *any thing*, on top of me. Imagine, then, my surprise when I heard Godwin begin a lecture on the price of tea! It is the ruin of many a household. The Exchequer has taken alarm at the country's annual expenditure for the commodity. Why, Mrs. Inchbald had calculated, to her amazement, that by avoiding consumption of both tea and coffee, she had managed on her savings in one year to contribute as much as twelve guineas to the poor of her parish. After a stunned moment, I said, in reply, that drinking tea and inviting others to drink it with me was an inveterate habit of mine—thus putting an end to the lecture. Godwin was staring fixedly across the room. I turned to see what drew him. But I could make out nothing that might rivet his attention. I asked if any thing was wrong. Nothing, he said, but were those, by chance, to day's news papers in the waste-paper-basket? I said they were; had he need of them? He asked if I bought a paper every day? I told him yes, some times more than one. He suggested that it surely was no use for him to buy in the afternoon what I threw out in the morning; that we should make an arrangement, living so close to one another, to share the news paper. I tried, afterwards, to read some deeper significance into the request, but must confess, this evening, that I trust what stirred his soul was the pure principle of thrift. I am, on retiring, some where between laughter and tears.

July 25, 1796

I *must* settle down to work. The play, seen by both winter managers, is not what is wanted. Perhaps Holcroft will read it and tell me honestly what is wrong with it. Mrs. Inchbald is said to earn over 400*l.* on a play. A novel brings considerably less, Robinson paying 150*l.* for her last. She has invested most of it in long annuities. She also wins lotteries. But then, I ask, does any of it give her the right to the pleasure of a simple cup of tea? Johnson, who has read my play, says the publication of it would do nothing but damage to my reputation; that I should set myself some task that has no relation to that particular obsession . . . as if my very life, my feelings, my experience, were a diseased part of me, wanting surgery. He says I might take up again my old "Cave of Fancy" and finish that for publication; but I care less than I once did for the allegorical form, which does not seem to hold up for any great length. Besides, taking up what one has left off nine years before is very much like continuing the work of a stranger, so much does one's sensibility change. "Mary" had a small sale. Times were different. If I put myself to the trouble of writing a novel, it would be for the money—and there *is* money in it now! Mrs. Radcliffe for her "Mysteries of Udolfo" is said to have made 500*l.* two years ago, an unprecedented amount of money paid for any novel. Last night from a towering stack of new novels on my table, all to be written up for the September *Analytical,* I began reading "Camilla," which is reputed to have earned Fanny Burney 2,000*l.* by subscription. It is an amazing sum! Not only is the novel now profitable, but there is the considerable advantage, at the moment, that Pitt's government does not consider such publication deserving of scrutiny for indictment of treason. I started scribbling here in this book—keeping a journal—with the express purpose of making notes for writing my life—but there is no use even starting, unless one can bring to it the utter frankness that Rousseau brought to his "Confessions." And how am I to do so, when, in the end, I must entrust it to the eyes of Johnson and his odious moralising? I will be who I am! My life, my loves, are what they were! Yet Johnson treats me so much as a pariah that he told the *Monthly Mirror*, it seems, when they requested a portrait of me to run with a notice of the "Letters," that the highest compliment they could pay me would be that of saying *nothing*. My own publisher! His sense of shame about me nearly cancels the spirit of friendship I once felt for him. Does a man, after loving a woman, have to hide for the remainder of his life? Then why should I be expected to do so? I must put my mind to writing some thing that distills my experience in disguise—for the sake of our hypocritical society. Think! Think!

This afternoon I visited Mary Hays. She is all bent upon the effort of writing a novel, her face grave as she speaks of its subject, which is so inextricably mixed with her life that I come away not quite sure which is which. The truth . . . ah, the truth!—who knows if the version lived, or the version dreamed and recorded in retrospect, is the more authentic? She is writing of her romantic attachment to Mr. Lloyd. I can understand the need, since I tried to do some what the same, making it, however, comic, while every thing in Mary Hays' expression lugubriously announces a tale of woe. I ask if perhaps the occupation doesn't salt the wound? Her shoulders heave with the most heart-piercing sigh, as we sit there in her little parlour, two lack-lustre ladies, abandoned and forlorn. She has asked why I don't change my name back to Mrs. Wollstonecraft? Fanny, she says, can continue with Imlay's name, but I ought to drop the name of a man so infamous in my life, as I have excised from my heart the love I once felt for him. Why not indeed? I could give her no satisfactory answer—since I am not completely truthful with her. Finally I left her sighing over her pages of closely written writing all on a downward slant; and I thought, what I often think of novels, that they are some times a melancholy pursuit, both to read and to write. Alas! Alas! Sweet tears of sensibility flow in copious showers down beautiful cheeks, to the discomposure of rouge . . . No, I do not at all like the sickly die-away languors that is the model for the sublime ideal of womanhood, nor do I care much for those who pander to it, writing novels to move the heart of a lady, while her hairdresser takes care of her head. Thinking these thoughts on the street, I became conscious of the fast nervous tap of my footsteps. I was almost racing

away from Mary Hays' parlour, in which, like a Vestal Virgin of
old, she protects with delicate sorrow the sacred flame of her lost
love.

> Unhappy sex! whose beauty is in snare;
> Exposed to trials; made too frail to bear.

M W   T O   W G

July 26, 1796

The weather not allowing me to go out about business
to day, as I intended, if you are disengaged, I and my
habit are at your service, in spite of wind or weather—

Tuesday   Mary

July 26, 1796

I had a note from Godwin saying that he cannot come to see me.
My one pleasure all day was filling my fire-place with some ever-
green branches that Marguerite had cut and which I arranged in
a great fan-shaped display. Taking my tea alone, I stared into the
greenery with an expression apparently so fierce that Fanny, stealing upon me for a kiss, burst into tears.

When she had been quieted and put to bed, I continued musing
by my fire side, Fanny still at the centre of my thoughts. Thinking
of my poor child, I was led, in the course of my reflexions, considering the current state of women, to lament that I had given
birth to a daughter. The wrongs done to women, who are the oppressed part of mankind, may be deemed necessary by their oppressors, but let them learn from my lips that they have made *all*
women suffer from such oppression. For a long while now I have
been considering writing a novel with the main object in view to
exhibit the misery, peculiar to women, arising out of partial law
and custom. In "The Vindication of the Rights of Woman"—
woman, singular, as a class, as a species apart, not a fully equal part
of mankind; when I hear my title corrupted to "The Rights of
W*omen*," it is as if it were imputed that only certain women are
oppressed by man-made institutions, rather than *all womankind*

. . . but I interrupted my train of thought, as I was about to say that in my "Rights of Woman" I took Rousseau to task for celebrating barbarism. While he tried to prove that all *was* right in the world, a crowd of contemporaries that all is *now* right, I said that all *will be* right. But experience has made me pessimistic! Easier was it to attack the sacred majesty of kings, than to question the inequality of the sexes. Did the Revolution in France, did the constitutional establishment of democracy in America, change by the slightest degree the laws governing the rights of woman? Where my philosophical tract, four years ago, had no effect on the hearts of men—to change unjust law and custom—might a novel succeed in moving hard hearts?

I shall have to pursue this line of thought.

July 30, 1796

Amelia Alderson of Norwich, one of Godwin's friends, came to call to day, so early that I had not yet put up my hair, which hung in a twist down my back. I apologised to her, saying one is some times forced to choose between one's looks and one's work—both of them as voracious as a pair of dragons in consuming time. But one need make no exaggerated courtesies before her, so charming and human she seems to be. When she sits, she swings one leg over the other like an active child. With a ready sense of amusement, she bursts out laughing in a most contagious manner. She drank tea in imitation of Mrs. Inchbald, as precise and *perfect* as a Swiss timepiece. And she tells extraordinary stories. *Ce n'est que les premiers pas qui conte*, she believes—as do I. She told me how a habit was formed, as a child, of throwing a penny over the wall of the city asylum for a man who would come clanking in his chains to catch it. She did so always with terror and trembling. Once he seemed to have admired a nosegay she was wearing, and from then on she brought him pinks, as well as money for snuff. Every kindness to him raised her feelings, in a way I recognise from my own childhood, when an act of charity would exalt me for days. The man, it seems, had been crossed in love. In fact, it is Miss Alderson's opinion that madness is not a physical derangement, but the result, in most cases, of moral causes. So affected was I, in listening to her, that Miss Alderson had to tap my hand with a light little pat to remind me of her presence.

I have exacted a promise that, next visit, she will talk about the treason trials which she regularly attended, having had a painful interest in them at the time. It is well known that, when Horne Tooke stood acquitted, pretty little Miss Alderson boldly approached and kissed him. Old Horne Tooke! And, it seems, he didn't blink an eye, only asked if ever again he were to be indicted, would she again kindly attend his trial. We practised exemplary discretion on the subject of our mutual friend Godwin—but I sense, on both sides, a readiness to exchange confidences whenever one of us shall make the first move that will spring the lock.

M W T O W G

August 2, 1796

From the style of the note, in which your epistle was enveloped, Miss Hays seems *plus triste que ordinaire*. Have you seen her?

I suppose you mean to drink tea with me, *one* of these days—How can you find in your heart to let me pass so many evenings alone—you may saucily ask why I do not send for Mr. Twiss—but I shall reply with dignity—No; there will be more dignity in silence—so mum.

I did not wish to see you this evening because you have been dining, I suppose, with Mrs. Perfection, and comparisons are odious.

August 4, 1796

At last the lock has sprung! It seems our sincere friend and philosopher Godwin, on the pretext of visiting his mother in the country—a pretext dutifully carried out, one must admit—set out to present himself at the house of Dr. Alderson to court his pretty daughter. I could not disguise my astonishment. With any one else, I might have attempted, *tant bien que mal*, to dissemble. Whether I could have done so successfully with clever Miss Alderson, who has a gift of seeing through to one's real feelings, is another matter, for I felt a shock run through my entire body and visibly jumped. What intrigued me was her jubilant reaction that together, she and I, we have uncovered Godwin's little game. For *he* told *her* of his attachment to *me*. He spared himself imparting as much to me! To add to the confusion, the principle within "Poetic Jus . . ." POETIC, indeed! My pen runs away with me. To add to the confusion, as I was saying, it remains to say that in his writings Godwin has avowed marriage to be a despised monopolistic practice. However, he has been courting Miss Alderson, on her say-so, since last summer—has known her for years and years, of course, but only noticed her nubility, as she terms her charms, on her last year's visit to London. He had alarmed her then by the pedantry with which he examined her opinions, but has since become more amiable and gallant. Before he left London last summer, declaring to her in dolorous tones that he was loath to depart, he asked if she would give him some thing to console him. She asked what he would have. He had seemed determined on endeavouring to ask for a kiss, but she watched his courage falter. Poor Godwin! How the two of us laughed at his expense! We were in the happiest conspiracy of laughter, rocking about on my great ungainly sofa, like two inhabitants in a row-boat upon stormy seas. When Miss Alderson could catch her breath and had wiped the tears from her eyes, she said he had asked to have her slipper, on the basis of once having had it in his possession, and having returned it, when her shoe had come off during a walk and he had put it in his pocket for a few minutes while they had rested. She had been completely taken by surprise when Godwin had asked her father for her hand—not her foot, *her hand!* Off she went again into breathless laughter. Well, he really does deserve it—a philosopher who preaches Sincerity! The proposal to her father was made, I dare say, around the time of his love letter to me. Possibly he was addressing another to Mrs. Inchbald. And who knows to whom else! It was only an additional source of wonder, as I confided to Miss Alderson, that he had threatened me with kisses so incendiary that they would burn me to a crisp. And has he kissed you? she asked with that level look of hers that I begin to recognise as a prelude to one of her uproars. In the light now of her experience and mine—both of us *unkissed* by him—we can only wonder if the philosopher has ever stooped to such a business.

August 4, 1796

I spent the evening with Mademoiselle Alderson—you,
I'm told, were ready to devour her—in your little parlour.
Elle est très jolie, n'est-ce pas? I was making a question
yesterday, as I talked to myself, whether Cymons of forty
could be *informed*. Perhaps after last night's electrical
shock, you can resolve one—

Marguerite, who is twenty-two, wears her practised air of innocence as she runs between Godwin and me. I wonder how she
interprets this strange courtship. I vouch the subject of her letters
to Paris must have some comment on the cold conduct of Englishmen.
Garrick's Simple Cymon, before love had given him eyes,
ears and understanding! For my peace of mind—since Miss
Alderson's revelations of last night, I can think of nothing else!—
Godwin is duty-bound to clarify the contradictions that he strews
on my path. Some times he appears at my door in the guise of St.
Preux, the ideal lover. Other times, carrying his folder of essays,
disembodied, abstract, musing to himself, he is completely blind
to my charms. All would be clear, if he had simply told me he was
in love with Miss Alderson. Then why play the gallant with me?
He can enjoy my friendship without pretending to be head over
ears in love with me. Does he think there cannot be tender friendship between a man and a woman; that he must come at me sidewise like some Tartuffe? I have many male friends. John Opie
often comes to joke, thereby to shake off the bitterness of his divorce proceedings. Certainly Mr. Johnson has been a friend, in
his time, with whom I could discuss any thing on earth, even the
old topic which so harassed me in those days, before I went to
France. There was kindness between us and no disguise, an openness that, in my opinion, friendship dictates. Godwin can claim
me as a friend, only under those conditions. It is merely a matter
of observing his own principle of Perfect Sincerity—any thing less
than truth serving to contaminate genuine intimacy. It confuses
me that his doctrines and their application lie such worlds apart.
And instead of adhering to reason, he tends to fall into a mutter

of self-justification. In answer to my note this morning, asking for an explanation, he said to Marguerite, *avec un regard déplaisant*, she said, that he cannot solve problems on paper, but would come to see me tomorrow morning on his way out. So I must wait! In the meantime, a prey to every sort of chimera of feverish imagination, I fear to go to sleep "and in that sleep to dream"—for in dreams one can be assured of no solidity nor orderly sequence in the universe, but only of the mutability of one thing turning haphazardly into another, oft enough into some thing it had not seemed capable of becoming: nymphs into streams, maidens into magpies, gods into bulls, snakes, toads—everything odd, repellent and unreal.

August 5, 1796

Godwin, quite gay, comes to call. He admits he *had been* enamoured of Miss Alderson, but that he is no more. He smiles, indeed smiling so generally that Marguerite, at one point, gets in the way of the beam of his radiance, which alters neither force nor direction, so that I must wonder now if he might be enamoured of *her.* He had simply fixed over his face a mask in which he would appear this morning—as if putting on a wig—and wore it with invariable rigidity. When alone once again, the door closed, I ask, as gently as I can, if I was to be given an answer to my note of yesterday. Had he not already answered that query, he asked, with a show of surprise. He had, indeed, felt an impulse to admire Miss Alderson, but now it was a matter of friendship that he felt. And intercourse between the sexes ought to fall under the same system of regulation as friendship, did I not agree? I did not agree. He shrugged, as if he thought me frivolous. Still smiling, *horribly unfeelingly smiling,* he gave the impression of some one considerably late for an appointment and departed, leaving me standing fully five minutes in the middle of the room, hardly knowing where I was.

August 6, 1796

I work at my desk in the gloomiest trance this morning, interrupted by Miss Alderson who comes through the door in a lance of sunlight, praising the beauty of the countryside that she has just passed, by way of Islington, from Southgate. Indeed, she sounds like a traveller who has risen with the dew—while I had hardly opened my eyes. I had been reproaching myself for having become a mere square-headed money-getter, only wanting to finish the tiresome business of the review I was writing. Immediately, however, I was put in spirits at the look of her comeliness and well-being, as she removed her Kashmir shawl, draping it prettily over the back of a chair, so that I might study its pattern. Then she fell on the sofa, giving a suppressed cry of pleasure when Fanny rushed in to be buttoned up. The three of us make a feast of greengage plums from an orchard behind the house in Southgate, where Miss Alderson stays with old family friends. She wipes Fanny's face and fingers with her handkerchief, both of them laughing, as gay as larks. It is when I see the monkey—made by Miss Alderson from a brown stocking, embroidered and stuffed, the most comical upturned grin on its face—that I settle irresistibly into a sprightly vein. My little damsel stands before me and so sweetly holds her monkey up for me to kiss that it charms away my cares.

We finally speak of the irksome topic. I confess that I have gathered from Godwin since Tuesday not one word of clarification on the subject of his feelings. She is astonished, then annoyed. She remarks, with that particular shrewdness of hers which I value, that it seems to her that he has been at great pains to answer only my query concerning his feeling for *her*, conspicuously neglectful of the other part of my question of how informed on certain matters he might be. She reasons that, to avoid the embarrassment of discussing his lack of experience between the sexes, he has decided to play the role of a man liable to strong feelings, but rather fast and loose. We both burst out laughing at the grotesque disguise. How salubrious to laugh at a subject which has caused me so much pain and sleeplessness! Why did he make me verses, why send me love letters saying how bewitching he finds me—if he does not wish to hold me in his arms? My imagination, apparently, travels swifter than his. But I am weak from guessing what his contradictions mean. Does he not dare to kiss me? Has he, as Miss Alderson in her wisdom concluded, never ever kissed any one . . . ? Impossible! Miss Alderson jumps up, saying it is useless to speculate further, when we might ask and have done with it;

that if *I* have not the courage to do so, *she will*. And so we put our two heads together to set the trap. She is to deliver the question, in my hand, and then exact the answer. When she leaves with my note to Godwin, I am in spirits.

William Godwin Philosopher

Not to be opened till the Philosopher
has been an hour in Miss Alderson's
company, cheek by jowl

August 6, 1796

Miss Alderson was wondering, this morning, whether you *ever* kissed a maiden fair—as you do not like to solve problems, *on paper*, TELL her *before* you part. She will tell ME next—year—

August 7, 1796

I can make no general principle from a matter that has been whirling in my head this morning, when, after looking out the window at an overcast sky, I returned to bed to think. I was wondering what to make of the fact that celebrated people so often seem less than we expect them to be—the fault lying surely within ourselves for endowing them with superior powers. I had always heard that Mrs. Siddons, off stage, appeared statuesque and sententious. Though curious, I was reluctant to go to gawk at her. But yesterday I let Twiss persuade me that she was neither as formidable nor as formal as her reputation makes her out to be. Miss Alderson had told me how, on first being taken to the house, she was so *sans gêne* that she nursed her infant while conversing. What, however, remains an unsurmountable obstacle is the memory of Mrs. Siddons, gowned in heavy black with a vivid broad border of crimson from shoulder to feet, a costume devised, they say, by Joshua Reynolds, when as Lady Macbeth she struck terror into one's heart in the night-walking scene. With that in mind, it is difficult to treat her commonly. And so, I suspect, revered as she is by all the world, she cannot easily drop her distinction borrowed from tragic heroines.

In her presence even her brother-in-law, poor Twiss, seems ill at ease. He once confessed, and perhaps regrets the indiscretion, that he had been passionately in love with her. He has, nevertheless, never regretted his marriage to her sister, an extremely agreeable woman. Indeed, what a great amount of charm there is to choose from in that household, the daughters, Maria and Cecilia, both delightful girls. In an oyster-white gown, embroidered with tiny roses, Mrs. Siddons sat on her settee with the tea-things before her. At one point I talked to Tom Lawrence. For my translation of Dr. Lavater, which never did get printed, he had done my portrait in perfect disregard of the coarse stuff of my clothes and the dingy surroundings of my rooms. I teased him a little about the drawing. He seemed to be forcing himself to pay attention. From under his long lashes I caught his look at Maria Siddons as she kissed her mother good night, and wondered if I read accurately the cause of his subdued spirits.

What struck me, ruminating in bed, as I let my mind wander over the evening, was the sudden jolt I had felt when, at a melodious chime from Mrs. Siddons' mantel-piece clock, I remembered that, at this very moment, Amelia Alderson, according to a plan which had seemed inspired, was delivering my inquisitive note. I had suddenly grown quite still in Mrs. Siddons' parlour, seeing Miss Alderson's lamp-lit scene, as in a theatrical piece for which one has poor seats, so that all seems diminished, remote and hard to hear. I imagined the white crackling note-paper slipped from under the brass base of a candlestick and handed to Godwin. I seemed to see his expression of curiosity hardening into anger. I felt weak with self-recrimination. It was a quiver, lasting only a moment, yet I determined to send a note, so that, rather than huddling his anger to himself, he might discharge it. I thought of running first to Miss Alderson's, but remembered that she had mentioned an early excursion, so there is nothing now to do but to face the consequences of having asked Godwin what I most want to know.

M W T O W G

August 7, 1796

I supped in company with Mrs. Siddons last night. When shall I tell you what I think of her?

August 7, 1796

I have spent the evening with Godwin. I have suffered much, and have seen him horribly suffer. Pride, shyness, sensitivity—all combine to make him obstinately try to justify his behaviour. I could not fail to observe how he burrowed down in the chair, like one of those animals who dig into the earth to hide out of sight till the footsteps of the hunter recede. It is hardly flattering to be made to play such a role. I wearily pointed out that strong feelings, implanted in us by instinct, depend only partly on volition, as any one who has cared for children well knows: that love is an impulse of the heart which cannot be denied. I no longer cared what I said. I no longer believed in the pleasing reveries of my imagination. I said exactly what was on my mind: how difficult it is for people to have any true understanding of one another; how much more difficult, because of conventional postures, for a man and a woman. I stood behind the blue chair with one arm along its back, and said I was tired of life, if life is to be all artifice—and Godwin, suffering, I could see, but thinking only of himself, appeared closed against me. All seemed lost. His feelings, in a luxuriance of wounded self-esteem, were devoted to defending himself. Both of us were worlds apart. I cannot remember quite . . . it was at the end of a prolonged silence that he said life might have been different had he fallen in love with me long ago at Hoxton. Instead he has been wretchedly alone—save for masculine friendship, with such as Mr. Marshal and Mr. Holcroft. Some times he has been so poor that he has been obliged to pawn his watch or his books for a meal. How then could he have hoped, given his ambitions, to have kept a wife? Only with recent literary success has he become interesting to women—only *now* has he women friends, only now the chance to experience, through their friendship and intimacy, some understanding of the female sex . . . but I am so sharp, critical and mocking that I laugh him out of countenance. The vision of Miss Alderson and I ridiculing him, as though he were some poor uninstructed fool, thoroughly mortifies him. He came to see me this evening only for fear that I would have added to my knowledge of his ludicrous inexperience the moral defect of cowardice. I did not think twice what I was doing. I moved towards him and stroked the lowered head, as if he were a child who had come home scarred from battle and was making every endeavour to be brave. We made an agreement: I no longer would use mockery as a weapon, and he will not sulk when wounded. I would not willingly give him pain. From mere playfulness, some times, I wound him. And yet, at other times, my cheerfulness and vivacity make him laugh—as later in the evening when telling him that I will always associate Mrs. Siddons with the scent of smelling-salts; for I recall in the theatre at Bath the physician rushing through the audience to administer to the needs of victims of sensibility, who were swooning and sobbing at every adjustment of movement from the tragic muse upon the stage. Thus, in my changing the subject to the gathering at Mrs. Siddons', Godwin's petulance—reminding me of Fanny's outbursts —was over like a summer storm. It must have cost him greatly to let fall all disguise but, for the remainder of the evening, I had an affectionate friend beside me. And we parted with the soundness of expectation that we might continue on this settled plane.

M W T O W G

August 11, 1796

Won'tee, as Fannikin would say, come and see me to day? and I will go home with you to hear your essays, should you chance to be awake. I called on you yesterday, in my way to dinner, not for Mary—but *to bring* Mary— Is it necessary to tell you sapient Philosophership, that I mean MYSELF—

August 13, 1796

Godwin visited yesterday—and the day before—staying long, reluctant to leave. To day I decide to surprise him in his lair. I have woken early and dawdled the morning away, crooning about the house the way Fanny does. Finally I dress myself, deep in thought all the while I choose the pale lemon-coloured dress he has seen only once. Should I wear a lawn cloak over it? Oh, heavens, how

many questions I put, before simply slipping into a dress and re-
garding myself in the glass. My critical eye, the one that leers,
approves of the auburn-haired maiden who looks like some
fresh-cheeked cowherd about to swing her milk pail up a path over
a hill and away . . . to see what Godwin's day is bringing
him. Fanny hides under the stairs. She pops out begging to
go with me, pointing outside, crying *out, out, out*—but cold-
hearted enchantress that I have become, by virtue of donning this
gauzy gown, I burst out laughing and leave her too stunned to
turn on tears. I call to Marguerite that I don't know what time I
will be back, and to cover my dinner with a dish if I'm late. And I
make my way down the street and around the turn, crossing when
I see the old flower-woman with her basket of daisies and corn-
flowers. I pay the poor old soul for a nosegay and get her Bless
you! in return. I *feel* blessed, blessed and happy and free, the blossoms nestled over one arm, standing thus before Godwin's door.
He gives a real start of pleasure. His nook smells so close I beg him
to open the windows and I stand, still cradling the field-flowers,
while he goes to find some thing to put them in, returning with a
sort of scrub pail, filled with water, at a loss what else to provide.
I go into his small scullery and unearth a bright green bottle, tall
enough for the daisies, a small honey-pot and a very nice white
jam-pot, into which I arrange the flowers and distribute them on
his table, at his fire side and on the window, where they bask in
sunlight. I sit looking out at a deep blue summer sky, layered with
clouds as evenly as those end-papers in books that seem to be
feathered. I can hear children bouncing their hoops over the cobbles. All smiles and gallantry, Godwin has seated himself in the
chair pushed back from a table strewn with papers. He has been
trying to rub off some ink from the broadside of his hand, but he
gives it up, saying he has some Vesuvian pumice which he once
bought in Fleet Street, the only practical remedy for removing
ink stains. He hands me a collection of verse translated from the
German and beautifully illustrated with coloured engravings that
I turn over. As I give back the book, our hands graze.
   A breeze is playfully blowing along the nape of my neck, my
head lowered, not now looking at Godwin, whose eyes upon me
burn with the intensity of a feverishly sick child, or like a child
dazzled by some splendid toy before his eyes . . . but, like a *good*

child, he does not reach out to grasp it. My rapture under the impression of his eyes takes my breath away. I look out the window, drawing a sigh. Well, Godwin? His gaze, not quite quickly enough to escape my comprehension, flinches from my heaving breasts to the book of verses in his hand, gripped so tightly his knuckles are white. I rise, saying I had only passed to bring him a brightness of flowers—and a God bless you! The door open to the street, I give him my hand, above which he bows.

August 16, 1796—Tuesday

Yesterday, the day being fair, Godwin stopped long enough for me to put Fanny's shoes on, the two of us hurrying to join him for a walk. We went along the edge of the wheat fields which have become a deep golden brown, and stand twice as high as Fanny who, none the less, raced into the long stalks of wheat after a dragon-fly. Her howl of indignation at finding herself lost, and unable to see her way out, brought Godwin wading in after her. It was lovely to see him holding her aloft, Fanny on his shoulder prattling into his ear, as he came striding from the wheat. We sat for a while in the shade of a towering tulip-tree. Godwin with his back against its trunk threw a stick to make a stray dog go away. But the dog ran to fetch the stick and bring it back, wagging a docked tail so amusingly that Godwin threw the stick once again and was bound to keep on doing so dozens of times. Later Fanny lay snug against his waistcoat, unbuttoned so he would not tear his sleeve out when he hurled the stick.

Imagine my surprise then that Godwin stood his ground before my house, when, leaving the door open behind me, I took it for granted that he would come to have his dinner with us. He held back, saying he had to go home to work on an essay he had promised to read to Holcroft this morning. I could not help the gesture of impatience that escaped me and a taunting phrase about philosophy. I seemed again to make fun of him without having intended doing so. To any stranger who might have seen us on our walk, we must have appeared the most ordinary domestic group, enjoying the summer sun. But Godwin seems to resent having passed his time so felicitously.

I am beginning to suspect that if he long remains unable to bend from the waist to kiss me, I will have to gently pull him down from his cloud of solemn thought. Nature, I expect, might instruct him on the rest of the procedure, when roused by the feel of my lips against his, all my body softly in repose within his arms. I longed for him last night. Is it possible he did not also long for me?

MW TO WG

August 16, 1796

I send the news paper before the hour, because I suppose you will go out earlier than usual to day.

Give Churchill to Fanny, if you can spare him, and, you may help her, if you please.

Entre nous, did you feel very lonely last night?

Mary

WG TO MW

August 16, 1796

I have been very miserable all night. You did not consider me enough in that way yesterday, and therefore unintentionally impressed upon me a mortifying sensation. When you see me next; will you condescend to take me for better or worse, that is, be prepared to find me, as it shall happen, full of gaiety and life, or a funny valetudinarian? Farewell, remember our agreement!
Tuesday

MW TO WG

August 17, 1796

I have not lately passed so painful a night as the last. I feel that I cannot speak clearly on the subject to you, let me then briefly explain myself now I am alone. Yet, struggling as I have been a long time to attain peace of mind (or apathy) I am afraid to trace emotions to their source, which border on agony.

Is it not sufficient to tell you that I am thoroughly out of humour with myself? Mortified and humbled, I scarcely know why—still, despising false delicacy I almost fear that I have lost sight of the true. Could a wish have transported me to France or Italy, last night, I should have caught up my Fanny and been off in a twinkle, though convinced that it is my mind, not the place, which requires changing. My imagination is for ever betraying me into fresh misery, and I perceive I shall be a child to the end of the chapter. You talk of the roses which grow profusely in every path of life—I catch at them; but only encounter the thorns.—

I would not be unjust for the world—I can only say that you appear to me to have acted injudiciously; and that full of your own feelings, little as I comprehend them, you forgot mine—or do not understand my character. It is my turn to have a fever today—I am not well —I am hurt—But I mean not to hurt you. Consider what has past as a fever of your imagination; one of the slight mortal shakes to which you are liable—and I—will become again a *Solitary Walker*. Adieu! I was going to add God bless you!—
Wednesday morning

WG TO MW

August 17, 1796

How shall I answer you? In one point we sympathize; I had rather at this moment talk to you on paper than in any other mode. I should feel ashamed in seeing you.

You do not know how honest I am. I swear to you that I told you nothing but the strict and literal truth, when I described to you the manner in which you set my imagination on fire on Saturday. For six and thirty hours I could think of nothing else. I longed inexpressibly to have you in my arms. Why did I not come to you? I am a fool. I feared still that I might be deceiving myself as to your feelings, and that I was feeding my mind with groundless presumptions. I determined to suffer the point to arrive at its own *dénouement*. I was not aware that the fervour of my imagination was exhausting itself. Yet this, I believe, is no uncommon case.

Like any other man, I can speak only of what I know. But this I can boldly affirm, that nothing that I have seen in you would in the slightest degree authorise the opinion, that, *in despising the false delicacy, you have lost sight of the true.* I see nothing in you but what I respect and adore.

I know the acuteness of your feelings, and there is perhaps nothing upon earth that would give me so pungent a remorse, as to add to your unhappiness.

Do not hate me. Indeed I do not deserve it. Do not cast me off. Do not become again a *solitary walker.* Be just to me, and then, though you will discover in me much that is foolish and censurable, yet a woman of your understanding will still regard me with some partiality.

Upon consideration I find in you one fault, and but one. You have the feelings of nature, and you have the honesty to avow them. In all this you do well. I am sure you do. But do not let them tyrannise over you. Estimate every thing at its just value. It is best that we should be friends in every sense of the word; but in the meantime let us be friends.

Suffer me to see you. Let us leave every thing else to its own course. My imagination is not dead, I suppose, though it sleeps. But, be it as it will, I will torment you no more. I will be your friend, the friend of your mind, the admirer of your excellencies. All else I commit to the disposition of futurity, glad, if completely happy; passive and silent in this respect, while I am not so.

Be happy. Resolve to be happy. You deserve to be so. Every thing that interferes with it, is weakness and wandering; and a woman, like you, can, must, shall, shake it off. Afford, for instance, no food for the morbid madness, and no triumph to the misanthropical gloom, of your afternoon visitor. Call up, with firmness, the energies, which, I am sure, you so eminently possess.

Send me word that I may call on you in a day or two.

Do you not see, while I exhort you to be a philosopher, how painfully acute are my own feelings? I need soothing, though I cannot ask it from you.
Wednesday

August 17, 1796

I like your last—may I call it *love* letter? better than the first—and can I give you a higher proof of my esteem than to tell you, the style of my letter will whether I will or no, that it has calmed my mind—a mind that had been painfully active all the morning, haunted by old sorrows that seemed to come forward with new force to sharpen the present anguish—Well! well—it is almost gone—I mean all my unreasonable fears—and a whole train of tormentors which you have routed—I can scarcely describe to you their ugly shapes so quickly do they vanish—and let them go, we will not bring them back by talking of them. You may see me when you please. I shall take this letter, just before dinner time, to ask you to come and dine with me, and Fanny, whom I have shut out to day. Should you be engaged, come in the evening. Miss Hays seldom stays late, never to supper—or tomorrow—as you wish—I shall be content—You say you want soothing—will it soothe you to tell you the truth? I cannot hate you—I do not think you deserve it. Nay, more, I cannot withhold my friendship from you, and will try to merit yours, that *necessity* may bind you to me.

One word of my ONLY fault—our imaginations have been rather differently employed—I am more of a painter than you—I like to tell the truth, my taste for the picturesque has been more cultivated—I delight to view the grand scenes of nature and the various changes of the human countenance—Beautiful as they are, animated by intelligence or sympathy—My affections have been more exercised than yours, I believe, and my senses are quick, without the aid of fancy—yet tenderness always prevails, which inclines me to be angry with myself, when I do not animate and please those I love.

Now will you be a good boy, and smile upon me, I dine at half past four—you ought to come and give me an appetite for my dinner, as you deprived me of one for my breakfast.

Two o'clock   Mary

WG TO MW

August 17, 1796

I left a letter for you at one o'clock. It was not till two hours later, that I suddenly became awake, and perceived the mistake I had made. Intent upon an idea I had formed in my own mind of positive pleasure, I was altogether stupid and without intelligence as to your plan of staying, which it was morally impossible should not have given life to the dead.

Perhaps you will not believe that I could have been so destitute of understanding. It seems indeed incredible. I think however you will admit, that it is no proof of indifference to a subject, when a man's thoughts are so obstinately occupied by one view of it, that, though you were to blow a trumpet in his ears, you would not succeed in giving him an apprehension of any other.

I have now only left to apologise for my absurdity, which I do even with self-abhorrence. The mistake being detected, it is for you to decide whether it is too late to repair it. For my own part, I have not the presumption to offer even a word to implore your forgiveness.
Wednesday

I had written the above before you called. I hesitate now whether to deliver it. You say you are calmed, so I would not for the world change that state of mind for a state of anguish. My disposition, however, to utter all I think decided me. Take no notice of it for the present.

August 22, 1796

Monday—

May heaven be my judge if I have ever passed so agonising a time. I could not go through such an experience again. My nerves are in such a painful state of exhaustion that I have given Marguerite orders to tell Godwin, if he should choose to call, that I plan to rest all the day. My hand is steady. The crisis is past! I give thanks for delivery from that ordeal from which, I believe, we mortals may die. Such, I am convinced, are the risks of daring to love and be loved. Surely it is the most considerable decisive action in the lives of men and women. At one false move, by one intemperate act, Fate overwhelms and destroys us. I am thinking, at the moment, of "Werter"; but I may as well have had in mind any of a score of tragedies, in literature or in life, even my own past dislocated passion, from which I despaired of recovery. Perhaps it is sufficient that things have ended well, yet . . . it seemed, as events unfolded, that they would end hardly well at all. Let me trace the course.

A week ago Saturday, when I brought Godwin flowers, I felt that, surprising him in his sequestered nook where he meditates, composes, writes—in a place *all his*—I seemed by my witchcraft to divide his nature into one part which fell a slave to my spell, the other silently, resentfully, cursing what he felt as all weakness and temptation. He shrank from me, feared me. So filled was I with the pleasure of enjoying the day's bright prospect that I was scarcely aware of the strange war Godwin was waging. Feeling blessed with a well-being that made me sing under my breath, how could I have comprehended so odd a resistance? We react so differently to pleasure.

Next day I sent Fanny with the news papers—and to bring back Churchill's satires. Did ever a love-sick lady in any novel sit under a green blind squinting over small print? Well, in life she may be obliged to do so. On Tuesday, Godwin dined out. In the evening, passing by his house, I saw a light on. I had imagined that he would likely urge himself as a sign of strength of character into passing Judd Place, continuing to Chalton Street, steeling himself to do so without a backward glance, nor the weakness of regret. How I must divine those imaginary conversations he carries on with himself in the streets, as he hurries here and there on his crowded schedule. My explanation for going to see him that evening was from a conviction that he longed for me, but was too proud to admit it to his own conscience—out of that seemingly odd determination of his to defy pleasure as though it were a snare. All day there had popped to mind all manner of things to tell him, so that, when eight o'clock drew near, I did not pause for reflexion, but rushed out of the house, barely holding inside my head, without spilling them, all the many things I had waited to tell him the whole day long. Expectation made me trot along the streets with no thought of the risk I ran from footpads. If one had been lurking with evil intent in the shadows, I feel secure I would have sung out a melodious good evening and gone right by, so bent upon my purpose was I. Marguerite thinks I am foolhardy to go about alone. She often insists on running to find me a hackney-coach. But at no time am I fearful of the three-minute walk between Godwin's lodgings and my own. Somers Town might be said to have some of the good character of a provincial village, such as Beverly, in York, where in my childhood I believed robbery and murder took place only in wonderful remote places; for so rare were such events in Beverly that the townspeople would speak a full month of some petty crime such as a gypsy stealing a sheep. What a heartless world it would be if, on my way to Godwin's, glowing as I was with optimism, I should have been struck down by a pike! At last, my heart jumping clear out of my breast like a toad from a tree-hole, I spied his lighted window.

You would never have thought we had seen each other the day before. To whom previously had I confided every thing droll or difficult? That ever there had been a time in our lives when we had not known one another! I had no sense, this time, of intrusion, but rather the feeling that he had been lackadaisically leafing through that mendacious book by the Duke of Orleans, reading it with half an eye and glad to be rid of it. The night was chilly. I'd wrapped my woollen cloak around me. Godwin laid a little fire and poured two small glasses of wine. He drew two chairs to the fire side, stood away to appraise their position and prodded one of them, a bit furtively, with his toe, till they touched. Every thing indicated his desire to establish the chairs in such a way as to enable us to sit as closely as possible. When we were seated, he raised his little glass to toast me, with a long rhetorical flourish which now escapes my memory, my attention having been taken by the way his hectic eyes were devouring me. Besides, rhetorical phrases spoil intimacy. I fall at such times, by contrast, into common speech. I said some thing of what a good boy he was to have been at home to receive me, how fine it felt to warm my feet at his fire, and my stomach with his wine. It did not register on me then, but I now seem to remember a look on his face not entirely cordial. Perhaps it was my lack of having praised his pretty speech —Mrs. Inchbald would never have neglected to do so. But I will not endure the fraudulence of flattery. It sounded to me like a guilty retreat from the intention of having put our two chairs together with specific erotic possibilities in mind. His eyes still lingered on me; I decided to take him at *their* word. I gave him my hand, which he fondled and kissed. He spoke of his longings for me. Our breaths intertwined and, at last, *at long last,* his lips pressed mine. He kissed softly, clinging, unwilling to release me from his embrace. I raised his hand in mine and drew it to my breast. I felt him give a start at touching, through the thinness of the stuff of my dress, the hard bud of my nipple. Self-absorbed, almost reverentially, in a profound rapture such as that of a person listening with all his might to some scarcely audible message, his open hand stroked my nipple, till he seemed oblivious of all else, his lips, from time to time, nuzzling my neck or cheek. He had become almost drowsy in his sensuality. Finally, certain signs made me understand that he had fulfilled and, for the moment, exhausted his desire. I wanted to hold him—but the hard wooden arms of the chairs were as solid an obstacle as Pyramis' and Thisbes' wall. His head was bent at such an angle that I might easily have reached out and caressed the tender nape of his neck, but I refrained from arousing him, saying in a voice from which all the breath seemed to have been struck, but sufficiently loud, I thought, for him to have heard, that I had never yet been allowed a view of his bedchamber. When, after a moment, he had neither raised his head nor responded, my blood ran cold. I gently withdrew my hand. And I repeated what I had said still once again, this time holding his eyes with mine. Strangely perturbed, he did not reply. I leapt up, hot with shame. He did not try to stop me. He was, when I again dared raise my eyes, running his hand through his hair. And some how, in haste, and humiliation, I departed.

On Wednesday I arose in anguish. I shut the door against Fanny, so that she would not see me weeping, and drank my tea, feeling too giddy to rise. Finally I sat down to write Godwin, without condemning his behaviour. On receiving my letter, he wrote a letter of his own, in equal agony. When he came to deliver it, Marguerite told him I was resting. He went away. I tore open the letter. At once, on finishing it, my demeanour of a condemned prisoner changed to transports of relief. I sang out for Fanny, who dragged up the stairs into my chamber with a tragic mask—so much does despair spread like some swiftly engendered epidemic. I caught her up and clasped her till she gave a wan little smile, not yet—nor was I—in full health. Yet she encircled her arms tightly about my neck, and lay her cheek so lovingly against mine that I took it for an omen that love had not completely flown from the house. I had sent my letter at noon. Godwin had left his for me at one o'clock. I took my reply around, to put him out of suspense, a little before three. I already felt quite calm. At the door, he looked like his own Caleb Williams, pale, drawn and gaunt. In the room the ashes from the fire of the night before were cold; the chairs, thank heaven, withdrawn from the fire side, rather than, like ghosts still there to revive my wounds. Miserable aspects of our former selves, we spoke softly, as though in the chamber of a convalescent trying to regain his strength. I said I did not wish to keep him from going out, but had thought I might bring him home to dine with Fanny and me, if he were free. He said he was on his way to dine with Mrs. Robinson, and only regretted that he had accepted her invitation—his words marked with that earnest struggle to say precisely what he meant, which had made me so long ago esteem him for his sincerity. I said I had come to demonstrate how remarkably his letter had calmed me; that, since he was on his way out, we would not speak further now, but should walk out together. He began hunting through his papers, then on the floor, for his latch-key. Finally he turned his pockets inside out, but found the key only when he gave up looking for it, his gaze haphazardly falling on a book into which he had slipped it to mark his place. Wishing to read the letter I had brought him, he begged me to wait as he read it in the other room. In the silence, I imagined his restoration—for who else was the convalescent that had made us speak in such hushed tones? I heard him stir inside and step lightly across the passage-way into the parlour, lighting up with a shy smile. He drew a sigh, as though he had strained every bit as much as I. He would see me to Judd Place in his way out, which relieved me—did he surmise the reason?—not again to be forced to hear the door heavily shut behind me. We sauntered through the steets. Here we were in ordinary reality once again. And we parted before my door—Fanny and I waving him off.

That evening Mary Hays came to read me her new pages. Her pointed, grim, little face, the curls tight against her skull which shows pink between each row of curls, makes me sigh with pity for the semblance of unhappiness she expresses, almost, I some times feel, an unhappiness she feels bound to express, as a soldier will flaunt a malevolent scar to give himself the occasion of boasting of battle. Early experience—her first love dying young—has set the tone for her entire life, producing the expectation that love is destined to be doomed. If not, why would she have fallen in love, at thirty-five, with a man of twenty? It has all the elements in it of hopelessness. Yet, I do not have it in my heart to blame her; for where is there blame in matters of the heart? It would seem that unrequited passion were a deterrent to love; *would seem to be*—if reason ruled the heart. Rousseau some where has written that people do not sufficiently consider the influence of one's first attachment in love that produces a long chain of effects, which continues to operate till death. If this is so, our choices are inescapable. It is futile to revolt. She cannot be reproached, but only pitied for having nursed such a wild, improbable, chimerical vision. An urge to write passionately long love letters recently overcame her better judgement. Not only did the object of her love answer them to fan the fire, but he also took to reading them aloud to friends to arouse their mockery. Her imagination had built such a structure of illusion that these public readings left her convulsed with uncertainty, and near madness. She was in such a pathetic state that, alarmed, I stayed with her all one night and managed to persuade her in the reasonable light of dawn to go and beg Mr. Lloyd to return her letters, with a promise that she would cease all further entreaties. The exchange decorously having been transacted in my presence, I asked them both to my house for tea—so that she might have the chance to demonstrate that, far from the lunatic which Mr. Lloyd must have conceived her to be, she was eminently reasonable. The contradictions of the situation confounded the intelligent, though cynical, young man, who meekly drank his tea, while listening to Mary Hays' most rational tea-talk.

In the novel that she is presently writing, the letters to young Mr. Lloyd find their rightful place. These letters—revised versions of the real ones—were what she read to me. Reasoning about love preciously suited my mood. I felt profoundly moved by the passionate avowals; at one point, in tears. Life—love—seem so very perilous, one's very happiness bursting as one grasps it. Mary Hays' thin voice rose and fell as she read, her eyes lowered so that the minute shadings of terror and relief that shook me from head to toe went unnoticed, as I recalled the dangers passed, scarcely even observed at their passing, so narrowly passed had they been. If I re-acted intensely, it was partly for having survived the treacherous vagaries of love. Not all the reasoning in the world can gain the heart of the person desired. Yet the affections must be exercised, for not to love is to be miserable, as Sterne so truly says. Mary Hays' reedy voice, a piccolo of a voice, sounded out its yearnings, as a song-bird sings—even where there is none to hear. To me it does not seem unreasonable . . . what I wish to say is that, if I were to have a choice between illusory sentiments, inspired by an active imagination, or the grosser nature of common sensualists, to whose appetites imagination has never lent its magic wand, I invariably should say that the true fire stolen from heaven comes from the imagination. No matter whether Mr. Lloyd once sat on my sofa or not, or what he thought, while he sat there; no matter even if there were *no* Mr. Lloyd—as there was, in truth, very little of him in the sentiments aroused—love was not less truly felt because his heart remained obdurate. One must love or be miserable.

I was observing her closely as she read: Half the sex, then, are wretched, degraded, victims of brutal instinct: the remainder, if they sink not into mere frivolity and insipidity, are sublimed into a—what shall I call them? She looked up. *Romantic*, I answered. She nodded; and *overrefined*, she said. As well as *unfortunate*, I offered. And, it seemed to her, *factitious*. She scribbled on the side of the page our descriptive phrases with a pen that was lying on my long table and which scratched, since I often neglect to mend my nibs. She then raised a face so lined with discouragement that I hoped the ruddiness of my complexion might some how remain obscure in the half light where I lay on the sofa. It was at such a moment that Godwin chose to enter.

He bowed to Mary Hays—I had warned him that, if he passed late, he might find me in company. With *sang froid* unexpected in the advocate of "perfect sincerity", he made a negligent bow in my direction. I, too, was caught up with stage-effects of seeming indifference. Since we were both playing our roles for the benefit of Mary Hays, I wondered whether she might not apprehend, if her intuition were sharp, the studied way we avoided any effusion of pleasure in our greetings. It occurred to me, as a principle to keep in mind for future use, that in wishing to deceive, had we acted as we truly felt, she might have more effectively been thrown off the track, thinking that we would surely never have behaved thus openly, warmly embracing, if there had been a secret relationship to guard. We are so constructed that we learn, in this society of ours, not to believe our eyes. But Godwin and I are not practised in throwing out false scents to escape the hounds. I had relit the essence under the tea-pot. Godwin has been reading passages from Mary Hays' M.S. since March. And I believe, although I have never questioned him on the matter, he is flattered to find himself pictured there as a wise old counsellor. It cannot strike him as undeserved that Mr. Francis is described as slender, delicate, his eye piercing, his manner impressive, the heroine's only "rational recreation"—by letter, that is, for every one must stand at a distance, so that the heroine can whip out her pen, like some Amazon warrior her sword, to wage epistolary battle against the world. Mary Hays has taken from Godwin's doctrine its pith to put into Mr. Francis' mouth. Despite his counsel, however, the heroine spends her time moping along the pathways of Morton Park, cultivating a sensibility devoted to idealising a hopeless love.

What amused me was that here, before us, as if by magic, stood our wise, impressive, delicate Mr. Francis. It put me into an ironic mood to have lifted from listening to letters from the fictional Mr. Francis to face the actual model, whom Reason had so totally abandoned the night before in the necessities of love—for we are all of us children, all vulnerable, all shivering and shaking within our souls, when it comes to these urgencies where Aphrodite, if we observe not her dominion, wreaks powerful vengeance.

"Mr. Francis . . ." I began, and entered into spirited raillery, which made poor Mary Hays weak with laughter. Misanthropic, as Godwin calls her? No, it is the burden of womanhood without the grace of beauty that has caused her to have to turn aside from commonplace happiness. In a better world . . . But, alas! in this one chastity is the calamity. How I made her laugh at my antic notions that her own fictional Mr. Francis had taken hold of our friend, like a puppet-master thrusting his voice and will and principle into inanimate wood. So extraordinary is it to see her in smiles, that it almost made me sad. How much more would it have instructed her, had she been aware how little, during these last twenty-four hours, Reason had been of service to our philosopher. In some ultimate evolution of humanity, Reason will surely reign supreme. But here and now, we must, I feel, give ourselves halfway over to the dark forces of life, where Reason fails us.

I had started on a conversation that I hoped would be a long, dawdling path, when—imagine my surprise—Godwin, who had barely addressed a single word to me, rose to take his leave. Thinking he might feel I suffered embarrassment from seeing him in these circumstances, I pressed him to stay. Over his face fell a look of terrorised indecision. It brought to mind some thing he had once said of himself: that by his fear he often produces the very thing he fears. The prospect of staying longer, of outstaying Miss Hays, was some thing he so desired that he could believe it nothing more than mere groundless presumption to think I, too, might wish it. While I tried to conceive of a way of signalling my desire, those two had fallen into a dispute over whether Juvenal is better in prose or in verse. Godwin was speaking very Mr. Francis-like. I saw he had made his decision. He reasoned that leaving would arouse less suspicion and thus please me. In the hall where he might have made some furtive promise to return, he spoke in a public voice. I closed the door with a swift sensation of disappointment. Within a quarter of an hour Mary Hays with her quire of paper was gone, leaving me alone, unable to sleep.

On Thursday evening Godwin called. Trying all the day to find some hint to his hesitations, trusting that they might be found within his letters in words so commonplace I had neglected to comprehend their literal meaning, I had reread them all, and discovered a theme running through them which previously had escaped my attention. "Let us leave every thing *else* to its own course . . . *all else* to the disposition of futurity . . . to suffer the point to arrive at its own *dénouement* . . ." It appeared that I might better soothe my friend by assuming to be less quick, open and affectionate. I do not enjoy disguising my true feelings, yet they seemed to account, in a manner which I had yet to determine, for his fearfulness. It was with an air more subdued than usual, therefore, that I greeted him. For all my good intentions, I cannot help a certain liveliness and laughter. I am not made of marble. I am ill at ease in the guise of primness and impassivity. Yet I hoped it might create a neutrality by which his nature could expand. However, apparently attributing the conciseness of my conversation to the lateness of the hour, he departed earlier than usual. I was left with the wonder of it all, and ended by going to bed with a lingering regard at the expectant look of puffed pillows and tight, smooth, clean white bed-sheets which Marguerite, at my bidding, had so freshly prepared. That was, as it were, the last straw! I wrote him the following letter:

August 19, 1796

As I was walking with Fanny this morning, before breakfast, I found a pretty little fable, directly in my path; and, now I have finished my review, I will transcribe it for thee.

A poor Sycamore growing up amidst a cluster of Evergreens, every time the wind beat through her slender branches, envied her neighbours the foliage which sheltered them from each cutting blast. And the only comfort this poor trembling shrub could find in her mind (as mind is *proved* to be only thought, let it be taken for granted that she had a mind, if not a soul) was to say, Well, spring will come soon, and I too shall have leaves. But so impatient was this silly plant that the sun could not glisten on the snow, without her asking, of her more experienced neighbours, if this was not spring? At length

the snow began to melt away, the snow-drops appeared
and the crocus did not lag long behind, the hepaticas
next ventured forth and the mezereon began to bloom.

The sun was warm—balsamic as May's own beams.
Now, said the Sycamore, her sap mounting as she spoke,
I am sure this is spring.

Wait only for such another day, said a fading Laurel,
and a weather-beaten Pine nodded, to enforce the re-
monstrance.

The Sycamore was not headstrong, and promised, at
least, to wait for the morrow, before she burst her rind.

What a tomorrow came! The sun darted forth with redoubled ardour; the winds were hushed. A gentle breeze
fluttered the trees; it was the sweet southern gale, which
Willy Shakespear felt, and came to rouse the violets;
whilst every genial zephyr gave birth to a primrose.

The Sycamore no longer regarded admonition, she felt
that it was spring; and her buds, protected by the kindest
beams immediately came forth to revel in existence.

Alas! Poor Sycamore! The morrow a hoar-frost covered
the trees, and shriveled up thy unfolding leaves, changing, in a moment, the colours of the living green—a
brown melancholy hue succeeded—and the Sycamore
drooped, abashed, whilst a taunting neighbour whispered
to her, bidding her, in future, learn to distinguish February from April.

Whether the buds recovered, and expanded, when the
spring actually arrived—The Fable sayeth not—

His reply:

August 19, 1796

I have no answer to make to your fable, which I acknowledge to be uncommonly ingenious and well composed. I see not, however, its application, either to
Wednesday when Miss Hays came, and when, as you
confess, my visit gave you spirits, or to yesterday, when
the presence of Margaret in the next room tortured me. I

had no reason to regard her as your confident, and was at
a loss how to judge. Your fable of to day puts an end to
all my hopes. I needed soothing, and you threaten me.
Oppressed with a diffidence and uncertainty which I
hate, you join the oppressors, to annihilate me. Use your
pleasure. For every pain I have undesignedly given you, I
am most sincerely grieved; for the good qualities I discern in you, you shall live embalmed in my memory.
Friday

Anger and discouragement have to discover some manner of expression—or one will burst. I did not estimate how cruelly
pointed was my fable till I had Godwin's reply. I wondered then
how we were ever to make an end to this misery. Only by the most
rigorously honest disclosure of true feelings did it seem to me that
we could extricate ourselves from this comedy of errors. I let a
day pass, for the full violence of his recriminations to wear themselves out in those inner dialogues one carries on to relieve distress. And next day I called on him with Fanny. He would, I knew,
control any expression of antagonism in her presence. I exacted
from him the promise of a visit in the evening—to analyse our dis-
agreements. I could barely ask more, since Fanny had lifted down
a volume from a low shelf and was murmuring a story to herself,
turning the pages with such vigour that I feared she would rip
apart the book. Godwin made some pleasantry about precocious
literary accomplishments. But whatever we said to one another,
there was a polite restraint to it.

Since Marguerite's presence had *tortured* Godwin—so he had
said—I sent her out. Wrapping in paper the warmest clothing
which Fanny had outgrown, I begged Marguerite to do me the
favour of taking the package to a young married couple who had
been kind to us in Paris and were now, as *émigrés*, living in great
distress with an infant on the south side of London. The prospect
of the visit put her in spirits, so I need not have felt ashamed of
the subterfuge, whose principal motive was to banish her from
the house for some three hours. I was, therefore, when Godwin
called, alone, save for Fanny soundly sleeping upstairs. She slept
throughout the storm. Not anger, but self-justification, raised Godwin's voice, as he strove to convince me of his rectitude, claiming

to be astonished that I—*the kind of woman I was*—made so little allowance for his scruples. I was ready to take offence at such a negligent description, but saw that very little gain lay in that direction, and kept silence. I do not believe, even had I tried, that I could have halted him, so vehement was his attack. *This* was the man who had brought a Chief-Justice low, when he had dissected the charges brought against Hardy and the rest. Just as he had written that attack—or spoken it, rather, for he has told me that he dictated the whole to Mr. Marshal—so now he railed at my injustices, pacing with a savage animation so uncharacteristic that I asked myself if he recollected where he was—so dramatic seemed his gestures, and so unguarded, as if he thought himself in the theatrical ambience of his own private imaginings. That slightly slanderous reference to me as *the kind of woman I was* turned out, on enlargement, to be a woman of understanding. At the moment, I confess, I appreciated little in his account of himself, except the desperateness of manner, as he strode back and forth and looked, when he looked in my direction at all, generally to one side or above me, as if I had become an aura, a priestess or, possibly, a judge, but not a discernible recognisable presence. My silence contributed to the liberty of his imagination. The logic of his discourse, as I say, escaped me. I heard him say I put him on his mettle . . . an expression that came through from a more general list of complaints. When I wondered at it, I realised that my *availability* was what put him on his mettle, and it brought to my cheeks a blush of shame. As quick as I am to anger, some inner regard for caution made me hear him to the end. After twenty minutes of tirade, his steps faltered, he faced me, stared, and let himself down into a chair. It was in a natural tone of voice that he said, without emphasis, but in weary conclusion, that a woman of my understanding must realise that he had fought his sexual feelings for so many years that now he was being fought by them. In dreams, he said, he conquered me with sufficient manly vigour. He had thought that his best chance effectively to realise his dreams was to possess me by surprise. But, each time he had tried, my complicity had panicked him. His dreams, false counsel, had prepared him for conquest of a woman, when, given his prolonged repression, such conduct was untrue to his character. He saw that his sole chance of success was to let himself be guided by me. He cast a look of apprehension at the door, as if some one might be standing behind it, listening. I assured him we were alone. He said he felt a fool at making such an unmanly confession. It was difficult enough to admit his inexperience without the dread of public exposure.

Last night, in his bed, like two children undressed, and shivering from cold, we clasped one another with such sweet pleasure, as I guided him to re-enact the spirit of his dreams, that never shall we know who was the sounder tutor—those dreams or my gentle guidance. A grey-streaked dawn struck his window, as we lay side by side, unwilling to be separated by sleep, speaking low, only dimly preserving in memory the considerable obstacle that had held us apart and which, upon sufficient pressure, like a wall that lists and sways, finally gave way.

My only concern to day—a day devoted to pondering—is whether my dearest friend has been subject to renewed castigations from his prevailing principles. I shall, now fairly four o'clock, have to write and ask.

MW TO WG

August 22, 1796

I am some times painfully humble—Write me; but a line, just to assure me, that you have been thinking of me with affection, now and then—since we parted—

WG TO MW

August 22, 1796

Humble! for heaven's sake, be proud, be arrogant! You are—but I cannot tell you what you are. I cannot yet find the circumstance about you that allies you to the frailty of our nature. I will hunt it out.

August 23, 1796

In the midst of our struggle, there seemed no way for us to speak simply with one another. We were caught in the confines of con-

vention's web. I do believe that until one can speak out openly
of sexual feelings, no one of us will have any but false ideals. It
also strikes me, not for the first time, how alarmingly vulnerable
and falsely instructed will be any sensibility formed by the common run of fiction. It caricatures human nature. It pampers
the passions. It overstretches sensibilities already weakened by
false refinement. I see now how the conduct of Imlay conformed
to a style of behaviour I was taught to admire, not by experience,
but by the example of idolatry in literary work—my predilection
for a man of his character all unconsciously prepared for by my
tears on reading "Clarissa." With Clarissa, seduced by Lovelace,
I formed a kind of readiness to recognise brutality and selfishness
as virile qualities conducive to heightened romance. No where—
no where in any single novel that I can think of, and I have now
sat racking my memory—is there the model of love between two
equal independent beings—such as, *I swear*, Godwin and Mary
shall be!

MW TO WG

August 24, 1796

As you are to dine with Mrs. Perfection to day, it
would be dangerous, not to remind you of my existence
—perhaps—a word then in your ear—Should you forget,
for a moment, a possible *accident* with the most delightful woman in the world, your fealty, take care not to look
over your left shoulder—I shall be there—
Wednesday

WG TO MW

I will report my fealty this evening. Till then farewell.

August 25, 1796

Thursday——
We have a language which only we discern. To be *kind* leads us
to *philosophise* and, when all is said and done, to feeling very *gai*.
Godwin last night had removed his spectacles, a preliminary ges-

ture to announce his rising ardour. I shall pass over the remainder of the scene a curtain of modesty, except to remark that, so piercing an outcry did I involuntarily utter near midnight, it brought hurrying footsteps into the corridor. It was Marguerite, put in mind perhaps of those bygone days when I would faint and injure myself, who had risen at my cry; but the remembrance of the ruddy good health of my appearance these last several weeks stopped her and made her tiptoe off—the light from her candle fading from the crack beneath the door of my bedchamber—her discretion provoking my smile upon the pillow. William had already half fallen into childish slumber, one arm outflung. I listened for a while to his even sonorous breathing; and shortly also fell asleep.

M W TO W G

August 26, 1796

I seem to want encouragement—I therefore send you my M.S. though not all I have written. Say when—or where, I am to see you Godwin.
Friday.

August 27, 1796

I enter the parlour to find every pillow overturned, windows wide, Mary with her hair tied up brandishing a feather-duster—so much disorder that I can barely make out a clear path to my work-table. Upstairs I find Fanny under the bed-covers with little Lucas. I ask what they are doing and in return get gales of childish laughter. To rout them out of bed, I have to promise they can play draughts on a little table at the bedside. Lucas has determined to teach the game to Fanny. It doesn't seem to matter to him that she is two and a half and he a grown boy of seven. She follows him in that precipitous way that worries me when, racing after birds or butterflies, I fear she will rush unawares under a team of horses or into the brook on the Green, so single-minded is she in the pursuit of a thing she fancies. It is more than a fancy she has for Lucas: he is the light of her life. Indeed, with every sign of budding male pride, he seems to know he need only strut by to arouse her admiration. In his fine straight carriage you can see he has sported in the open air, raced in green fields, climbing trees, leaping streams, practising his strength in all sorts of strenuous ways. His grandmother in Devon can no longer keep him, having suffered an attack of dropsy in the chest; so Mary—who has come to keep house for me, since it is more than Marguerite can manage —has begged me to let her have the boy with her till she can settle on where to apprentice him. My household grows. Failing, because of it, to find even a small corner to myself this morning, I decide to go out for air and exercise. Godwin says he prefers to walk with a purpose, and that we might pay some calls together on foot, which, really, except for a matter of phrasing, amounts to the same notion.

MW TO WG

August 27, 1796

The wind whistles through my trees. What do you say to our walk? Should the weather continue uncertain suppose you were to bring your tragedy here—and we shall be so snug—yet, you are such a kind creature, that I am afraid to express a preference—lest you should think of pleasing me rather than yourself—and is it not the same thing?—For I am never so well pleased with myself, as when I please you—I am not sure that please is the exact word, to explain my sentiments—may I trust you to search in your own heart for the proper one?

Saturday morning   Mary

WG TO MW

Your proposal meets the wish of my heart: I called at half after two yesterday to obtain this point from you.

August 28, 1796

Some times, listening to Godwin recount his round of visits, I am amazed that he has a chance to think, let alone to feel, in a day so teeming with society. I need blank space, untolled hours, when I want to think. On the contrary, he thrives on time diligently spent in the study, followed by a round of visits, which he says provide effective stimulation to his thoughts. An idea generating in his mind is borne from one friend to another, and yet to a third till, by acceptance or resistance, the notion becomes as smooth and clean and sparkling as a pebble that has been rolled in the tides of the sea. Discourse in this useful manner first became a habit when he conceived of writing "Political Justice"—speaking it to the publisher Robinson, to Holcroft and to others, before settling down to the writing. I am used to hearing about the virtual parade of young men who call in the hope of finding moral improvement at his feet, and who go off huddling their benefit behind refined, reflective faces. There is an entire brotherhood of them. I can't seem to sort them out by name—Stoddart, Hazlitt, Coleridge, Dyer—since they bear as much of a family resemblance as peas in a pod, but I plan some day to make a thorough examination to distinguish them. Godwin pays his feminine friendships conscientious attention. He dons a ruffled shirt and is off in a quick no-nonsense stride that eschews dalliance till his destination is reached. Once there, gallantry, philosophy and tea all blend in one exquisite aroma. All his women seem to write: Mary Hays her novel; Amelia Alderson a play; Mrs. Inchbald, the queen of the lot, of course, the most famous writer among them— I refuse to say *us*; a certain saintly Mrs. Reveley distinguishes herself solely by reading what the others write; I have not yet met her, nor Mrs. Fenwick, who is also writing, though it is not clear quite what. But, of them all, it is the celebrated Mrs. Robinson who is Godwin's plum: the most beautiful woman on whom he has ever laid eyes.

With the wind whistling, we determined yesterday upon a destination that would provide both utility and pleasure, Godwin deciding he would present me to his famous friend. We started off at a rapid pace that made me wonder if she might, had we tarried, vanish into thin air. Despite all the disadvantages of woman's clothing, I kept up, arriving panting at a large door, painted white, with an enraged lion clenching a brass ring in its jaws. From his extravagant eulogiums I had expected some still visible sign of physical beauty but, and it only adds to the sweetness of his character, it is more a moral perception of beauty, and the effect of still considerable charm that meets the eye. Ravages from illness and the use of laudanum are hard to hide; not to speak of time's hand. Her daughter, a pretty girl of twenty named Maria, let us into a room crammed with French furnishings so ornate that, at first, I failed to make out that there was any one there, save a white hound that had pricked up its ears at our entrance and lifted to look us over. On a sofa, in a dress of pale lilac lustring and a profusion of lilac ribbands, lay Mrs. Robinson, quite still, watching us approach.

So it was here that Godwin, chin in hand, comes to listen to a tale of life's persevering malignity from lips as delicate as a rose-bud, in a voice faintly lisping, distinctly *vieux style*. For all his egalitarian views, he has a weakness for wealth, power and prestige. I have heard him extol the virtue of what he calls *sitting loose to life,* in readiness to sacrifice every thing one possesses to the public good; he swears to all his ardent young men that such conduct will prove an uncommonly exquisite source of happiness. Yet how he sits loose to *luxury!* I am more fiercely a leveller than he, for finery brings to my mind the misery of the general populace; not that I am unfamiliar with luxury, but am unfriendly to it. I had to force myself into the conversation, with a French phrase here, a bit of literary allusion there, as if to give me *body*, as mantua-makers say, when they line some limply hanging silk with stiffening. I wished, I suppose, in just such a way to *stand out.*

Above us, from all four walls, portraits in heavily gilded frames gazed down. A moment more, I thought, and I shall be *écrasée*. I raised my glance to a pair of eyes which seemed to have been directly gazing at me and, with a start, recognised Mrs. Robinson, in muff and bonnet, fair and young. It would seem, from the style of the portrait, painted by Romney, who always has a way of catching his subjects *sur le vif*. Could she have been at the time of the portrait more than twenty, the age her Maria is now? Indeed they have a similar softness. What in heaven and on earth had I expected to find? Certainly not such a frank and unsuspicious regard, nor open, guileless gaze; not from a woman of fashion; not from Garrick's once breath-taking Perdita; not from one whose Florizel had been no less than the Royal Prince. Up there upon the wall sat a lovely, still young woman with vivid complexion, caught eternally as once she had been—while down below lay an ill, middle-aged, abandoned woman.

I felt a seizure of shame to have appeared so stiff, when it might be seen as a sort of flaunted moralising manner. Unwittingly I had behaved in a way that reminded me of Mrs. Siddons or Mrs. Inchbald. For to avoid any stigma attached to the stage, they are conspicuously reserved where there is a breath of a suspicion of scandal. What would they have made of Mrs. Robinson? Lifting their skirts as they wheeled round, turning their backs, would have had some thing reminiscent of the way one saves one's hem from mud in crossing streets: they *cross life* in such a manner. Mrs. Siddons, of course, is bound to keep up appearances for the sake of her daughters. In such roles as Milwood, the wily courtesan, which I hear she plays with all the allurements of a supreme seductress, she must guard a reputation so absolute that no one in her audience need hiss through a fan. But such constant concern, it seems to me, must finally take away from one's humanity. Was I not in every bit as false a position in life as Mrs. Robinson? Who of us can cast the first stone? I felt ill at the thought that my silence might have given the least twinge of pain to a woman whom I had no reason to despise.

But by this time, in order not too much to tire his friend, Godwin was ready to depart. The tiny hand slipped into mine seemed very frail indeed. And the narrowness of the close-set grey eyes gave me the impression of some one about to swoon into lifelessness. On the street, Godwin confided that the opulence of the quarters, in which Mrs. Robinson and her daughter live, is built on sand. Installments of her pension of 500*l.* have been so long suspended that she is head over ears in accommodation bills and, at this very moment, 1,200*l.* in debt. She must daily contrive to keep bond creditors from falling upon her like a pack of wolves. The Prince refuses communication. Appeals for the continuance of the pension capitalising on her royal amour is to be taken up by Parliament—in the meanwhile, she is hounded by tradesmen.

All the world once craned its neck for a sight of a woman who now gallantly keeps up her spirit by scribbling. Godwin gives what practical literary advice he can—perhaps only flattery, for he is unable to be heartlessly honest, where it concerns the fair.

Thus for our visit.

August 29, 1796

Monday—

I had Marguerite prepare for dinner yesterday a *gigot* with broad
beans, such as was my standing dish among the Havrais, and a rich
batter pudding with gooseberry jam. Godwin was on hand and
our mutual friend Twiss who, tall and emaciated, would seem to
have no appetite for any thing but snuff, which he immoderately
consumes, all the while nervously conversing in his high, nasal
whine of a voice. He is a type that we English produce, like some
rarefied long-stalked plant cultivated for its orchidaceous bloom.
When not quoting Shakespear, whom he has reduced to knowing
by heart—for he is an actor *manqué*—he loves to recount back-
stage gossip. But it was not Drury Lane gossip this time that was
under discussion, but the subject of marriage. I have always known
Twiss to be against all principles of monogamy, but yesterday,
warming to his subject with the wine, he gave Godwin and me
certain precise anatomical details in proof that sexual union can
never be governed by the state. His libertinism finds, of course,
no agreement in Godwin. Twiss is deceived if he assumes that a
man, who would innovate the current moral standards placed upon
the union between the sexes, must be a libertine. I felt helpless
at the turn of the conversation. I managed, however, by a remark
that broadened the topic, to halt Twiss from hurtling down the
by-ways of the Vale of Tempe, like some maddened, cloven-
hooved creature. With redeeming good sense he perceived his
mistake and, covering his chin in his long bony fingers, inaudibly
mumbled some thing sounding like an apology. I could see that
Godwin was wondering how to make the conversation more general. He did so by offering his opinion that mankind ultimately
would reach a point when, as I had so nicely expressed it in the
last line of my novel "Mary," *there is neither marrying, nor giving
in marriage*. I had meant, of course, in heaven. But Godwin took
its meaning in the sense of his own strongest assumptions. He
foresees, in some utopian time to come, that mankind, having
reached the limit of population, will refuse to propagate. We shall
then not have to begin at the beginning, but, living by reason,

shall live for ever. Death will be an accident. Sexual union will be unnecessary. An exclamation broke from Twiss. To soothe him, Godwin hastened to add that it was only an enlightened ideal, in no imminent danger of realisation. We went together, all three, to Mrs. Siddons', where Twiss with a goatish leer dallied with a young actress upon a window-seat in full view of the company.

MW TO WG

August 29, 1796

I will come and dine with you to day, at half past four or five. You shall read your tragedy to me, & drive clear out of my mind all the sensations of *disgust*, which I brought home with me last night.

Twiss put you out of conceit with women, and he led my imagination to trace the fables of the Satyrs to their source.

Monday   Mary

MW TO WG

August 30, 1796

I send no Amulet to day: but beware of enchantments —Give Fanny a biscuit—I want you to love each other—

August 31, 1796

Such a charming letter this morning from Amelia Alderson—the Belle of Norwich, as Godwin says she is called—who had to leave London a fortnight ago at a call from her father who had fallen ill. She writes of an amiable clever friend of hers, on the point of bringing forth her first child, who is desirous to know in detail my means of inuring Fanny to thin clothing in our cold climate. She says complimentary things, that give me a glow of pride and pleasure, about Fanny's admirably strong, well-formed limbs and florid complexion. One day, walking together in the fields, Fanny tore from my grasp to race after a butterfly. It led her a merry chase. And it made, for us behind, such a pretty scene: the child reaching in vain for the winged creature, her hair streaming, her light frock billowing out and the pink ribband round her waist like a porker's tail. It was then that Amelia Alderson first asked me what principle of child-rearing I followed. I said *my own*. It seems only natural to me to wish my child to be free and untrammelled. Light muslin does not hamper her movements, nor turn her into some overswaddled, shambling invalid. How horrified I was in Sweden at the sight of babes overloaded with flannels in the height of summer. I had wondered at seeing so few children in the villages. Indeed, they appear to have been nipt in the bud, rendered feeble by the continual perspiration they were kept in by the mistaken tenderness of mothers for ever spinning and knitting.

North American Indians raise their children, as I remember reading in Charlevoix, the missionary who shared their fire side, by letting them run free and scramble naked, even in the snow. Their bodies grow robust and supple. Freedom, always freedom, is the rule! The severest discipline the Jesuit Father could recall was when an Indian mother flicked a few drops of water into her child's face. There is no whipping. They are never made to sit still in silence, like a prisoner, as I remember being forced to do for hours on end; nor were the children at too young an age expected to behave like their elders. And yet, when grown, they are said to be remarkably disciplined. I have never believed in violent methods of breaking either children or horses. I do not see the necessity of force, when humanity and steadiness prove more effective. The rearing of children has the purpose of laying a foundation of health in mind and body. Fear shall never achieve that result.

How tragic it is that here in London almost half the infants die before the age of five. My eyes begin to well with tears, remembering how my own poor child was stricken by the distemper at four months of age. Her fever rose so high that my hand on her brow burned as though I'd touched an oven. I sent the servant running through the streets of Havre for the doctor. When he came, he said I was to watch to see whether the fever decreased, at which time he would give her a potion. I was in despair. It was early in the morning. The doctor had said he would return the following day —but my child would be dead before he came back to succour her. Where I heard of the treatment that I then tried, I cannot say, but I determined to nurse my infant through her illness. I was brought basins of warm water into which I plunged her. Whether from prayer or these ablutions, the fever was low next morning and the child resting easily by the time the doctor returned.

I have heard of treatment which is said to be taken by the Turks, almost by way of diversion, as we take the waters in our country, that has rendered harmless the pox which is so fatal among us and, when not fatal, disfiguring. Old women, whose trade it is, come about after the heat of summer among parties of children, made up for the purpose with a nutshell full of the best sort of small-pox, putting as much as can adhere to the point of a needle into the veins, which they open, but which is supposed to give no more pain than a common scratch. On the eighth day the children, who have been playing together, are seized by the fever and have running sores. But in two days they are well again, without scars.

I wonder how society can expect healthy offspring, when it condones the fashion of mothers sending their babes at birth to a nurse to be suckled, thence straight to boarding-school. To be a good mother a woman must have common sense—or she is liable to bear close resemblance to those ignorant village women all over Sweden who, spinning and weaving, by their very maternal tenderness murder their children.

I wanted my child to be free. I wanted her to be a free citizen in a free country. In the conviction that the cities of Europe have become stagnant and artificial, I wished her to grow in the simple rural life of America. In our little house in Havre, before Fanny took ill, even before her birth, I thrived on an imaginary project which consoled me for all the suffering of those unstable days in France. When alone in Imlay's absence, whenever he went away, dedicated to alum or soap or whatever, I would sit idly by the fire or lie abed late, reverting to a dream of our future family happiness, when all these separations would be over. I dreamed then of America. I saw us with our child in a settlement on the Ohio River, the slow brown moving stream of water reflecting straightly planted poplars on the banks, where our rustic house would stand amidst a luxuriant garden. I had heard so much of the territory. And I had, in furious endeavour, read accounts of discovery and settlement by such as Filson, Brissot, Charlevoix, Crèvecœur, Cooper, Jefferson, Franklin, to enable me to write from such

knowledge a book whose proceeds sent my brother to Philadelphia
and myself to Paris. Like a bird building its nest, one must have
bits and pieces to construct a desired reality. I was, as much as any
bird building its nest, determined to make a home for my child.
I took for straw almost any thing at all I had heard in conversation
at Barlow's of the business scheme he had been engaged upon—
selling tracts of land in the territory to aristocrats fleeing from
France: it was the first time in its short history that the United
States Government had been persuaded to sell land. Barlow as
agent of the Scioto Company had expected to gain millions in
the process, exciting at one time an equal expectation in Imlay
—the two of them plotting their transactions together like a pair
of scalp-merchants. I told myself that some day Imlay would grow
tired of the desire to amass an immense fortune, and be happy
with an independence—for it appears to me absurd to waste life
in preparing to live. Money, taking into account the future comforts it can procure, may be gained at too dear a rate. We lost
our dream into the bargain. And yet some times, even now, I find
myself glimpsing in my mind's eye that rustic cabin on the banks
of the river, as though it were a memory of an experience lived,
rather than a vivid contrivance of the imagination. The future in
store for us became almost more real than the life we lived together . . . which makes it seem to me that no one can tell the
story of another's life as well as the one who lives it. For what
transpires in the imagination, though it may be closed to others,
can be the determining part of one's existence. A young girl's love
is thus. She may appear milk-and-water—all the while building castles in the air from the vitality of feverish desires. It is my conviction now, on looking back, that some moments passed in France
were only bearable because of my dreams, when, on the one hand,
yawned the terror of my being recognised and arrested—particularly after the execution of Brissot and Condorcet, and the imprisonment of Paine—and, on the other, my fear of some thing equally
terrifying occurring to Imlay, whenever he was absent. During the
worst of it all, I was nourished by the intensity of building our
idyllic nest. That it never came to be, does not diminish its constructive influence upon a time that might have been bleaker, but
for those dreams. My poor mother had it in her head to emigrate
with her family, and used to tell us tales as children of the way

life would be, when we finally would be together in the new world. Thus in both her life and mine, America was the lure that allowed us to live with courage through hardship. A little patience, my mother would say. "A little patience," she said, a moment before she died.

MW TO WG

August 30, 1796

The weather, I believe, from the present appearance will not permit me to go out to dinner—If so you will call on me in your way home—will you not? You need not write—I shall take it for granted—

MW TO WG

August 31, 1796

Since you think that I mean to cheat you I send you a family present, given me, when I was let loose in the world—Look at the first page and return it—I do not intend to let you extend your skepticism to me—or you will fright away a poor weary bird who, taking refuge in your bosom, hoped to nestle there—to the end of the chapter.

The day is dreary. The Iron Chest must wait—Will you read your piece at your fire side or mine? And I will tell you in what aspect I think you a *little* unjust.

On second thoughts, I believe, I had better drink tea with you; but then I shall not stay late.

Yours,
Wednesday   Mary

September 1, 1796

Thursday
All day long, yesterday, I had been carrying on a pumped-up debate, as absurd an occupation as that of little Lucas when he plays draughts by himself in a corner of the kitchen, without pleasure,

since he can never enjoy the complete satisfaction of winning, but must lose each time as well. I am very put out with myself for having got into such a calamitous state. A passing remark of Godwin's, when he visited me the night before, had provoked my pique. I felt what he had said to be unjust. And all this dreary day I have wriggled and struggled to escape the trap of an adamantine chain of destiny which seems to bind me.

He had come to me bringing me the prompt book of "The Iron Chest," which he'd got from Sheridan. Last winter Kemble paid the dramatist Coleman 1,000*l.* to make an adaptation of Godwin's Caleb, leaving out all politics, but—either because of its length, as Godwin claims, or as Coleman claims because Kemble was so dosed with laudanum when he came on stage—the play died the death of a red-hot poker in water—one long hiss. Coleman has now taken it away from Drury Lane to give it to the Haymarket. Of course Godwin sees not a penny of the proceeds. He says, with hind-sight, he himself ought to have made a theatrical adaptation of his own novel, rather than to have let another make a fortune from it. The humiliation of having been in the theatre last March to witness what I have heard was a lurching, mumbling, unforgivable performance from Kemble—who, in his defence, says he rose from a sick-bed—urged Godwin to keep cosily at home with me the night of the Haymarket opening on Monday. Next morning I hastened to unfold the *Times*—before him, as is my habit—to see that there had been a crowded house whose general decision was of triumph for the new version of the play. I immediately sent round the paper, folded open at the review. And soon after, Godwin went out to get us seats for Saturday.

All of this has worked on his imagination in such a way as to make him wonder if he might not turn his hand to writing drama, while continuing the essays which grind laboriously slow, some times advancing only a page or a page and a half in an entire morning. He has begun to plot some scenes of a tragedy, bringing them to my fire side to read aloud. Having one afternoon browsed in Aristotle, after waking from a nap, sleep having overcome him, for sleep is never some thing gained, in his opinion, but rather some thing lost, he remarked that tragedy is a higher form than the epic, since it can say more in less space. Such condensation, he went on—now on his own, without the authority of the ancients—requires *a masculine state of mind*. He was striding up and down my parlour, as he likes to do to stimulate his thoughts. I was sitting under the lamplight, still holding "The Iron Chest." I felt—I cannot say why—a slow rise of anger.

I had yesterday sent Mary to Godwin's in the afternoon to scrub and polish, since his regular bed-maker is suffering from rheumatism in the knee. I am not overly fastidious, nor do I go in for finery in either clothes or furnishings, yet a certain amount of order soothes me. Godwin had lit the fire to take the chill from the air and turned up the lamp. After having dined with his publisher Robinson, he had called on Mrs. Inchbald, and then on Mary Hays. His little attentions in both their houses have made him an indispensable friend. It is curious how differently he characterises himself with each, as if the various parlours, large and small, into which he makes his entrances have become theatrical scenes, requiring an adjustment of roles. With Mrs. Inchbald he is an admiring gallant of the variety of large feathered hats that seem to be as much off the head, in slapping flourishes, as on. With Mary Hays he plays the somewhat gruff truth-teller, bassoon to her piccolo. While at Mrs. Robinson's he smooths his surface and subdues his voice to be a looking-glass of refinement. Amelia Alderson, most malicious where she knows it can do no harm, said to me once that Godwin is *a man after his own heart*. I know what she means: he will act according to principles which often ignore another's wants—but is pleased with himself, all the same. Last night, we were in very different moods, he all sparkling with vigour, while I drooped in a sickly qualm before the fire, chin in hand, and stared into the flames, as I listened to the wet logs hiss.

I had been quick to anger, the night before, at his saying that tragedy was too strenuous an exercise for females. Not that I deny the statement—*but must we for ever sit and listen to what all females are like?* We are apparently indistinguishable to men, though even grains of sand be infinitely variable in the eyes of the Lord. Godwin is unaccustomed to domestic intimacy—except for his mother in Norfolk, and his unmarried sister Hannah who lives in London. Yet his lack of experience does not seem to incapacitate him from making pronouncements on women that uphold every superstition about us which society seems to support. His obstinacy on the subject reminds me of Voltaire's sorry remark on the death of Mme. de Châtelet: "I have lost one who was my friend for twenty-five years, a great man, whose only defect was being a woman."

So much for philosophers—!!

We women who think are forced to choose between two absurdities that limit our actions and condemn our efforts: either we are different from men, hence inferior; or we are the same as men, only less able, therefore again inferior. Does difference necessarily mean deficiency? By a human standard that allows for variability, it would not be so. A quality such as "delicacy" would be seen as a positive quality, rather than be found wanting against the masculine attribute of "vigour." Why should "vigour" not be put against a standard by which "delicacy" is the desirable attribute— and thus be declared *lack of delicacy*? Yet neither, in truth, should be an absolute standard whereby to judge the other.

One would think that, if reasoning and logical analysis were the philosopher's art, philosophers would have swept away in the fresh wind of the exercise of their powers all the miserable prejudice binding women. But, no, their philosophy is meant for only one half of the human race. When Rousseau writes: *Man is born free, and every where he is in chains*, my heart, inasmuch as it is human, leapt in awesome recognition. Yet was I not to be told a few pages further on that man, meaning mankind, excludes women; that this separate species, a slave by nature, is meant to be subordinate to man? How could I then have been so in love with Rousseau?—why only, denying my sex, by reading what he said as having relevance *to me*, whether he wished it or not; and, for the rest, by treating what he said on the subject of women as nonsense. Dr. Johnson said Rousseau knew he spoke nonsense. "Why, Sir, a man who talks nonsense so well must know that he is talking nonsense."

I have known men who made the immense effort, against two or three thousand years of tradition, to reason away inherited prejudice. Tom Paine was such a man. His political convictions did not stop at the door of home or church. Every where, he said, women were adored and oppressed. Perceiving that the state of their education was largely at fault, he exhorted me to come to France with him to effect a national policy for equal education, pursuing the very great victories of the Revolution, convinced that what happened in France would have universal application. So much faith did he have in the new France that the 10,000*l*. he earned from "The Rights of Man" he donated to the French nation. And Condorcet, a kindly man, encouraged by his wife, hoped at the time to enact legislation for granting women full political rights, but his voice rose, singularly alone, without an echo. He was sadly disheartened by the adamant resistance to all his efforts. Yet in conversation he continued to turn away every common prejudice, saying, when it was said that women had not the reason of men, that *they had, however, their own*. Thus have I met men whose rational faculties conformed to justice. But more often, when I have known a man well enough to presume reasoning powers that would lift him above all vulgar prejudice, some small incident, some spontaneous remark, even a witticism by which he expected to arouse laughter, would cause my aspiration for mutual understanding to evaporate like dew before a scorching sun. No man, it seems, can imagine how our self-confidence vanishes at the pointed finger which ridicules our *human* efforts. A gallery of misogynists is for ever on the watch. What made my head so heavy in my hands, as I stared into Godwin's fire, was the thought that still once again, here where I had so comfortably nestled, yawned the oubliette of all hope.

I had written in my note that I thought him a *little* unjust. He now begged me to state my case, placing in my hand a cup of tea —for I have been a decidedly corruptive influence on his manners. I began by saying that a certain attitude seemed to run throughout his general conversation. Had he not been aware of wounding me when, on the subject of tragedy, he had felt obliged to point out that it was a form of writing in which no woman could compete? Godwin looked astonished. He said, guilelessly, that no woman could write with the magnitude of a Sophocles or a Shakespear—that none had. I agreed. Few men had. We sat on, in silence. But if you are in accord with me . . . ? he questioned. And I hastened to say that I was. For how could woman, poorly educated as she generally was, kept in the house, when men were free to roam wherever they fancied, forced to think that the end of all learning was merely to please a man—how could she possibly be an equal to genius? But to blame woman for what man binds her to be . . . ! Drawing himself up on a subject about which he is supposed to have some authority, Godwin said that, inasmuch as women receive a less intellectual education, they are more unreservedly under the empire of feelings that are liable to become a source of erroneous thinking. Did I not see that false sentiment must always follow a partial education? I did see—with a sense of injustice that brought tears to my eyes. Arguments will always end thus. We are educated only partially because we are physically weak; and then that very neglect in education unfits us for intellectual distinction. I winked back tears. Nothing would enable me to jump the obstacle of that traditional belief that *all men*, brazenly partaking of the genius of Shakespear and Sophocles and who-all-not, shall always be defined as reasonable, controlled, logical, knowledgeable, unemotional, courageous and consistent . . . whereas, *all women* . . . but what is the use of reiteration? Men wish to keep us in the dark—slaves and playthings.

September 2, 1796

I have been recollecting the time I had to go to Hull to find a vessel for Sweden. Finding one, I was forced to wait while it loaded its cargo, so that I spent some three weeks there, six days of it riding at anchor, waiting for the wind to change, surrounded by mist and water, while the ship sat heavily in the tide, weighed down with lead from Derbyshire, butter from North Riding, cheeses brought down the Trent, and corn from several outlying counties. The fleets from Hull were frequently a hundred sail at a time. I remember as a child the excitement of inspecting the barrels and bales on the docks, trying to imagine whether they contained Muscovy yarn, fish from Greenland or tobacco from the West Indies, imagining that I stood at the very confluence of the world—such is the grandiose notion of childhood. One day at Hull the physician and his wife took me in their carriage to Beverly, where I had lived till the age of fifteen. I found that many of the inhabitants in the town had remained in the same houses ever since I had left. I could not help wondering how they could thus have vegetated, while I was running over the world of sorrow, snatching at pleasure, and throwing off prejudice. Time had stopped in Beverly; the same old woman was sitting at the corner beyond the ironmonger's working on her bone-lace. The town appeared diminutive. Still the very familiarity of the streets elated my heart. When I came to the Common, I could have kissed the chickens that pecked the ground; I longed to pat the cows and frolic with the dogs that sported there. I gazed with delight at the windmill, and thought it lucky that it should be in motion at the moment I passed by. Entering the dear green lane which I had often gone down, I anticipated and then delighted to hear the familiar sounds from the rookery, even while my eyes sought the spire that then appeared over the withered tops of the aged elms. Then I thought to myself: Ah! if only I might return to childhood once more, regain the sanity and purity of feelings I knew in this little village . . .

It is woman's fate to live by an illusion that romance shall lead to happiness; then, not finding it, to sentimentalise childhood. We women are idiots. For ever in bondage, we end up perpetual minors. How on earth shall I instruct Fanny to live a life in which her mind—what mind is left to her to have—will not be imprisoned in its own little tenement? Shall I, like Lady Montagu, worrying over the future of her grand-daughter, hold her to the one absolute necessity, which is to conceal whatever learning she attains, with as much solicitude as she would hide the crookedness of a crippled limb; for attainment in our society can only draw down envy and hatred. Am I to teach my child that the female sex is in so unfortunate a state that the only means of making herself and others happy is by complaisance, subterfuge and all that sort of thing? The evils women endure degrade them so far—as almost to justify men's tyranny.

When a woman is married, she must bear every thing, for she is her husband's property. Yet what alternative has she? What profession is open to her? Schoolteacher, governess, milliner or mantua-maker, to make fans, artificial flowers and stays; or she may keep house for an aging father, or for her brother, if he will have her. When I left Bath to attend my mother in her illness, and when she then died, I imagined I might earn my bread by painting or needlework, and that my sister Bess and I, with economy, might together live on a guinea a week. My angelic friend Fanny, so dear to my heart, who was to live with us, thought our chances best if we could somehow raise the money to stock a small haberdashery.

The uncertain employment of artistic work seemed to her a plan with little chance of gaining the subsistence of even half a guinea a week a piece to pay for furnished lodgings, where the three of us could pig together. The following spring Fanny married. And my two sisters and I started the ill-fated school. When it failed, nothing remained but for us to look for our livelihood to the position of governess. And what can an unmarried woman of the poorer class do?—why, wash, if she can get it, from one in the morning till eight at night *for twenty pence a day.*

I have written "The Rights of Woman," now I shall write of their wrongs, to show how flagrant is a system of law that makes a woman unable to divorce an unprincipled man, nor lawfully to obtain custody of her child. She cannot even keep from her husband—who may be a drunkard or gambler—what money she earns by her own exertions. When my poor sister Bess was driven by a condition near madness to leave her husband, she could not take her child—for she would have been hunted down like a felon. As it was, while I accompanied her by coach from her husband's house, I was afraid she was going into one of her flights. Losing all presence of mind, she chewed her wedding-ring to bits. Like an outlaw, she then had to hide for months. If she had appealed to the law to sue for divorce, the pronouncement that would have been given, I can well imagine.

Judge: How's that? Now, what did she say? We want no new-fangled notions here in our court, if you please. I won't have it. We do not want French principles in either public or private life, if you please. Why, heavens, if women were allowed to plead their feelings, as an excuse or a . . . heavens! palliation of infidelity, it would open a flood-gate for immorality. What virtuous woman ever thinks of her feelings? It is her duty to love and obey the man chosen. The conduct of the plaintiff does not appear that of a person of sane mind. Not at all, as a matter of fact. No, no, I will listen no further. Why, never could too many restrictions be thrown in the way of divorce, if we wish to maintain the sanctity of marriage. (*Benign smile.*) And though the law might bear a little hard on a few, a very few individuals, it was (*raising his hands in benediction*) evidently for the good of the whole of society. APPEAL DENIED!

September 3, 1796

This morning being a lovely Saturday, the sun is shining through my windows—one of those unaccountable fortunes of Judd Place is the way the sun rises and holds in sight all morning, and half the afternoon. By mid-morning the sun is sufficiently high to be out of my eyes, yet brilliantly floods the Bowling Green across the way. I would never be one to work with my back to the window. One would miss too much of life. I can sit and watch, in perfect absorption for minutes on end, whomever passes. My mind floats from subject to subject; at one moment, seeing a chip cap and apron on an elderly woman, my thoughts are captivated by fashion; another moment, spotting some gesture or slight change of expression on a passer-by who has no notion of being watched, the pain of living becomes my theme, my own sighs finally rousing me. But now I must cease dreaming and, in the little time left to think, put my ideas into order, must try and see in cloud-like formations the substance of a book. Maria, at the heart of it, has my sensibility, and poor Bess' circumstances. Of her marriage it may be said, as Mrs. Siddons put it, when she played Calista: "Hearts like ours were paired . . . not matched." Once married, she finds her husband does not wish to become either friend or confidant. I shall take as the basis of character of the husband the most outrageous aspects of Imlay, even some of his business dealings. In the same way that it took time to begin to understand the extent of his fraudulent speculations, so Maria will at first ignore her husband's swindles and spendthrift habits. I shall put it all in—how he used to buy goods on credit to sell for ready cash. And the promissory notes! He required such stimulus of hope and fear, produced by wild speculations, to enliven his spirits. The libertinism of his habits had jaded his senses. Yes, I have the husband out of whole cloth; I know each stitch of him like a Spitalfield weaver his wares. But that the world may not seem too black, I have drawn an uncle, infinitely kind and loving, who sees Maria's marriage as the abject condition it is; as I write of him, he begins to resemble no one as much as Mr. Johnson. At the very centre of the book is Fanny, who when not bounding into the room to pull on my sleeve, begging me to play, dwells in my heart. This book will be written for my unfortunate girl, that she may know what transpired between the two creatures, man and woman, who gave her life. Some day she shall read what I have written and understand. But I hear her pounding down the stairs. In another moment she shall fling herself upon me—for I promised to take her to the Green, together with her monkey. And *my* promissory notes have bottom, so . . . away!

Saturday night——

We have been to see "The Iron Chest." We went with Miss Hays and several of the virtual parade, one of whom uttered not a word all evening, looking on from large, liquid eyes. Godwin wore his green coat and crimson under-waistcoat. He bowed to those who waved and leaned over the side of the box to shake hands, till by quarter past six it seemed no one cared if the curtain went up or not. Many of his friends had come, for this, I believe, is the second performance, few reasonable men having risked the first. Godwin sat striking the program, rolled like a baton, into the palm of one hand, his ears buzzing with excitement, for when I posed a question, he answered me in a way that made no sense at all. Ever susceptible to praise as he is, there has seldom occurred such a public display of it. He sat there, a meaningless smile on his lips, and waved, in a way that reminded me of the time I saw the Prince of Wales acknowledge his subjects through the window of his carriage. Mr. Wilcooke, sitting on my right, presented me to a Mr. Dying or Dyer, who had stepped into the box to greet Godwin and who struck me as having a conspicuously bright and wicked eye. Godwin's good friend Holcroft rushed up with his usual energy and cheerfulness, by his rapid banter making Godwin break into smiles, despite himself, for he had been making every effort to school his demeanour into an appearance of philosophical sobriety. Holcroft's blunt manner is not to be schooled; nor his words which run like a river, and sparkle with poetic passages. He is an original and curious man. Godwin tells me he is suffering from a terrible depression over the difficulties of getting his plays produced—but then what magnanimity in his exuberance over his friend's success!

Both have suffered these last two years from their politics. Holcroft's "Man of Ten Thousand Faces," presented in January by Drury Lane, played only seven performances, its success impeded, his friends say, by the public's prejudice. How cruel an injustice has been done to him by being released prior to standing trial! Having been accused of high treason, it would have been only just that he be publicly heard in his own defence. As it is, he is every where branded *an acquitted felon*, his name an object of suspicion and alarm. But he will not be silenced—believing the stage the surest means of teaching moral and political truths. It would be so, I dare say, if the Lord Chamberlain were not standing in the way. What times we live in! That writers, and those who publish their writings, should be so singled out for these flagitious charges. Godwin was spared only because Pitt saw no possible popular influence from any book which cost as much as three guineas—the price of a copy of "Political Justice." The stage has no business with politics, Coleman has written, when he wrote to tell the public how the play, when first staged, came to fall to pieces, after four days' wear; he has the temerity also to say he hopes Godwin will discover no intentional injury in the omissions, compressions and alterations made to fit the story to the stage. What can one say to such brazenness!

Only Ellison's presence as Sir Edward Mortimer—all an uphill part, in the Green-Room phrase—brought life to the exertions on the stage. I peered once into Godwin's face, but, for all I could tell, he sat as equably as if sitting to Romney or Reynolds. I suppose he was pleased. I was not. The part of the novel that stays in mind with an excess of horror is when, unable to prove his innocence, Caleb is cast into prison. How a man in such circumstances was to live day by day, without external sources, solitary, having nothing beyond the stores of his own mind and memory, was a unique act of its author's invention. The theatre can express none of this—only melodramatic stage-effects in a dreary chain of events. It would have been treasonous to have exposed what lay at the heart of the book—that it is impossible in our society, with things as they are, for a poor man to obtain justice.

To make room for those who came to pay their respects to Godwin during the first intermission, I asked Mr. Wilcooke to accompany us outside the box. We made a slow promenade up the red rug. I was wearing a plain silk dress with a white lawn cloak, bordered with lace, for to dress violently neither suits my inclination nor my purse. It pleases me none the less to be a spectator of some of the exuberant displays of women of fashion. I saw one young woman dressed *à la Turque* and admired the freedom and grace of the loose trousers, for it is a style that is catching on. A joke makes the rounds that compares the freedom the fair sex may enjoy in such easy, graceful dress to the danger that men may take a hint from Turkish customs and attempt to deprive women of some of the freedoms permitted them, and shut them into harems. However, I have heard the women of that particular country defended by one who has lived among them, and who thought them the freest in the world, having even visited them in their *bagnios* where they loll about in a perfectly natural state, and where they seemed far less ludicrous than Frenchwomen with their curled, short hair, powdered white round faces, shining with red japan, rather like the faces of sheep. The Revolution got rid of the excesses of such artificiality. Fear of invasion in France made the women stand by their men with muskets, dressed for the advent of danger. I did see amazing styles of dress during those days, all hampering contrivance of costume thrown off until, inevitable as the coming of winter, Robespierre abolished the bands of women, as he abolished so much that was truly revolutionary. From such experience I predict Turkish trousers will go the way of most freedoms—ridiculed out of style.

Earlier this week, according to the *Times*, Mother Windsor with three of her *pupils* had appeared in one of the most conspicuous boxes here in the Haymarket. Once seated, there was little the box-keeper could do. Men of the world, not above consorting with prostitutes privately, made an uproar at their public appearance. Not only is the presence of *impures* the subject of general complaint against the summer theatre managers—the winter managers handle such things better—but also every where lounging puppies lean against the columns in the vestibule, making loud, impertinent remarks to one another. Two of them, flamboyantly dressed, not even bothering to speak behind their hands, made a distinctly vulgar comment about Mary Hays' dress, which was of shell pink, cut low, and cinched below the bosom. She made a pretence of having heard nothing. But as we were climbing some stairs to return to our box, one of the young men pressed up against her, as if by accident. To evade his insult she made a sudden sidewise motion, landing on the edge of the step in such a way as to twist her ankle. Once seated, we saw that it had begun to swell. Such indecent conduct begins to be general, not only in the corridors, but during performances which, time and again, are interrupted by jeers audible to all. I am going on at some length about the events of the evening because of some thing said by Godwin which arose from these social circumstances and which, baldly stated, would lose all meaning.

We had gathered for the second half of the play. The performers held my attention, because I feared if I looked away an instant, letting my thoughts wander, I would never again pick up the thread of the action. The sombrousness of the last act must have pleased the taste of the audience for, when the curtain fell, they united in loud applause. I said to Godwin, when I thought I could be heard, that even with all Coleman had left out, there was still enough left *in* to make a stirring narrative. Mary Hays leaned forward to add her compliments. Godwin then said—to one of us, I know not which—that his strong conceptual groundwork had outlasted all permutation, whereas, he added—and needn't have —our work, meaning Miss Hays' and mine, was so largely personal that it would not have outlived such a transformation. He may have made the remark in jest. It was really all he said. Once again we were surrounded by well-wishers. But he had said some thing similar to me when he had called for me.

It had not been the most appropriate time to start speaking on the subject of my M.S. Already late, we had had to rush to a hackney-stand. Godwin had let his head roll back against the cushions to regard the pedestrian traffic through the little window, his face turned away, as he spoke. He had just finished reading the advice given my daughter, on the supposition that death might snatch me from her before I could properly fortify her mind. He had found the form exquisite. Some of the poignant passages about my early youth had reminded him of "Mary," as well they should, since in both instances I draw from my own precious experience of childhood—though there is less transposition or invention in the present M.S., motivated as I am that Fanny should know the absolute truth of things which concern her. For her I wrote of the cruel restraints of my childhood and of the warm sunshine of romance which so dazzled eyes blinded by illusion. I even drew on Imlay's history in America, when he had had a commission in the Army, and referred to the life of libertinism he'd lived in London. I am not the first woman, I am sure—though I have never seen such a description in any novel—whose husband, as she is his legal property, tried to turn his wife over to the use of another man *to pay off a business debt*. I imagine I have drawn a picture of marriage more realistically than usually portrayed—it was my pride to have done so. Godwin, in a voice turned avuncular, expressed doubts, not at the exactitude of the novel's correspondence to real life, but that the picture it drew was too personal, singular and, he was led to believe, sentimental. There was no universal principle governing it. I was telling a story on the presumption that such personal revelations might interest and inform the general public. But my tale was too paltry—too paltry and too personal. There was a flaw in the very concept of it. He suspected I had flung words on paper without necessary preliminary preparation. He would have me make a rational plan in advance, which would afford scope for my narrative, by situating it against a background of dramatic social circumstances—perhaps using the French Revolution, a background about which I had some direct experience, or the events that had transpired in America.

But that is not the book I want to write!! I want to write of a woman's marriage to a man under our present system of legal bondage. I cannot suppose any situation more desperate than for a woman of sensibility and education—or, at least, if not education, a mind avid for improvement—to be bound for life to such a man as I have described. It is a subject personal *to millions of women*. What is usually termed "great misfortune" in novels may more forcibly impress the mind of common readers—with stage-effects to raise the hackles of the hair—but what I have in mind is to show the lack of liberty in the lives of ordinary women. The French Revolution can wait! *And* America! Marriage is in such a sorry state that it must find a voice raised in protest. To be a woman is to inhabit territory infested by mephitic fog.

Our language is hesitancy. When we speak from experience, we are told to speak of other less trivial things. In the end, we conform to what is expected of us, resigning ourselves to silence; or, like slaves, exchanging our stories in secret among ourselves—changing nothing in the every-day world. This is the way it has been for as long as history—but avaunt! ye waking dreams! it need not be so!

Sitting here under the lamplight in the silence of the night, when all are abed, I falter and grow afraid. For an hour no carriage has passed. With half an ear I had been listening for the clipclop of horses' hooves that might have brought Godwin to me from Mary Hays'. It is true that her ankle visibly swelled and grew inflamed, but it seems to me that she exaggerated her incapacity, quick to take advantage of Godwin's offer to see her home. So successfully have we kept from her, and others, the truth of our liaison that it begins to be an inconvenience. I would have liked to continue the conversation begun in the carriage. But to keep up appearances, I had to smile and say a good night to the hobbling invalid, leaning on Godwin's arm, with her look of a cat who has swallowed a canary. It irritates me that she intuitively understands all, yet makes the pretence of concealing understanding, in order to spare herself from a truth which might be painful —in the same way that she refused to acknowledge overhearing in the vestibule of the theatre any ridicule. Once and for all I must clear up the ambiguity, for it serves her purposes too well.

M W T O W G

September 4, 1796

Labouring all the morning, in vain, to overcome an oppression of spirits, which some things you uttered yesterday produced; I will try if I can to shake it off by describing to you the nature of the feelings you exerted.

I allude to what you remarked, relative to my manner of writing—that there was a radical defect in it—a worm in the bud, etc.—what is to be done, I must either disregard your opinion, think it unjust, or throw down my pen in despair; and that would be tantamount to resigning existence; for at fifteen I resolved never to marry from interested motives, or to endure a life of dependence. You know not how painfully my sensibility, call it false if you will, has been wounded by some of the steps I have been obliged to take for others. I have even now plans at heart, which depend on my exertions, and my entire confidence in Mr. Imlay plunged me into some difficulties, since we parted, that I could scarcely do away with. I know that many of my cares have been the natural consequence of what nine out of ten would have termed folly—yet I cannot coincide in the opinion, without feeling a contempt for mankind. In short, I must reckon on doing some good, and getting the money I want by my writings, or go to sleep for ever. I shall not be content merely to keep body and soul together—By what I have already written Johnson, I am sure, has been a gainer: and, for I would wish you to see my heart and mind just as it appears to myself without drawing any veil of affected humility over it; though this whole letter is a proof of painful diffidence, I am compelled to think there is some thing in my writings more valuable than in the productions of some people on whom you bestow warm eulogies—I mean more mind—denominate it as you will —more of the observations of my own senses, more of the combining of my own imagination—the effusions of my own feelings and passions than the cold workings of the brain on the materials procured by the senses and imagination of other writers—

I am more out of patience with myself than you can form any idea of, when I tell you that I have scarcely written a line to please myself (and very little in respect to quantity) since you saw my M.S. I have been endeavouring all this morning; and with such dissatisfied sensations I am almost afraid to go into company—But these are idle complaints to which I ought not give utterance, even to you—I must then have done—

Sunday morning   Mary

Sunday night——

A Sabbath rest. And a walk *en famille*. Mrs. Inchbald joined us. She is handsome, I admit, about my height, yet with no more bosom than a boy, and a stiff walk without the least sway or softness. Since her fair complexion freckles at the mere touch of the sun, she wears large-brimmed cambric or calico hats, her hair negligently tucked up underneath, drawn back from her face which is a perfect pale oval; the eyebrows the same sand-colour as her hair give a curious impertinence to the eyes. Feature by feature, she is delicate, even interesting, with indisputable presence. She is also the liveliest of conversationalists, stammering, I notice, only on words that have a negative implication, as if reluctant to contradict others. Fanny, who mimics these days like a monkey, said in no uncertain terms, as I covered her, fortunately waiting till I put her to bed, that she would *n-n-n-n-n-n-not* go to sleep. I scolded her most sternly, though secretly admiring the shrewdness of her observation. There must be a key to understanding why one can run trippingly on and then be abruptly halted—at one point rather than another. There is a mystery to it which, try as I may, I cannot decipher, although I am convinced it would give me a handle to her character. Amelia Alderson has a theory. She says it is all due to those early years on stage, when playing Cordelia to Mr. Inchbald's Lear, from which she consequently suffers incestuous guilt—taking the act for the deed. It does seem madness that she chose to go on stage. The ultimate effect of her handicap was to prevent her from advancement in the profession, and she finally gave it up. But having been undeterred by the volley of eggs, potatoes and even broken bottles that are said to be the usual salute of displeasure for strolling players in country places, helped to provide her firmness of character. What I have never been able to harmonise in her personality is the prudishness, on the one hand, and the vivacity of a veteran flirt, on the other, till I learned she is Roman Catholic. One can flirt if one's senses are so schooled that never would one dream of serious consequences. Yet rumour has it that for years she has had a partiality for John Kemble. He, the Siddonses and the Inchbalds, all together, shared bread and cheese on their knees as they lumbered by fly from one inn to another in a travelling company of players, when all of them were young and unknown. And, indeed, Mrs. Siddons is similarly prudish, both women holding, as steadily as they would a spear on stage, moralistic principles which, to my mind, seem overly scrupulous and of excessive strictness. At one season such airs are said to arise from Popery, at another from Puritanism. There is an offspring of the two tendencies described as *Puritan Papist*: I had heard of such a collusion—but never before met a living example.

We were walking in Green Park, where the fashionable world takes its promenade summer evenings, now that St. James's has lost its prestige. The architect of the gardens of the Tuileries held the opinion that the King's Park in its rural, wild character was more grand than any thing he could contrive; so that, to this day, we differ from the French by a wilful lack of artful regularity. So popular is it to promenade for an hour or two after Sunday dinner, that our little group was caught in the tide of a massive, moving stream of people. The paths swarmed with citizens of all ranks, the lower orders, tradespeople, as well as the *beau monde*. Such a sight is it that those whose windows give on to the park sit there in their windows like theatre-goers in their boxes, even to the extent of passing opera-glasses among themselves, the better to distinguish the celebrated and the elegant. There was such a crush that poor Fanny, having a view of nothing but a forest of legs, began to sob and drag on my arm. Godwin led us across the great broad Mall through an opening in the iron railing to the canal in St. James's, where we could sit and rest awhile—for we have imported the French idea of putting chairs inside the parks—in view of an alley of old lime trees that always delights me, and the open water on which drift all varieties of waterfowl. Old Jack, the gigantic and venerable swan of the vicinity, we could see sunning on a far-away rock amidst reeds and rushes.

Godwin had pointed out the exact spot, as we passed, where, last October, the King met with the mob. The royal coach was heavily pelted with mud and stones—the plate-glass windows of the coach now replaced by copper panels—while on every side had come denunciations of the war against France and remonstrances for peace. "Peace!" and "Bread!" were the cries. The mob managed to halt the carriage just under St. James's Palace garden wall. It gave me an icy chill to see an ordinary bit of roadway and wall, and bring to mind a scene of violence, such as I had too often witnessed in France—having once seen from the window of the house, where I was staying in Paris, Louis XVI sitting, with more dignity than I expected from his character, in a hackney-coach, in silence except now and then for a few strokes on the drum, going through absolutely deserted streets, to face trial; soon after, death. A heedless attack on the British monarch, instead of progressing the people's liberties, has been a signal for greater oppression. It has served the government as a pretext for the passage of the gagging bills. They are beginning to call Pitt "the British Robespierre"—for he maintains authority by keeping the country in a constant state of alarm over plots and conspiracies. One can almost conclude that the rabble who stopped the King's carriage were recruited from our prisons to act as provocateurs. Such is Godwin's theory of Pitt's methods. Unable to write about the present circumstances, Godwin has been contemplating a study of Robespierre, written *à la Plutarch*, on the assumption that the public will draw parallels to the present upheavals. Mrs. Inchbald warns of the personal danger in such a project, saying that if the reading public can have such understanding, so can the government. All our aspirations must be tempered by thought of the risks we run. Treason is no longer an overt act, but, newly defined, printing, writing or speaking that *intends* harm to the Sovereign, or incites others to do harm, is now considered treasonable. We are to be judged by our intentions. How they can be determined remains a mystery. But the result of the new legislation is that we cannot write what we please, nor find a printer to print what we write, nor, if we manage the first two, is it a simple matter to persuade a bookseller to sell our literary labour. When two harmless tradesmen were judged for the crime of seditious treason for having sold copies of "The Rights of Man," the government rested content that they had provided a strong lesson to others. Godwin reiterates the remark Fox made in the course of recent debates: "You may prevent men from complaining, but you cannot prevent them from feeling . . ."

Perhaps because she considered it imprudent to speak so openly on the subject, at a place where we might easily be overheard, Mrs.

Inchbald rose and took a few steps to the edge of the water to toss on its surface bits of bread she had thought to bring with her inside a tiny silver-mesh reticule. Her white muslin, against the dark waters and distant feathery willows on the far bank, gave her the appearance of a shepherdess—milkmaids and shepherdesses all the style these days. Returning to her chair, which borrowed the benefit of shade from an elm, she listened at length to Godwin's observations on the performance of "The Iron Chest," nodding from time to time.

At one point, she asked after my work in, I thought, the compassionate way one asks after an ailing relative. Prudent people, unwilling to mention my wicked book on the rights of woman, praise the travel book, feeling it sounder, safer territory for discussion. In asking *par politesse* after my work, I thought I saw her brace herself against a possible polemical reply. I answered, saying only that marriage as despotism was my subject, nothing more. She then spoke feelingly of how grossly disappointed she is in the public reception of her recent novel; her first, though well received, had been ten months, unceasingly, in the writing and had resulted in a period of ill health, low spirits and a long train of evils; her health suffering during the confinement, her spirits upon publication. Besides, she had frequently obtained more pecuniary advantage by ten days' labour for the theatre managers than by her entire ten months over "A Simple Story." Now she was again using the heroine of that book—a woman of fashion with a heart, having a bright understanding, yet little power of reflexion—a role she was fitting to Miss Farren, who wished to play the part of a fashionable lady of the present day, a lively, amiable and clever character, rather than the more elevated roles into which she has been cast. The subject of the new play could also be said to be about marriage, but in a comic vein—presenting the contrast between an old-fashioned matron from the country and a young unmarried woman whose spirit was untrammelled by convention. And would not the younger become the older *in time?* I asked myself. I did not bother to express such reservation, conscious that the seriousness of the theme must be diluted for the stage. The current audience—or the managers who choose the plays—require melodramatic and violent simplification, not fastidious argument. "The Iron Chest" underwent just such a transformation, the novel's distinction of subject—a living picture of what it means to be poor—translated into wild ravings and terrific posturings. For all the Gothic horrors in the motley collection of novels I have been forced to read over the summer, some still cock an eye at the daily habits of ordinary human creatures. I vow my Maria—and a poor, uneducated servant I have only lately begun to create—shall be troublingly real. But Mercy and Goodness!—as one of Mrs. Inch's characters might exclaim—how far apart we are in our received opinions and sympathies. I strain to change the way things are. How is it she does not? She, too, has known penury, injustice and struggle. Even now she allows herself but thirty-four shillings a week on which to live—I should *die* on that!—which necessitates walking up I don't know how many flights of stairs, even having to lug her own water and cinders. The savings that ensue are sent to a sister who is not well off, and to the poor in the neighbourhood. She stints on clothing, wearing unadorned muslin, head held high in the pride of one who exerts free choice, preferring liberality to others over capricious spending on herself—another instance of what I take to be her practice of extravagance in the pursuit of virtue.

Godwin had properly propelled us across perilous ruts and slippery grass, seeming to marvel at the sight of two of his _____, a term I hesitate to write, though it is commonly spoken without hesitation in kennels. He has so praised Mrs. Inch, that she seems almost too fine to be looked at, as an amateur of porcelains is supposed to have said of his Dresden.

Her examination of me under her light eye-lashes appeared to evaluate my character with the exactitude of an old-clothes dealer making an appraisal. Nothing escapes her. She can seem to be lost in thought, or be gazing at a far distant point on the landscape, yet enters the conversation with an almost musical perfection of timing. Godwin admits she is in love with him. It is hard to determine, for the degree of control she exerts over her feelings. I hardly hoped to surprise some involuntary regard. Nor did she speak to him in any familiar way that would have implied intimacy; if any thing she addresses him with a formality that conforms to the style of mere chance acquaintances. But there is one unusual effect. She heaps upon him an amount of flattery that is almost of too Christian a kind of humility for my taste, uplifting him as she abases herself. Then he will turn a phrase to compliment her—the game consisting in who can grovel lowest. I watched in wonder. It is an inverted sort of manner of loving; but, indeed, it did seem to me to be a mysterious code of the language of love, which we know to be infinitely various. She spoke her love for him, in this manner. While he, unaware of the passionate resonance behind the words, spoke back with a certain fluency, but by rote, like a schoolboy speaking French.

MW TO WG

Sunday night

I have spent a pleasant day, *perhaps*, the pleasanter, for walking with you first, with only the family, and Mrs. Inch—We had less wit and more cordiality—and if I do not admire her more I love her better—She is a charming woman!—I do not like her the less, for having spoken of you with great respect, and even affection—so much so that I began to think you were not out in your conjecture—you know what.

I only write now to bid you good night!—I shall be asleep before you—and I would leave you a God bless you—did you care for it; but, alas! you do not, though Sterne says that it is equivalent to a—kiss—

Past ten o'clock!

MW TO WG

September 8, 1796

I received an apology this morning from Mrs Newton and of course you did. I should have called on you in my way home, an hour ago, had I not taken it for granted, in spite of my fatigue—and I do not like to see you when I am not half alive.

I want to see you—and *soon*—I have a world to say to you—Pray come to your

Mary

September 10, 1796

Life too often seems a labour of patience, like rolling a great stone up a hill. Day follows day, each browned by care. How often have I puzzled the means of living in some thing of a settled style. However much one will endeavour to try for resolutions, they occur in their own good time, or not at all; but, when they do, seem effortless.

Yesterday was a day that started like any other—an early walk in the fields holding Fanny by the hand; breakfast at nine; the door to my study closed at ten; sitting till two over "Maria." I cannot seem to make a sequence of it. I throw all my energies into creating my characters. It is easy work to write of some one with a sensibility like mine. But the story of Jemima—poor, uneducated, brutalised by life—how living in the lower orders corrupts the soul, and the manner in which injustices heaped on her are passed in kind to others—this cruel life of London that is all around us demanding attention. All one need do is open one's eyes and observe. Let the look of faces passed sink deep—do not push them aside for more pleasant thoughts—and they will germinate a world of misery within the imagination. I have not yet got it in mind under what circumstances Jemima shall tell her story. But one cannot do every thing at once, and, when this glow of creative power infuses me, I have full confidence that I shall solve all remaining dilemmas—tomorrow, the next day, no matter.

I open my note-book this morning—a healthful habit of tuning up the mind and sharpening the nib—to remind myself, when all seems gloomy, how easy life can be—happiness, like unhappiness, a habit of mind, often based on very simple sustenance. When I stay at home too much, my brain becomes a bedlam of groans and sighs. But when I am active, in company, the day seems filled with benevolence. I feel on the path to some steadiness, yet, where it concerns feelings, the method is often too obscure for words. Curiosity some times bears me up in a breezy manner from my incessant worries; and observation practised for its own sake, as a form of education, a stimulant to the imagination. Godwin, in theory, says he does not agree; for him books are the sole source of learning. He says so, but his habits do not bear it out. For he is as pleased as I to walk the streets and absorb the sights and sounds that abound there. When he insists it is not in the category of true learning, he is only practising philosophy; if he did not do so, he would be like any one else, and so, to show his profession, he must contradict, the way the egg-woman with her basket of new-laid eggs must cry to show them off—in just such a way does Godwin make a show of his philosophical wares. Yesterday he was as eager as I to go on foot to Mary Hays'. I had promoted the notion of going there together, to give her, once and for all, visible proof that some thing binds us. I still feel a sting of anger at the way, leaning on Godwin's arm, she looked over her shoulder to see my reaction. I do not like this sort of female competition. I do not intend to disturb her steady friendship. But if she desires an exclusive attachment, I'm bound to reveal the state of things as they are, in order to douse the flames of her imagination. I know how liable she is to take her fancies for a mirror of truth, and I would spare her that humiliating deception.

I had worked till two, then gone over expenses with Mary—prices for the most common necessities, such as candles and soap, having risen extravagantly—ill health in the body politic always expressing itself in a feverish rise in the cost of things. I had promised to make up a tale to tell Fanny before dinner. She did not want a *new* tale, she desired again the one of yesterday, and, with her large dark eyes fixed on my face, hung on each twist and turn. I wondered if I ought not write it down. My "Original Stories" were quite popular at the time they were printed eight years ago; perhaps I ought to speak to Johnson of the possibility of writing more. And yet, for some reason, Fanny gets cross when I go to get Mrs. Trimmers' tales for children from the bookcase. She does not want a book—unlike Godwin—but my own voice, my eyes not lowered upon a page, but open upon her face; she will insist upon it with her small wilful force—in just the way she exacted from me the other day a penny ice from the Italian's barrow, obtaining it by sheer obstinacy, for I gave in, against my better judgement, out of admiration for the tenacity of her desire. On other days she passes the barrow with barely a glance. We must not always make a rule and arbitrarily hold to it, merely to revel in our own firmness. Fanny and I dined on boiled beef at our usual four o'clock dinner hour. And Godwin came at five; at six we were expected in Hatton Gardens.

Godwin strode across Bowling Green, intending to take his usual path, when I stopped him. I have a particular horror of passing the Foundling Hospital—the cold stone building affects me so unpleasantly I have to look away to nip in the bud a constriction of the heart at the thought of so many motherless children languishing inside, or, far better, avoid the street entirely. When Godwin heard this, he slowed his pace, letting me choose the route. My way is to go straight to Gray's Inn Lane Road. Godwin is amused that my feelings are hardly aroused by St. Andrew's Burying Ground, nor the House of Correction—but that massive edifice of blind building stones at a distance never gave away its purpose, my ignorance keeping me from reflexions about the misfortune of its inhabitants. As for St. Andrew's—as Mrs. Burney once said to Dr. Johnson: "We may look to a church-yard, for it is right we should be kept in mind of death." As I was explaining my posture in answer to Godwin's amused enquiry, we fell at the turn of the King's Road into the midst of a flock of geese driven by a distracted young man, who followed close behind, his crook for picking a goose up by its neck for a prospective buyer, the better to see it, held languidly over one shoulder, as he scanned the upper windows of the houses, calling: "Buy a live goose." Godwin's recoil of surprise must have frightened one of the geese, for it flew off the ground, raucously scolding Godwin who, in the end, was left with several soft white feathers on his breast. When I'd plucked him, I held a little nosegay of plumes, holding them all the way to Mary Hays' to whom I presented them for a new goose-down pillow. She took them from me without the least spark of amusement, Godwin and I still breathless with laughter at the reminder of the way the flock had hurtled out of King's Road, quacking and waddling, furious at the interference of a pair of half-boots and breeches, which was all they could see of him, although *he* would consider himself the top half, beginning from his head, rather than from his toes.

From that moment on, we went more slowly, for the street, from that point, grows crowded with barrows and baskets, donkeys' paniers heavy on either side of their haunches. Some of the costermongers are familiar by face. A hundred times or more I have passed the chair-mender with the peg leg, sitting on the cobble-stones with his bundle of rushes to one side as he mends the seat of a chair. I particularly love the old-clothes man who goes by with several hats on, one on top of the other, and is bearded in the fashion of the Jews. Each trade attracts a certain nationality: the milkmaids all either Irish or Welsh; Fanny's icemen Italian; those who sell the fine white sand for cleaning pots and pans, and for sprinkling on bare floors, coming from Cornwall. Godwin says his favourite cry is from the fellow who grinds knives, scissors and razors. He followed him around for near half an hour once just to hear his cry. It soon recommended itself as the only way to shout out lustily the word *scissors*, which necessarily becomes *sithers*. Godwin and I tried *sithers* some dozen times, no doubt appearing out of our senses to passers-by. We halted to gaze at primroses, two bundles a penny, and fine bigarroon cherries tied to a stick, which Godwin would have bought for Fanny, except that I didn't want him to be burdened all the way to Mary Hays' and back. The good woman showed us her loose black and white heart cherries, fourpence a pound—"full weight, all round and sound"—dropping a handful into one of the tin bowls of her hand-scale. There being all too short a season for them, Godwin would bring a pound to Mary Hays.

To reach Hatton Gardens—which earlier this summer was redolent with the fragrance of small wild strawberries, which come to mind, even now, in passing—I generally turn at Baldwin's Garden straight to Leather Lane, where I like to watch the cobblers' apprentice boys hammering away, a mouthful of small copper nails making it impossible for them to speak as they work. From there it is but a step further to Kirkby Street, where Mary Hays has lodgings.

She has been in suspense these days, while Robinson is taking his decision on whether or not to print her M.S. Godwin has spoken highly to him of one who is well known as part of his seraglio. I did not know in what mood we would find our friend, and feared it might be with head in hand and heavy sighing; so that I was pleasantly surprised, after giving her the soft, snow-white flutter of plumes, getting in return no more than a speculative glance, to see, as Godwin and I were squeezing through her narrow corridor, a visitor sitting in the high-backed chair. He rose swiftly when I entered. It was Cristall. I have heard of him from Opie. As a young man, it is said, he began painting in the potteries till he could afford to come to London to study at the Royal Academy. He has a strange growl of a voice, but an illuminating smile, ingenuous dark Celtic eyes, and reddish skin from his habit of sketching out of doors.

It is curious how Mrs. Inchbald can appear in sixpence-worth of muslin, draped here and there, to make one catch one's breath at her entrance into a room; while Mary Hays, no matter how industriously she labours for an effect, will hang all awry, and be for ever tugging or pulling, never in repose. Then there are those disconcerting expressions of hers: abruptly remembering that the water must have reached its boil, or that she has forgotten to pass the Bath buns, her eyes will glaze over in sickly distraction. She is better company when alone—then she will simply let the water boil for ever till none is left, and it is all to do over again; and will not bother that her wrist is bare to the bone, that sharp prominent bone that seems to blister up under the pale skin. When she had gone inside for the tea-strainer that she had neglected to put on the tea-board, I asked Cristall if he had known Opie in Cornwall, but he had not. Cristall says he likes best to wander into rugged nature with some paper and a black lead pencil. Among his first subjects was a shipwreck on the rocky coast of Cornwall—he has a preference for coastal scenes—and, although he has some times had to finish in the figures in a landscape for some older artist, he has little taste for portraiture. Opie now asks a hundred guineas for a three-quarter portrait. Romney got thirty. Godwin asked whether Cristall agrees with Northcote that Opie is the first painter of our time. Ay, he replied, and, though we waited for more, it was all he was going to say.

We had whiled away a pleasant hour, when I rose. Godwin got to his feet. If we had not made a sufficient point by arriving together, leaving simultaneously, I thought, must make its unmistakable impression on Mary Hays; but—madness to report!—I saw her blink back the comprehension that, for a split second, had widened her gaze. She had hobbled with us to the door—for her ankle is still severely weakened. I did not ask her to come to tea later in the week. And Godwin, who abhors long conversations in narrow draughty corridors, was unceremonious in his farewell.

We were already on the street when, wondering at a pressure over his heart, he discovered his paper horn of cherries. We ate them on our way to the hackney-stand, spitting pips with the abandon of children let loose from school.

M W   T O   W G

September 10, 1796

Fanny was so importunate with her "go this way Mama, me wants to see man" this morning that you would have seen us had I not had a glimpse of a blue coat at your door, when we turned down the street—I have always a great deal to say to you, which I say to myself that 'tis pity you do not hear one—

I wanted to tell you that I felt as if I had not done justice to your essay for it interested me extremely and has been running in my head while the recollections were all alive in my heart—you are a tender considerate creature; but, *entre nous*, do not make too many philosophical experiments, for when a philosopher is put on his metal, to use your own phrase, there is no knowing where he will stop—and I have not reckoned on having a wild goose chace after a wise man—you will ask me what I am writing about—Why, as if you had been listening to my thoughts—

I am almost afraid on reflection that an indistinct intuition of our affections produced the effect on Miss H— that distressed me—she has owned to me that she cannot endure to see others enjoy the mutual affection from which she is debarred—I will write a kind note to her to day to ease my conscience, for when I am happy myself, I am made up of milk and honey, I would fain make every body else so.

I shall come to you to night, probably before nine— May I ask you to be at home—I may be tired and not like to ramble further—should I be later you will forgive me— It will not be my heart that will loiter—By the bye—do not tell any body—especially yourself—it is always at my lips at your door—

The return of the fine weather has led me to form a
vague wish that we might *vagabondize* one day in the
country—before the summer is clear gone. I love the
country and like to leave certain associations in my memory, which seems as it were the land marks of affection.
Am I very obscure?

Now I will go and write—I am in a humour to write—
at least to you—Send me one line if it be but—Bo! to a
goose—Opie left a card last night—

WG TO MW

Bo!

Mr. Merry boasts that he once wrote an epilogue to a
play of Miles Peter Andrews, while the servant waited in
the hall. That is not my talent. So, as you once said, I
shall cork up my heart; to see whether it will fly out *ce
soir* at the sight of you.

Saturday

September 12, 1796

I had, of course, heard of Thomas Cooper—Godwin's educational
experiment. But I had heard of him in such a way that I could
never have envisioned the buoyant young man who, this morning,
stepped into my parlour. His father had been ship's surgeon to the
Army and had died in Bengal. As the executor was about to bring
back to England his effects, a great storm swept over the land. As
a result of all financial accounts having been destroyed, the family
was left indigent, when the boy was twelve. Godwin, a second
cousin, took him to live with him, and undertook to educate him.
But he was too severe with the boy, too unyielding, which he himself has come to realise. Instead of gently leading the youth to a
recognition of right conduct, he humiliated him and made him
obstinate. It was before Robinson had made his offer of a publishing contract of 1,000*l.* for "Political Justice." Godwin had no more
than a hundred pounds a year from his earnings, living in mean
lodgings which he shared with his friend Marshal. One can imag-

ine the effect of two struggling literary men, rather chop-fallen, upon a boy whose high spirits exploded in a racket of mirth and, finally, defiance. Godwin never laid a hand on him but, in the close quarters in which they lived, he often grew violently eloquent in castigation. He had read "Émile." And he had fancied that he, too, would create a new man from the soft clay of youth. But human nature is stubborn stuff. For all that he lashed out at the poor boy, he grew more secretive, stubborn and proud.

From my knowledge of Thomas Cooper's training, I could scarcely have anticipated the young man brought to meet me to day. He has a dark shock of hair that is thick and curly and which he tries to tame to one side, but it is far too springy and full of electricity, giving his shining, young, exuberant face a dramatic frame. He looks at one from blue eyes as if savouring the description he is going to make in a coffee-house among admiring friends. Even while telling me of difficulties suffered these last four years, he could not resist presenting them with an air of self-deprecating amusement. At sixteen he had joined John Kemble's company. Given some small role, he started to declaim so passionately in rehearsal that he was then given parts in which he uttered not a word: the second witch in "Macbeth"; one of the bearers of Mrs. Siddons' train in "The Mourning Bride"; a Senator in "Othello" scowling and silent in a black cloak, and so forth. When he had finally worked up to playing Malcolm in "Macbeth," a role that has the play's closing speech—having to do with calling home all exiled friends who had fled the tyranny of "this dead butcher and his fiend-like queen"—the phrase *fiend-like* slipped his mind. He desperately searched his memory, while trying to make out the prompter's cue, which he couldn't hear for the tumult behind the scenes. The prompter was almost shouting at him, the audience hissing, and finally, the curtain ringing down, while he still stood on stage trying to collect himself, cracked him on the head. Kemble came over—the dead butcher arisen—and in ringing tones declared Cooper unfit for the profession. As a friend he advised him to return to London—they were in Edinburgh—he stretched his arm, pointing the way to London. We laughed at Kemble's familiar posture and inflexion.

Cooper then had joined a company of strolling players—as Holcroft once had done—at four shillings a night, travelling bag-and-baggage across the country. Now he is about to start for Bristol to find a ship that will bear him to America. Holcroft is of the decided opinion that the offer made by a Philadelphia manager should have been rejected, that it will lead only towards extinction; and Godwin yet thinks that Cooper might have withstood the temptation of the money *on principle*. Yet now, for good or for ill, he is making ready to sail.

I can well comprehend Godwin's apprehension, having felt similarly for Charles, when he went to seek his fortune in the new world—though now I am embittered that, when there is need in the family, he answers neither Johnson's plea nor mine. Perhaps one feels, once in the new world, that one has arrived not only on another continent, but on some remote star. I held young Cooper's warm hand in mine, with a sense that I might never again look into those morning-blue eyes of his, and imagined that at Bristol the ship would lift sail and cut through swelling seas to that far other world where so many of our "exiled friends" never think of return, but harken to the beat of a life which makes the past vanish—and we for them like dead souls, buried at sea, it seems.

I had uncorked the ink bottle and had drawn out a sheet of paper to write a letter of introduction for Cooper, but, head in hand, after they had left, I dreamed an hour away. I promised Godwin to write a letter which Thomas Cooper might carry with him to Philadelphia, but sat besieged by all kinds of troubling thoughts. Why did Rowan not answer a letter of mine written to him in January? I sent the letter, I remember, with a young clerk of Imlay's who hoped to find a better situation in life in America. I could not be perfectly explicit in writing of Imlay's unkindness and cruelty—I did not wish others to be privy to the baseness of his conduct—and, to add to the necessity for secrecy, was my own agitated frame of mind, so I cannot be accountable for the coherence of my communication. I had purposely sent my news to Rowan, to Rowan rather than to my brother Charles—also in Philadelphia, but to whom I wished not to have to explain my present circumstances—because he once had seemed to feel for me. Perhaps he has found a way to be re-united with his family and has long since left his adoptive country. He cannot return to Ireland, nor to England, with the state of public affairs such as they are in both countries, in a posture scarcely to assuage private difficulty. It occurs to me to begin to wonder if some lack of delicacy on my part, in opening my heart to him, when alone, wounded and unhappy, can have provoked such silence. Or could it have appeared to him that, stating my heart-broken condition so freely, I might be seeking a favour in return for those I'd tended him in my little house at Marat-Havre? No, surely not. He is too finely attuned to read into words what isn't meant.

Those former days come back to me now with a swift pang of nostalgia—Rowan appearing at my door, one morning, dressed as if he had come round to deliver a sack of meal from a barrow, standing before my door bare-headed, in dusty boots. When I understood who he was, I drew him inside and sat him down. He had a letter which I quickly read, for I was eager to hear in his very own words how fared our friends in Paris. One was in prison; one had died; others had found their way back to England. After a cheerless time in Paris, he had come to try to seek passage to America on any ship that would take him. He had become skilful in the part of posing as an American, even to growing his moustaches in the fashion made popular by the American Revolution. Friends in Paris had advised him that Mr. Imlay might know of a captain of a ship about to debark for either Boston or Philadelphia. But Imlay, it happened, was in Paris, having left two days before. And I was to join him there, if his business exigencies did not let him return by the end of August, so that I awaited word to make my plans. I knew no course of action to suggest, to an exiled man with a price in England and Ireland of 2,000*l.* on his head, but to accept our hospitality. Perhaps it would be only a matter of days until, through connexions of Imlay's whom I might trust with such a matter, I could secure him safe passage from France. In the meantime, I sent the servant to beg shirt and breeches from her *beau frère*, who was a head taller than Imlay and nearly as tall as Rowan. I was jolted into action from fear. I could only hope that Rowan had caused but slight notice in the town. Wandering around, conspicuous for his gigantic proportions, not speaking a word of French into the bargain, he would hardly have escaped attention. He appeared in my eyes alarmingly like a French aristocrat who, fleeing France, was trying his best to disguise himself as an American. The spirit of the

Havrais in those days was such that *à la lanterne* preceded any reasonable investigation into the identity of strangers.

Our time together, stretched to a fortnight, was one of the most pleasant experiences of my life, for we found ourselves in an immediate accord, the more so for being flung together in a situation of danger. He would accompany me to the markets and in the afternoon into the nearby countryside to the crest of a wind-swept hill-top, from where we could scan the ships in the harbour, including ships of war which often, crippled from fighting in the Channel against our fleet, would make for port, the way birds with broken wings on a last spurt of effort will slip under the safety of foliage. Evenings he sat with me over tea in the little parlour with its three solid oak beams and would entertain me in his musical Irish voice, broken by deep laughter at the ironies of fate. With Fanny, whom I was still nursing, he was particularly gentle, holding her in his strong arms, rocking her and lulling her in his low voice, till she grew tractable and calm. Cradling her might have given him some relief from the torment of missing his wife and eight children back in Dublin. All his efforts to obtain the emancipation of three millions of his countrymen through parliamentary representation—by force of arms if need be—had failed. But never had he meant to excite insurrection. For he believes, in the spirit of Locke, in a power in the people to provide for their own safety by a new legislature, when the old has acted contrary to trust; and that such power is the best fence against rebellion, and the most probable means to hinder it. He had joined the Catholic struggle as a member of the United Irishmen. Tried and sentenced, his only path lay then in escaping, which he did in a small pleasure-boat hardly equipped for a Channel cruise, but skilfully handled by smugglers who knew both coasts, and who proved loyal to him, even when they discovered the size of the price on his head. It had been they who had brought him safely to the shore of Brittany in France.

I wonder now at Rowan's life in America where, a friend of his reports, he lives like a recluse in a one-room house, tilling his few acres, solitary, industrious, preferring to keep to himself rather than have intercourse with the townspeople, whom he considers blood-chillingly commercial, as they trade in slaves and speak cold-bloodedly of their transactions, without the least moral repugnance, the making of money their supreme concern. "Good God!" he wrote his friend. "If you heard some of these Kentucky people talk of killing the natives! Cortes and all that followed him were not more sanguinary." It strikes me as a strange outcome, after so many flights and pursuits, that the democratic life so idealised—on all our thinking such a potent influence—should in reality and at close range prove but a race of men meanly satisfying their appetites, without any humanising morality, the lack of which leads them to glorify their own most piratical exploits.

Perhaps I had had a glimpse of this native greed from Imlay—and from his conduct with Barlow. Indeed, no man was ever higher in my estimation, nor sunk lower, than did Joel Barlow. With his wife, Ruth, I had formed a close friendship, meeting her some times at eight in the morning at the baths, afterwards dawdling over breakfast. We were intimate first in London, again in Paris, when she came from America to rejoin her husband in '93, at which time I was living with Imlay, the connexion between the two men binding us all the more closely—a handsome, thoroughly civilised, generous and gentle person, whom I some times contemplate in memory, another of those lost to me across the seas on that distant continent. Joel Barlow gives an arresting first impression, with his diminutive, refined presence, reflective air and deferential manners. He had come from a most aristocratic family in the state of Connecticut, which I am told is one of the most aristocratic of all the states. Often he has held us in thrall with his stories of the Revolution, having taken part in many battles, notoriously in the Battle of Long Island. A less creditable addition to his history, however, is when he sailed to Europe for the Ohio business. Neither we British, nor any other government that I know of, has ever conceived of making public land a basis of revenue; but the American Congress—to kill two birds with one stone—thought it useful both to develop settlements from wilderness and to make a profit from lands formerly free. Barlow came to Europe for a company that had wild tracts of government land to sell and hoped to sell them to French emigrants. From what I could understand of the business, Barlow's company pocketed their gains, without ever making good to Congress—the entire affair smelling of swindle and corruption, not to mention that, in the end, the company blockhouse was attacked by Indians, all the French in the first party killed or captured. Those remaining scattered to older settlements, although some of them did commence a cultivation of vineyards on their four-acre tracts on the banks of the Ohio River, which I have heard extolled as a perfect earthly elysium. Barlow has ever lived in a customary sort of negligent spendthrift manner, sublimely indifferent to any necessitous provision for the future, but I cannot say if he pocketed money not rightfully his, or if that entire Ohio venture was, from its inception, simply a case of mismanagement and disorder. He is not a man well put together. High-minded in parlour and pamphlet, in the conduct of practical affairs all principles fly out the window. His pamphleteering always seemed to me a consequence of ambition. Johnson published a pamphlet of his, in which he expresses the sanguine thesis that all human benefit will arise from representative assembly, the past but a prelude to the American achievement. All of this makes him much respected in certain circles. But there is in his character a division that kindles my suspicion that what he says is from a desire for personal enhancement, rather than devotion to the truth. For example, I have seen him grow stony whenever there is mention of slavery—the Achilles' heel of the democratic principle—which I consider a system of degradation, feudal, barbarous, unnatural and obsolete; he contends agreeably that it is indeed a corruption that offends all reasonable men, saying so with a blandness that lacks all heat of moral fervour. A man such as Thomas Paine acts on what he feels, putting his heart and soul into a measure. Convinced that slavery has no justification, he draughted words to that effect for the Declaration of Independence. It was Jefferson who chose to omit them; had he not, such outrage against equality would for ever have been outlawed in the land. Paine is the old sort of revolutionary. Barlow is part of a new rising faction in America, who, forgetting first principles, contemplates government as a private monopoly. Once the Ohio land sale looked unlikely as a source of making him a personal fortune, he switched his interest to Louisiana.

At first I barely comprehended the import of the whispered conferences between the two men, who would plot and scheme between themselves, while Ruth Barlow and I talked easily before a fire on the far side of the room, in that cheerful parlour of theirs in Paris, before their pear-wood chimney-piece that was carved like the façade of a Greek temple. I had assumed Louisiana was the same sort of affair as Barlow's Ohio scheme, but some fragmentary phrase that happened to reach my ears gave me a notion of some thing decidedly more sinister. I remember a quick glance at Imlay lounging back, his legs in long boots, one crossed atop the other, his hand over his chin, as he tested the bristles of moustaches which grew thick and dark, long on either side of his mouth, in the shape of a sickle. It was a characteristic way he had of listening, his eyes bright with attention, as Barlow appeared to be laying before him some elaborate proposal. The two of them were joined in their passion to amass a fortune, a bond in common like the vice of gambling. In other respects they are dissimilar: Joel Barlow small and bright and quick to Imlay's more sluggish and self-dramatising manner. Barlow's temperament made him stay awake into the small hours with chimerical schemes produced by his teeming intellect, but they might all have remained hypothetical, had they not engaged Imlay's more restless and practical energies—and his unwillingness to leave any new danger untried. The scene at the Barlows' which comes to mind must have been during the very first of the year of '93, for it was in January, I remember, that Brissot was preparing his report for the Assembly on the possibility of wresting control of Louisiana from Spain. That wintry evening at the Barlows' when Imlay snapped at the scheme, jumping to his feet from his slack position on a chair, I did not pay strict attention to the context of the discussion. There comes to mind then his silence, one June evening, when he came to me in the country at Neuilly, where I later was staying for safe-keeping. At a barrier guards checked one's papers. I would often wait there for Imlay's return in the evening. On this particular day he had come into the house before I expected him. I hurried down the stairs to see him standing looking out a window open on the garden. When he turned into the room, I knew he had some frightful news. I asked if it was Brissot who had been taken, and he nodded . . . but, wait, I am confusing, am I not, news of Brissot's arrest with still another evening, in October, when Imlay, standing within the same small room, dull with early dusk, his voice low in disbelief, recounted that, by Robespierre's orders, the Twenty-two, all Girondists, had one by one mounted the guillotine. As he spoke, I seemed to see them standing at the foot of the gallows—then all went dark. When I recovered consciousness, Imlay was placing a pillow under my head; he made a startled sound that I was able, only afterwards, to interpret. The impact of my grief had been so acute that it had caused a paralysis along one side of my face. When Imlay informed the physician called to my bedside that he had been breaking tragic news—unsure of the physician's politics, he had avoided any more precise definition—he had replied that it was common for sufficient shock to cause a stroke. I wept all night—not for Brissot alone, but for that good and kind man Condorcet as well, and all the others of the Girondists who had been the very spirit of the Revolution, killed by a madman who wished to rule without the interference of either moderation or humanity. Imlay sat by my bedside, puffing his pipe, reflecting on the cruel fate of our friends and their desolate families, fearful for what the following day might bring. From the moment of Brissot's arrest, there had been no further thought of working to secure the territory of Louisiana for France. Now with Barlow and a man in Gothenburg, Imlay was forming a business to procure articles for the French Government: blockade-running with grain, iron, soap, other such essentials. Barlow was to stay in Paris, Imlay to supervise the shipments from Marat-Havre. He had already made a trip to oversee initial arrangements. Now he wondered at my bedside if, next day, despite the French Government's official gratitude to American revolutionists he might not walk through the Neuilly barrier straight to gaol. We went over his past actions to see whether they could be subject to interpretation of traitorous conduct. I did not know when I had fallen unconscious, that I carried Imlay's child. But I understood, with all too melancholy a presentiment, that events were arranging our lives, independent of any desire for peaceful domesticity. That night was a turning point in our destiny. After that it was *crack! crack!* and off he would be on his own affairs, which, to my impatient complaints, he would insist he must carry out for the security of our future happiness and, shortly after, for the sake of our child. It was never the same between us. Robespierre's revolution was a world of difference from the aspirations in the hearts of our friends. From then on Terror ruled.

September 13, 1796

I am at my desk early, my hair undone—Godwin having gone only moments ago to his study, with an order that I was to work without interruption till we meet to go to Clifford's Inn. He agrees with my method of alarming the mind and making it run by writing in one's journal, although less inclined to think it worth while to note one's personal sentiments than to say some thing of the public face of things. I would do all my William wishes me to do but, filled with sluggish sleep, and the delicious temptation to creep back into a warm bed, I cannot hope to try, so early in the morning, for subjects of piety or politics. I can write only of what is uppermost in my mind, and hope thereby to dissipate the cobwebs and begin to perceive things steadily in the clear light of day.

I have been uncertainly speculating on the past. Having written to Rowan started a long train of thought that is not without its bitterness. As memory animated scenes that once took place in France, I was again reminded how Joel Barlow became my tormentor. But I begin to wonder if I did not make him bear too much responsibility for my misery, in order to spare blaming Imlay, although the two of them, it now seems to me, were a matched pair. Barlow's immoderate desire for wealth, his continual whirl of projects and schemes, the whole labyrinthine crooked business, seemed imperceptibly to draw Imlay in against his will. Hating Barlow as I began to do, laying at his door alone the contemptible avidity for money, made me able to continue to love the man I trusted as a friend, husband and father of my child. In my innocence, or blindness, or lack of cunning, I warned Imlay against the gulf into which he was being dragged; and, even at the very last, found it hard to believe that I alone did not know him better than any one else, and have superior knowledge of his real and true nature. Had we not together formed the prospect to bound our views to his gaining a thousand pounds to procure us a farm in America? Did I not accurately read a suffusion of tears at the thought of our future comfort? He liked to speak of our being permanently together amidst six children, once he had earned an independence. I believed then that it was paramount to his every other consideration—why should I have not? Ought I to have been forewarned? Could I have foreseen his utter lack of principle? I some times ask myself these questions. Certainly he had been used to—and now is bound to—a more cunning woman than I. I was entirely deceived by a certain artlessness in our earliest meetings, when I would appear with what he called my barrier-face, as I waited in sight of the guard-house at Neuilly, some times with a basket of grapes over one arm, some times, he said, looking like the Maid of Orleans, always his humbled, most affectionate own dear girl, who would scold herself for the least caprice of sensibility or quickness of feeling; who would promise to be cured of her querulous humours, to be both reasonable and good . . . ah, yes, to be *good*, that I may have deserved to be *happy*. I feel a warmth creep to my cheeks, even now, as I recall on what basis lay that happiness. For his caresses, and the rapture into which they plunged me, I had to learn to be mute in misery, fawning in his presence and, in his absence, acquiescent. I would scold myself for my quick-coming fancies, as a child—indeed, as a child who is taught by the strap to restrain every expression of what it truly feels. In order to avoid vexing him, I would display a docility, for which I would then be praised—tamed to a mere plaything, a slave-girl.

To have felt love for such a man is now mortifying. Yet when novelists or moralists praise as a virtue a woman's coldness and want of passion and make her yield to the ardour of her lover out of compassion or to promote a frigid plan of future comfort, I am disgusted. Heartless conduct I shall always believe contrary to virtue. What we can hope for in this world is to avoid a love which makes of a woman an outlaw, when heart and reason are in discord.

M W TO W G

September 13, 1796

You tell me, William, that you augur nothing good, when the paper has not a note, or, at least, Fanny to wish you a good morning—

Now by these presents let me assure you that you are not only in my heart; but my veins this morning. I turn from you half abashed—yet you haunt me, and some look, word or touch thrills through my whole frame—yes, at the very moment when I am labouring to think of something, if not somebody, else. Get ye gone, Intruder! Though I am forced to add dear—which is a call back—

When the heart and reason accord, there is no flying from voluptuous sensations, I find, do what a woman can—Can a philosopher do more?

Mary

September 14, 1796

The rumour of imminent invasion by the French has become the subject of conversation in almost every company. Thus, we found ourselves at Clifford's Inn in a heated argument over whether this fear of invasion is a mere matter of fancy or a real possibility. Northcote had invited to dine with us a naval commander, who has had no small experience in battle. All the French harbours, with the exception of Cherbourg, seem to be such as are termed *tide harbours*, which is to say they are dry at low water, and at high water navigable for too short a period of time to get out a sufficiently large fleet. But several such harbours might be used, one detachment standing out to sea till it is joined by another, and so on, till the whole force is collected. Commander Browne said such a force might manœuvre undetected across the Channel under cover of clouds and the concurrence of favourable winds. When he had been commanding the *Venus* frigate in the Channel Fleet under Lord Howe, he had endeavoured to intercept an American convoy of merchant ships ladened with corn, by which the French Government hoped to relieve the people's suffering from a disastrous harvest. His frigate had reconnoitred the harbour of Brest, where twenty-five French sail of the line were lying at anchor, waiting to join the convoy to cover it from attack. In a fog, unseen, they had managed to pass close by and evade the British by taking advantage of changeable winds and hazy weather. Lord Howe was in pursuit for more than a week to engage them. The encounter finally took place with the French fleet to windward. Since it is impossible to attack from leeward, the

British had been forced to tack for two full days to try to gain the weather-gage, once again succeeding in losing sight of them. If such a situation were to occur in the event of an invasion, the French fleet, slipping by our superior armament, could surely land troops on our shore.

Accustomed to storm and shipwreck along his native coast, having been raised in Plymouth, Northcote remains skeptical. He does not believe that an open, wide, treacherous body of water such as the Channel is so easily crossed. I had occasion to study him as, with a scowl of contemplation, he was rolling a bit of bread between his fingers, as he spoke. He is a small, intense man, perhaps fifty years of age, so lean that one is aware of the bony structure beneath the skin. Godwin, who only some few months ago made his acquaintance, has developed the habit of visiting him at his studio, where he sits watching him filling into a painting those details for which he does not require some one to sit—working on the fine hairs of a sable collar or the drapery of a satin gown—all the while that he is fully able to carry on a vigorous conversation. Godwin would like to sit to him, but does not know how to ask him his price. He is hoping an occasion will arise of itself, for once he has expressed a desire to have his portrait done, he would not like to haggle. As I was examining Northcote—disjointing his features to analyse the composite, according to the rules of physiognomy of Lavater's system: the prominent, bony, broad brow denoting superior intelligence, the fleshy overhang of the outer edges of the eyelids said to signify strong affectionate feelings—an impatient exclamation burst from his lips and he held up the bit of bread he had so energetically been kneading between his fingers.

Bread!—there lay the trouble. Did we not think it absurd, Northcote asked with feeling, to concoct a mixture of India corn or potato or barley or horse-chestnuts—or whatever other odious adulteration they might next think up? It did not relieve the shortage of grain. Nor would the continuance of a prohibition against distilling wines and spirits ameliorate conditions; nor would they be improved by preventing starch being made of flour; nor by making it criminal for aristocrats to powder their wigs, though a full pound a day is required to whiten a wig. None of these strictures got to the cause of the scarcity. And that was the practice of jobbing—corn jobbers hoarding against higher prices, profiting from the distress of their fellow countrymen. This might only be alleviated by the government setting up granaries for the poor.

Godwin hastened to point out a natural sequence of events, rather than a single cause, for the crisis. In January, the year before, there had been in Britain such a frost that the death-rate had *doubled*. It had affected the harvest. Prices had risen. Crowds had broken into premises where a steam-engine had been grinding corn, soldiers killing one man on the spot. Immediately there had circulated a call to arms against the cruel oppression of the government. But Pitt had been content with dilatory and delusive measures, such as forming still another committee to review the situation, until the people, outraged, voicing cries once heard in France, had stoned the King's carriage. The attack—by the people or by *agents provocateurs*, as the case might be—had been on October 29. On November 3 severe restraints of constitutional rights were proposed, so swiftly on the heels of the outbreak against the King that one could not avoid the suspicion that such restrictive measures had long been in preparation, needing only some such occasion for their proposal.

Godwin believes Pitt is at the heart of these rumours of invasion. It is an alarm rung to terrify the people into compliance, a scheme of the Ministers which has gone to unimaginable lengths. In Norwich irrational fear of an invasion has nearly produced the closing of the Cathedral, for word has spread there that it shall be set on fire as a signal to the French to invade. No one can trace how such a belief was started, yet every one is looking every where for the culprit who shall light the torch.

What Godwin wishes in his heart—a heart less cynical than mine, I often think—is that no man in the kingdom shall have a hundred loaves of bread, while any has none. Property belongs *by right* to him who has most need of it. It is an idea I have heard him espouse in company—dubiously received by men of fashion, but often ardently by younger men, standing about with hectic glances. Northcote stirred at the familiar Godwinite phrasing, cleared his throat and declared some thing to the effect that political justice might come to be, when philosophers were kings;

but, for his own part, he believes in the perpetuation in power of fools and scoundrels.

We had consumed a pike roasted with a pudding in its belly and a veal pye with plums—which Northcote says was Dr. Johnson's favourite dish—and were waiting for the boy to bring more wine. One eats well at Clifford's Inn. Tucked away in a corner behind St. Dunstan's Church in Fleet Street, it has, however, a gloomy prospect that always reminds me as I enter its squat doorway . . .

September 15, 1796

I interrupted my description of Clifford's Inn at a piercing outcry from Mary, whose little Lucas had tilted the soup-kettle, badly burning himself. We bandaged his arm and put him to rest in a corner of the kitchen upon numerous pillows, fussing over him till he managed to cast us a wan smile of gratitude and to close his eyes to slumber. While in another part of the house Fanny had been having a tantrum and, when none of my caresses soothed her, was left to cry herself to sleep.

How can a woman write—except in bits and pieces, making a pattern somewhat in the way odd pebbles accumulate to form a picture, though one standing close-by might not immediately see the composition. Demands—human cries for help, for kindness, for courtesy—would seem to have us so hop up and down as never to compose the sort of sentence that will roll to a stately, slow and solemn period—those orotundities relished like late apricots. When Godwin wants me, mornings, to reflect upon public events, I can only answer that it is not my way to sit back an hour contemplating before I lift my pen. I need rush to write down what I can, lest it be lost, for, subject as I am to so many tugs, my style grows bent, of necessity short, urgent, on the wing and passionate. If our *minds* are not different, men's and women's, our duties are.

And so it was yesterday that I was halted from giving a full account of our dining out in Northcote's company, conversation ineluctably drawn to fellow poets and painters—finally to Lawrence, who lives as if money burns in his pockets. A house in Piccadilly purchased last year cost him 5,000*l.*—imagine!—and now he has bought himself a Rembrandt which every one has gone to see. It is of Bathsheba at her *toilette*, a full-length, seated, three-quarter nude. The only painter in all of London who has not gone to see the painting is Fuseli, who refuses to acknowledge merit in others, as if to say to the world that nothing is good enough *for him*. He has actually been heard to say that he wouldn't go across the way to see it. Godwin said he was not surprised to learn of his indifference—it is how he makes himself superior. As for Lawrence, Godwin often beseeches him to assume more frugal habits, for he seems to be heading by extravagance to paupery. Northcote soothed his fears, recalling that Reynolds, spending a fortune on paintings, always called them the best sort of wealth. As a boy from Plymouth, Northcote had come to London to work in Reynolds' studio. I asked him, therefore, whether it were a true report that the sister of the artist had been a skilful, though little known, portraitist. Smiling, he recalled that it was the one subject that always infuriated Sir Joshua. Miss Reynolds' portraits were an imitation *of his defects*. Every one dreads a mimic, Northcote explained: for though there be a difference between an imitation and the original, it is not great enough to make one feel at ease.

Poor Fanny Reynolds! I sit here this morning musing on her fate. Where else could she have learned to paint, but from her brother's paintings. She had not spent years in Rome, as he had, copying the treasures of the Vatican. The only woman I have ever heard of who received any sort of education as an artist was Angelica Kauffmann, whose father had to dress her in boy's clothing when he sent her to learn to draw. I sit in a silent fury of sympathy, imagining young Angelica Kauffmann, dressing before her looking-glass in a theatrical transformation that alone would gain her entry into studios where she might study the human form. How senseless it seems to me that we women may go to Lawrence's studio in Piccadilly to gaze upon "Bathsheba at Her Bath," but any woman, wishing to be an artist, will have to put on breeches, jack-boots and waistcoat, even perhaps feigning a gruff tone of voice, to be let in to see some ordinary woman sitting nude upon a studio bench. Poor Fanny Reynolds, sister of greatness, with only her brother's paintings to draw from, becoming for her efforts his grotesque shade. I sense her house-bound, silenced existence. How had she dared pick up a brush that men alone

are said to have the right to wield? Why, she had dared from such
a desire to paint as makes one think talent bestirred her.

Tuesday, four o'clock

I have been a prisoner all the morning. If I do not
hear from you, I shall expect you to tea. Dyson dines
with me, and, alas! if I do not command him to depart,
he would probably stay with me alone till midnight.
When you come, I trust he will soon withdraw. Will that
do?

He tells me you are in high health and a flow of spirits.
Intelligence, how welcome!

W G T O M W

Mercredi, September 14, 1796

*Il faut que la visite soit chez moi ce soir, n'est-ce pas?
Et à quelle heure?*

*Je ordonne à vous que vous écrivez ce matin, et avec
génie étonnante! comme assurément vous pouvez si bien.*

M W T O W G

September 14, 1796

I have no genius this morning. Poor Fannikin has the
chicken-pox which I am glad of—as I now know what is
the matter with her. Business takes me to Mr. Johnson's
to day. I had rather you would come to me this evening
—I shall be at home between eight and nine; but do not
make a point of interrupting any party. I like to be near
Fanny till she is better.

M W T O W G

September 15, 1796

The virulence of my poor Fanny's distemper begins to
abate, and with it my anxiety—yet this is not, I believe a
day sufficiently to be depended on, to tempt us to set

out in search of rural felicity. We must then woo philosophy *chez vous ce soir, n'est-ce pas*; for I do not like to lose
my Philosopher even in the lover.

You are to give me a lesson this evening—and, a word
in your ear, I shall not be very angry if you sweeten gram-
matical disquisitions after the Miltonic mode—Fanny
at this moment has turned a conjunction into a kiss; and
the sensation steals upon my senses. N'oubliez pas, I pray
thee, the graceful pauses, I am alluding to; nay, anticipating—yet now you have led me to discover that I write
worse, than I thought I did, there is no stopping short
—I must improve, or be dissatisfied with myself—

I felt hurt, I can scarcely trace why, last night, at your
wishing time to roll back. The observation wounded the
delicacy of my affection, as well as my tenderness—Call
me not fastidious; I want to have such a firm *throne* in
your heart, that even your imagination shall not be able
to push me from it, be it ever so active.

Mary

WG TO MW

I conceived this to be a day fit for our excursion, and
regretted its lying fallow; but you know best. I shall expect you.
Thursday

September 15, 1796

I am torn between the two—Fanny who is sick and William who
sulks. He did not in his note this morning send even one word for
Fanny. Our walk, upon which he counted, has been spoilt—but
what can I do? She has need of me. I shall insist later, when we
dine, that he make plans with a friend for tomorrow, my weather-
eye telling me this balmy brightness shall prevail. But how unfair
is he to be jealous of Fanny's claim to my attentions; and then,
wounded, to wound me by remarks such as those inconsiderately
made last night. He had been musing upon past decisions in the

course of making his way in life, speaking to no purpose which I could comprehend, while, I confess, my mind kept rushing back to my poor little darling's flushed face and burning brow. I cannot even explain what started the train of thought that led back more than ten years ago to a proposal by Sheridan to pay him a regular stipend, from funds set apart for political purposes by Fox's party, for the editorship of the *Political Herald*. Sheridan once said that Godwin ought to be in Parliament. I asked how such praise had made him feel. Unmoved, he said, indifferent—as he had been to any activity not dictated by the promptings of his own mind. But to day, bored by the slow labour of literary work, drowsy and discontent, he had begun wondering how he would have replied, had he known the difficulties of the life he was choosing. His imagination wandered away, with pleasure, to alternative lives. He sat before me, breathing through his nose, like some heavy, disconsolate stranger. To rouse him, I asked teasingly if he would truly go back in time, at the cost of losing all he had gained. He said he thought he profitably might. I winced at his thoughtless cruelty. Did he mean to be cruel? Or was he so fixed upon his goal that he was blinded to all else? He seemed stuporous. I could not catch his attention. The thought inevitably overcame me that he might wish to roll back time in order to detach his heart from mine.

I have had to go through a nine-hundred-page novel to finish up a review of it for the *Analytical*. I went myself to Johnson's yesterday, rather than send Marguerite, in order to speak on behalf of Mary Hays. She has begun to lose all hope that Robinson will print her M.S. I thought I might be the means whereby she renewed acquaintance with Mr. Johnson, who had once brought out a book of hers, but remembers her only vaguely. And so I went to St. Paul's Church-yard to set a day for our visit—only to find, on my return, a note to say that she is finally out of suspense with Robinson, who will do the novel, after all. Well, thus stands our engagement, all the same, not for this Sunday, for Johnson is to go to the country, but for the Sunday following. By the tone of her note, I gather she is offended by my silence. I shall send her the fourth volume of "Tristram Shandy," which she had asked to borrow last time I saw her. And I still have, unread, though glanced at, the M.S. written by her sister, dreariness itself, I'm afraid—yet I must think of some thing gracious to say of it.

September 17, 1796

My poor Fanny is not so well as I expected—I write with her in my arms—I have been trying to amuse her all the morning to prevent her scratching her face. I am very glad, I did not stay from her last night, for I find she did nothing but seek for me the morning before and moan my absence, which increased her fever.

Opie called Tuesday evening—from a message which he left, I am *almost* afraid that the Devil will call this evening—

September 18, 1796

What a *contretemps!* It seems almost, on waking, the memory of a comedy witnessed from a side-box at Drury Lane. Fortunately, I had warned Godwin of a possible visit from Fuseli, so that, coming for tea, he might not be taken by surprise. I did not choose to tell him of Fuseli's conduct when I met him by chance the other day in Johnson's office. Reading with his arms crossed over the pages of a book, his chin lowered upon his hands, a snuff-box for a weight between the pages, he did not immediately withdraw his attention, so that my first sight of him was of the whiteness of the hair upon the crown of his head. When I entered, he cast up his eyes, peering from his low angle of vision, *a frog's perspective*, as he calls the device he so often uses in his paintings, and which, in the case of women, gives him a pleasant sense of the rotundity and weight of the bosom. He stared in that familiar and irritating manner of his that derives, I suspect, from the habit of treating living models as if inanimate. I stared back into his sullen, saturnine face. It was, I believe, the first time, since returning from Sweden, that I have found myself alone with him. However, he has often dined at Johnson's, when I have been there, usually arriving late, announcing his approach from the foot of the stairs.

Johnson, who dotes on him, once told a guest, who had no previous knowledge of the procedures of the house, that she was about to meet the most ingenious foreigner, but that if she wished to enjoy his conversation she must not attempt to stop his torrent of words by contradiction. How right of him to caution her! If he has not every one's undivided attention, he will sulk and spit insults. His gaze as he looked up, his chin sharp on the back of his long, thin, conjurer's hands, had the cold impassivity of expression that I have observed on his features when he is enjoying the study of his collection of drawings of insects; his large, pale, blue-grey eyes bored into my person with just such scientific coldness. At last he recollected himself and rose to greet me.

He was intrigued by my nonchalance. Heaven knows that when I would have wished to pique his interest, I could not have feigned indifference to get it. In "Mary," I once characterised him, with those strong lines of genius in his face, as a thinker who delivered elegantly and in a musical tone of voice notions infinitely superior to every one else's. His admirers say he is the equal of Michel Angelo; his enemies that he cannot even draw. I think him a genius, and a devil. Once when I accompanied him, his wife and Lavater to a masquerade at the Opera House, a devil came howling up to us and began jabbing about us with his pitchfork. Fuseli told him to go to hell. The admonition did not make him leave us in peace, but inspired such dramatic raging that I had a sense, in watching Fuseli beat him off, that part of his own soul had been magically drawn from him to stand visibly manifest in the form of that costumed devil; it was his angelic side battling the demonic in his own nature. I have heard him boast that he is called *Painter in Ordinary to the Devil,* saying that if he cannot be Prince of Heaven, he will rule in Hell.

I had the desire to leave my pages there on the desk, for I had been told Johnson was out. But, on second thought, I would not have wanted Fuseli to think he had frightened me away. Thus I took the chair by the window, intending to wait. As I sat down and glanced out, the great bells of St. Paul's struck the hour, their reverberation startling a flock of pigeons which lifted into the air and wheeled circularly—one would think they might become indifferent to the hourly tintabulation of the bells. I gazed up at their changing patterns against a blue and cloudless sky, as they whirled about the great bell-tower, a gratifying accompaniment to its intonation. Fuseli, smiling, was making some comment. I gestured him that I could not hear, to postpone what he had to say till the bells left off when, at the last stroke but one, Johnson opened the door, glanced from one to the other of us, restraining astonishment. Thus whatever Fuseli had been trying to communicate during the jubilant striking of the bells was for ever lost. I might then have gone upstairs, staying to dine, but the thought of poor Fanny's discomfort prohibited me from any further dalliance.

As I hastened along Fleet Street to the hackney-stand, I happened to catch sight of my reflexion in the glass panes of a shop and endeavoured to imagine my appearance, when I had been standing in the door to Johnson's office. I had dressed my hair that morning with some attention. From time spent in the fields with Fanny—for I insist she have sufficient exercise—my hair has lightened to a golden shade of brown. I was wearing a plain muslin gown, a silk turban, and carried, besides my paper folders, an embroidered reticule that Everina once had made for me. My air of confidence perhaps was what caused Fuseli's almost quizzical expression, as if he puzzled to define an unknown element which had altered a familiar composition. I wonder now if he might have recollected how once he'd told me I resembled a milkwoman, meaning that my garments were no better than those of some slovenly Irish girl, who will stand in Stephen's Green with her cow and milking pail, in a habit of coarse cloth and black worsted stockings, bits of hay in filthy hair hanging down her back. It was at a time when even the necessaries of life were hard to come by, let alone any pursuit of luxury, my plainness the result of privations—not to mention that earning a livelihood leaves little energy to devote to coquetry. When I first came to work for Johnson eight years ago, it was the seed-time of life, when I might store my mind with knowledge. I did not complain of the necessity of labouring; on the contrary, I was thankful to draw my pleasures from such employment. Yet, however much I struggled, I was over my head and ears in debt. The *old topic* of incessant family worries was one about which I could speak only to Johnson. I had no disguises with him. Some times when he bade me be calm, I thought him unkind, unfeeling—for when a creature is perpetually tormented, broken-hearted, half mad to the point of being unable to rise from bed or, rising, so violently affected in the pit of the stomach as not to be able to lean over a tea-pot, it is unfeeling to be told to remain calm in the face of adversity. Such reasoning —from a man whose emotions are as tidy as the top of his desk —was scarcely a good bracer, for I had already been reasoning a long time with my untoward spirits. I believe that until one is able to form some idea of the whole of existence, one is tossed about as if in a rudderless boat. I idolised Fuseli—his instruction my one firm sign-post in life—so that he could cast me into deliriums of self-reproach. A word, a mere look, would be enough to make me weep or dance like a child. It was humiliating to be so dependent upon his least observation. I prayed, I reasoned, I wished I could knock my foolish head against the wall that bodily pain might make me suffer less spiritual anguish—all to no avail. I danced upon a string held idly in his hands. I was desperately searching for some thing serious in life. But how can one live tranquilly day by day, when the shape of one's life remains obscure? I had no control over my existence. I wondered what I was meant to do, agonised to determine if one step or another might ultimately lead me out of the painful impasse. Johnson advised me to end my attachment to Fuseli, since he was a married man, warning me that continuance would remove me from the common course of life—but I could not do without seeing him, nor even hope that a day would pass in which I might not hear his tantalising voice.

How intimately I know the sound of his footsteps—and fancy as well that I even recognise his knock at the door, knowing precisely how he lifts his silver-headed cane to give three rapid taps, then glowers at the door, head thrust back, eyes level with where a pair of eyes will momentarily appear. I have gone visiting with him and know his ways; I have also sat in my rooms in Store Street, my heart in my mouth, listening for his footfall. Although expecting him yesterday evening, I was, however, unprepared when Marguerite let him in, a little after six. There he stood on the threshold of my parlour, over which he gave one of his sweeping glances, then entered, with an insouciant salutation, and took into his hands the black basalt library bust of Rousseau made by Wedgwood that I have had by me for many years—my single treasure!—and set it lightly back on the bookcase with the comment that he was pleased to see that his countryman looked on less of a scene of disorder than he had in Store Street, his way, I suppose, of complimenting me on the greater spaciousness of my new rooms. He threw himself into the seat of my blue wing-chair—it gave me a turn to see him so familiarly seek it out—and scowled intently into my cavernous chimney-piece, in which lay a thin layer of ash, for the previous evening had grown chill and, alone, to cheer myself, I'd lit a small fire.

I asked if it were a true account that he refused to go to see Tom Lawrence's Rembrandt? Perfectly true, he said. He'd always loathed that Dutchman's disgusting naturalism, his swampy excrescences in painting the female form, while all the male models were the crippled produce of shuffling industry and sedentary toil —not even to speak of the local vulgarity of the style of painting them, nor the ludicrous barbarity of the costumes they are made to sit in. True, no one out-tells Rembrandt in recounting a story, and no one excels him at chiaroscuro—"that infernal machine," as Blake calls it—which certainly produces picturesque effects but —how many times have I heard Fuseli on the subject!—art, classical art, has an impersonal character, serene, detached, without any obtrusion of personality. He wished me then and there to see the newly finished painting in his Milton Gallery. When I replied that Fanny's fever prevented me from going out, nothing would do but that he recite by heart whole passages of Milton, that I might enter the spirit of the argument he had been wholly absorbed all day in illustrating. I lowered the lamplight, for the pulse in his temples had visibly started to jump beneath the skin, as he howled at me speeches out of the mouths of Moloch, Mammon or whomever else, playing all of them at once. He was Satan as a flying fiend, who:

> Puts on swift wings, and towards the gates of hell
> Explores his solitary flight; sometimes
> He scours the right hand coast, sometimes the left,
> Now shaves with level wing the deep . . .

I found myself falling under Milton's powerful spell. Or Fuseli's! Might he still with hypnotic voice and sleight of hand entice me to throw myself headlong, in palpitating ecstasy, before the altar of his art? I looked at him hard as he strutted in his short rapid strides between the window and the cold grate in the chimney-piece—and suddenly a repulsive feeling for him crept over my skin, chilling me through and through, making there rise to my features a fish-eyed look of contempt for—what *he* likes to call—*that poor forked thing* upon my rug. I am still, I believe, so liable to his influence that, even as I looked at him in an effort to remove myself from his dominion, the cynical expression upon my face was one that had once been borrowed from him, a lesson indelibly learned. As I said to Godwin half in jest to day, I came out of the school of Fuseli more of a cynic than I went into it.

When Godwin arrived, I adjusted the lamp, stirred to make him his dish of tea and observed him gazing at Fuseli in friendly, yet timid curiosity, for while he admires his store of knowledge, he yet fears his caustic turn of mind. As if butter would melt in his mouth, he inquired of Fuseli how the project with Cowper was proceeding. Fuseli had worked with the poet on an edition of Homer that Johnson printed; now Johnson wishes to bring out a new edition of "Paradise Lost" which Cowper is to annotate, while Fuseli does a series of drawings. Fuseli answered, quite off-hand, that were Cowper not to go completely out of his mind, their common cause might see the light of day, but that he has no need of him to complete his Milton Gallery, as he now calls the work. It is ordinary knowledge among Johnson's circle that Cowper suffers annual seizures of madness that coincide with that time of year when, long ago, his cousin rejected his proposal of marriage—a madness reserved, some say, to the frosts and fires of February. It is feared, each time, that, like a voyager, subject to storms and shipwreck, he will be lost once and for all.

> Your sea of troubles you have past
> And found the peaceful shore,
> I tempest-tossed and wrecked at last
> Come home to port no more.

When Godwin recounted that Milton is said to have earned from the sale of his masterpiece no more than 13*l*. 9*s*. 6*d*., Fuseli replied that Milton had not written for money—but for immortal reputation. But Godwin insisted on his point: had British copyright laws that then existed functioned to benefit an author and his family, Milton's daughters might not have lived out the remainder of their lives in such bitter penury. Since copyright is restricted to only a few years, it is the booksellers who make a fortune—descendants of authors, on the other hand, live in obscurity and distress. In France an author or his heirs receives payment each time his play is acted in the theatre. Fuseli waved one hand in the air to discount all such considerations. My sentiments are with Godwin. England boasts of her geniuses, and uses them ill.

Fuseli has invited us to visit his studio to see a painting he has completed of Milton teaching his daughters—a painting far superior, he says, to the one on the same subject by Romney. In Romney's painting all the light is on the daughter to contrast her youth with Milton's age, her bright eyes with his blindness; while in his own painting he has balanced the sublimity of Milton's intellect against the girl's simplicity, her lowered attention as she writes against a lectern balanced against the blinded upward gaze of the poet. He had done the scene twice to try for the effect of transcendence above all earthly concerns. In one of those short-tempered phrases he uses, he said: "Nature puts me out." What he had wanted in the representation was the ideal of Milton. He has begun sketching a youthful Milton dreaming of a beautiful Italian woman, materialised beside the sleeping youth. For Fuseli our world of dreams is all to be explored, not only the visible world. It is what he means when he says *Nature puts me out*. I can never forget the impact his "Nightmare" made upon me. On the body of a sleeping woman there squats a hideous, dark, leering monster, while through a window a stallion blindly gazes on the scene. Whenever I have heard Fuseli asked what it signifies, it so angers him that it leads me to suspect he no longer knows what the forms express, forms which once tormented his imagination. When pressed, I have heard him say one thing one time, something quite contradictory another. Often, in various connexions, he speaks of our loss of control when we fall asleep, of a dream world of uncanny monsters, of desires magically realised, of terror magnified, and of what he calls the uninterrupted undulation of outward forms that inwardly originate.

When I glanced at Godwin, arms crossed immovably over his

chest, which is a manner he has, I have noticed, whenever he would restrain himself from displaying feelings of unease, he was listening—or pretending to listen, I could not discern which—while Fuseli, who had risen to his feet, paced back and forth and finally struck a pose as if warming the back of the calves of his legs at the chimney-piece. There was no fire in the grate. Perhaps he took such a stand to remain the centre of attention. I myself had been neither listening nor participating. For some moments I had been thinking to myself: that one standing there is the man to whom I once gave all my heart, this one at present the object of my particular affection; the first made me fiercely unhappy, the other who perhaps does not touch me as deeply—or perhaps only does not hurt me so terribly—accompanies my days, and nights, and, what is more, leaves me in peace a good deal of the time. I can remember feelings for Fuseli of a rawness and anguish barely describable—how I hung on his words, on his looks, on the least little life-line of benign notice, grovelling for an expression of love. Such a passion humiliates one's soul, while with Godwin there is a tenderness that allows me to be . . . I was about to say: *my own man*—I mean, of course, in the specific sense of keeping my head, though my body stirs to passion.

The evening ended in farce. Neither made a move to leave. It had become a contest. I yawned discreetly behind one hand, but neither made the least pretext of comprehension. Inquiring where Godwin's quarters were, discovering them to be merely a few steps away, Fuseli offered to walk him home. Seeing there was little chance of Fuseli leaving us alone, Godwin made his docile exit—only to creep back some three quarters of an hour later with the remark: *Impossible man!* and clasp me in his arms.

MW TO WG

September 19, 1796

I am a little feverish to day. I had full employment yesterday; nay, was extremely fatigued by endeavouring to prevent Fanny from tearing herself to pieces; and afterward she would scarcely allow me to catch half an hour, of what deserved the name of sleep.

I could have wished to have spent a long evening with

you, instead of a flying visit, and I should have been myself again. Why could you not say *how do ye do* this morning? It is I who want nursing first, you perceive—are you above the feminine office? I think not, for you are above the affectation of wisdom. Fanny is much better to day.

Monday noon

September 21, 1796

Yesterday, late in the day, I went to Godwin's. I thought, as I walked the dark streets, that I saw some one lurking behind me; whether a fitful imagination produced the fear of pursuit or whether the incident itself, which made my heart begin to beat, exhausted my nerves, I could not, on seeing Godwin, raise a smile. Nor could I restrain myself complaining against his conduct. Sunday, when he had stopped in his way to dine at Horne Tooke's, he had scarcely been able to contain his desire to be off. Monday I was paid an equally unceremonious call. It demands greater restraint than I possess to withhold criticism of his neglect, when I have had my hands full with Fanny. He seemed unfeeling. I was seated in a chair drawn to the small round table—we had been about to take tea—while Godwin stood hesitantly. The account of my injuries brought stinging tears to my eyes. He looked, I thought, as much as I could tell from my misty view of his features, penitent and sad. He said that when he'd first seen Fanny with her face flushed crimson, her swelling sores suppurating, her eyes fanatically ashine from the fever that inflamed her small wracked frame, as she lay limply in my arms, he had been subject to feeling faint. Fearing that I would have two patients to nurse, he had thought it prudent to withdraw, not to add to my burdens. It had not been the first time such a fit had overcome him. What produced such an effect was the sight of wounds, bodily infliction or pain. He did not understand the connexion of such an infirmity with his character in general, but—reticent and eager to give an impression of equable strength—he had felt it best to conceal such a weakness from me and had stayed away, during Fanny's illness, to avoid another such episode.

I sat there before the tea-board, my hands over my face. I heard a pair of chair legs scrape across the bare floor as Godwin rose, then felt him stroking my arm, speaking incoherently, a softness in his murmuring, soothing voice that made me weep the harder —as if such tenderness, though I had hungered for it, brought more vividly to mind my deprivations. When I had recovered sufficiently to excuse myself for such a silly display, Godwin was sitting in his desk chair. In a slow, distinct, self-examining manner he said that he had recently come to the conclusion that tact was one of his weak points. By some inherent deficiency that he was unable to correct, he seemed also to have a singular want of foresight as to the effect of his actions on others. Then in a self-castigating spirit, he spoke of his incapacity to begin conversations. Though he may be considered talkative, initiating a topic of conversation has always been a matter of much embarrassment to him, so much so that on one occasion when he met in the street an acquaintance of his, who happened to be liable to the same infirmity, they had stood looking at one another for the space of several minutes, each ready to listen to what the other was about to say, but neither able to take the initiative. Thus they had parted without uttering a single word.

I burst out laughing at the absurd picture. Thus for the remainder of the evening I was in spirits, and am to day feeling apologetic for my quickness of feeling. I have to agree with Godwin when he says that previous sorrows in my life have so destroyed my trust in others that, from an insignificant slight, I am liable to construct a universe of injury, indignity and resentment. Well, I am often silly and shall say so to my dearest, kindest friend.

M W T O W G

September 21, 1796

Though I am not quite satisfied with myself for acting like such a mere Girl, yesterday—yet I am better—What did you do to me? And my poor Lambkin seems to be recovering her health and spirits faster than her beauty —Say only that we are friends; and, within an hour or two, the hour when I may expect to see you—I shall be

wise and demure—never fear—and you must not leave
the philosopher behind—
Wednesday morning

WG TO MW

Friends? Why not? If I thought otherwise, I should be
miserable.
In the evening expect me at nine, or a little before.

September 27, 1796

Mary Hays has returned the "Tristram Shandy"—without a line,
so that I take it she is hurt by my seeming neglect. I shall have
to write her to deny, or to expostulate, rather, that friendship which can change without cause would be of slight texture
and—idle to go into my complaints that night at theatre!—that
I have no cause to change my opinion of her. True, my actions
could have led her to believe that there was a misunderstanding
between us, for I have neither called on her nor asked her here.
And there is that matter of a book I had promised to lend her and
forgot. Well, I shall have to plead business or the weather or whatever. And, as for our mutual friend Godwin, who has got the both
of us into such a bother, if truth were told (and it *cannot* be, not,
at least, in so many words) it would be a balm. The trouble is that,
without putting myself at the mercy of her discretionary powers,
I would still like to make things clear between us. Poor Godwin,
in bed to day with fever—for all of his hot forehead and reddened
nose no object for such eager competition! I shall tell her he has
been ill and that I've been nursing him, that I've been frequently
with him to see that the things proper were got, as well as to
amuse him—that should present a picture of unmistakable intimacy. And, in case such a sight brings her rushing across the city
to add her comforting ministrations to mine, I must add that he
had rather not see any company for a few days, so that she will
gather that, though she is *company*, I am not. I do not consider
such treatment cruel, merely hygienic.

Godwin has told me of an incident that took place last winter
when, wishing to visit her as he had promised, going to her rooms,

he walked into the parlour to find her stark naked before the fire.
Instead of quickly departing by the door through which he had
come, he closed the door behind him, intending to go into the
adjoining room to wait, thoughtlessly proceeding to carry out his
plan, which entailed taking a path into the parlour towards her,
while she stood paralysed, without even the power to conceal herself behind one of the garments she had been about to put on.
Sensing by her look of panic that she wanted him to go away and
was unable to say so, he began backing off, unable, however, to
remove his eyes from her rouged figure in the glancing light of a
flickering fire. When he had gone, she quickly dressed and went
to the landing to call him to come up, then went downstairs in
the expectation of finding him waiting in the office of the landlord. But blaming himself for the blunder, he had hastened away
in confusion. He recounted the story to me as an example of the
sort of catastrophe that unwittingly happens to the sort of man
he is, with a mind so continuously reflective that it leaves him unprepared for adventures where quick thinking alone might have
saved him embarrassment. It was obvious to him, after the event,
what he ought to have done: turned and gone straight out the
door. I sympathised with his remorse. Yet some thing nagged me,
some inexplicable thing. When had the occurrence taken place?
Godwin thought it might have been in March and, when pressed,
at the end rather than at the beginning of the month—*after* our
tea with the faithless Mr. Lloyd. I wondered if it were not a case
of jumping from the frying-pan to the fire: that having given up
Mr. Lloyd had left an imagination sufficiently vacuous in which
to germinate the hope of kindling a passion in the heart of her
good friend and counsellor Godwin. I cannot say she consciously
wanted to arouse him by the sight of her nakedness in the fire-
light, but I am led to suspect the scene of being staged. Did she
think that an inadvertent sight of her charms would turn friendship into passion? Would he, falling to his knees, in murmured
lamentation, let loose his true feelings? In novels it occurs in just
such a style—and Mary Hays, victim in my medical opinion of a
glut of novels at too early an age, her mind heated with incredibili-
ties, as Dr. Johnson once phrased it, would have imagined just
such an answer to her prayers. Such belief alone would have made
her stand all pink in the fire-light, like a sacrificial swine. It is, of

course, unfair of me to ridicule her love. But that she thought to wind Godwin in such tricky meshes . . . ! The episode has contributed to my conviction that she has designs on him, and is willing to play every wile to ensnare him into her possessive arms, where in her imagination he already lies. (She is reading my copy of "The Monk" which certainly has in it the feverish evils of confused yearnings—an unwholesome porridge if there ever were one.) So where am I in this reasoning aloud of mine? Ah, yes, that it is less cruel to insinuate the truth than to perpetuate falsehood.

I rushed, earlier this morning, to Godwin's bedside to see how he had slept. He was very sweet, as I sat on his bed to keep him company, before running off on errands. He said he had had, all night long, perplexing dreams. He asked if I believed in the biblical Joseph's ability to predict from dreams. I said I do not, though often I have been either entertained or appalled by the constructive power of the imagination as it reveals itself through our sleeping mind. He said he was often puzzled by the meaning of his dreams. He had been dreaming, he told me, of a Miss Pinkerton, whom he had only met once quite casually at the home of a friend: that she had in his dream beseeched him to look into her face to tell her what he saw there. Slowly, as is the way of dreams, he turned and did as she had bid him and, as he did so, a darkness seemed to lift as instantly as when the sun slides from behind a cloud. Immediately he saw her transformed in a radiance of light, while laughing and stroking his hand in gratitude, as happy as a child. He asked what I thought of his dream and did I perceive any significance. I could not say that I did. I confess that Godwin in his wrinkled night-dress, speaking through his nose, was hardly in the posture of a passionate swain who turns glum girls gay. He was insulted by my making fun of him and returned to his reading of "The Monk," he, too, absorbed in the tale as, I suppose, has been for months now all London Town.

M W T O W G

September 28, 1796

I was detained at Miss Hays', where I met Mrs. Bunn, as it was necessary for me to out stay her. But this is not the worst part of the story. Mrs. Bunn was engaged to dine at Opie's, who had promised to bring her to see me this evening—They will not stay long of course—so do as you please. I have no objection to your drinking tea with them—But you—should you not like it—may I request you drink tea with M. Hays, and come to me at an early hour. Nay, I wish you would call on me in your way for half an hour—as soon as you can rise from table. I will then give you the money.

September 28, 1796

My Wednesdays are frantically spent dashing from one bookseller to another to see what books have been printed and put between boards. I then travel high and low to see that a volume is placed in trusted hands for review. I some times send it off with a note scratched out in a corner of Johnson's office. Often it is a tiresome business. Other times it provides precisely the sort of spirited exchange I most relish, and I will dally to extend a conversation beyond the mere necessity of commerce. To day was such a day. I went from pillar to post, carrying packages of books to spare time. I had left with Johnson a new volume on the life of Lorenzo de' Medici for Fuseli, who is signing his reviews these days by the initials Z.Z.—as previously he signed them R.R. or Y.Y., so childish, going, as Godwin says of him, to strange lengths to appear out of the ordinary. I had a new novel, "The Gossip's Tale," that I thought Mary Hays might do; to drop it at Hatton Gardens seemed a nicety for which I might trouble myself, in order to heal wounds still somewhat raw. I hesitated only because she is at times dilatory in finishing a piece, and the one in mind must be quickly done, since Johnson is in want of materials for next month. I shall also have to take her to task, as gently as I can, for a habit of hers which I once had to cure in myself: that is, alluding to things in a work which can only be understood by those who have already read it. One must give an account of the incidents on which the interest turns, to enable a reader to have a clear idea of a book which they have never heard of before. It is a technique that can be easily learned, once the rudiments are clear.

In a hackney-coach to Hatton Gardens I lay back, gazing with half-closed eyes upon the tumult of the streets, sinking into revery; soothed, serene, conscious of an extraordinary sense of rectitude in the universe, with no one single discernible cause for such elation. Money which I had determined to borrow from Johnson to enable me to pay off certain small debts was safely within my pocket. Certainly having it eased my mind. Yet it was, as I say, a general sense of well-being, one of those reckonings one occasionally has, like a glimpse from on high, of one's small self resolutely manœuvring in a world of pitfalls—with some self-esteem at the sight of frailty triumphant. It was such a feeling. Thank God for it. For in another moment, all such philosophical benefit was lost in the frantic *va-et-vient* in Mary Hays' rooms.

She was not alone. Mrs. Bunn was there, Opie's wife—who shall no longer be his wife, once Parliament has passed his Divorce Bill. I was somewhat prepared for her by Opie's description: a woman of small stature, bright eyes, pretty, singularly direct. Opie said he could never have given her the things she wants in life—social position, constant diversion—although her Irish Major might manage it. I like it that she did not throw me any of those little, cunning, sidelong glances to try to detect what I might think of her; rather she turned on me a beam of frank curiosity—on a woman, the sight of whom had made her once crane her neck over a crowd of heads, when I had been at theatre one night with Opie. Not having wished to make me uncomfortable, he had resisted telling me that his wife was in the theatre, so that there had been no chance of *my* having had a look at *her*. She was dressed in the style of Irish gentry, overdressed, that is, for the time of day at which we met, yet there was such a studied plan of colour and of well-placed bangles and brooches that the whole had its own air of naturalness, like the vari-coloured plumage of some small tropical bird. It was not clear what she was doing at Mary Hays', but I was at once seized by dread that, having insinuated so much in my letter of yesterday, had Mary Hays rancour towards me, she might susceptibly allow to be drawn from her, were Mrs. Bunn to ask about me, all that she now suspects of my present attachment. Before I knew it, there would be just the sort of speculation which I want at all costs to avoid. Now I saw that I was obliged to stay as long as Mrs. Bunn, and a little longer, to pledge Mary Hays to secrecy. When I returned home, I dashed a note to

Godwin to come immediately, not only for me to give him back the money he lent me last week, but to impress upon him the necessity of going at once to Mary Hays' to bind her to our urgent need to keep the connexion between us secret. Once it becomes the common currency of gossip, tars and feathers cast upon me for my conduct will certainly stick to Godwin as well. These reflexions raced through my mind, all the while that I was holding a conversation with Mrs. Bunn. I enjoyed the guileless expression of her eyes—which once more proves the point that women, whom gossip may paint with the blackest pitch, are often seen to have the rosiest complexions and very best of manners. I could see why Opie found it impossible to resent her, or to banish her completely from his life. By the very oddest coincidence in the world, he had been planning to bring her to see me, she had heard him speak of me so often she had requested the meeting. I insisted that she keep to that very plan, promising to be home this evening for their visit. She rose at once, smiling and extending to me a hand scented with patchouli.

I removed from my sack the volume I'd brought Mary Hays, which she took without meeting my eyes, going to a corner of her settee, turning pages to try to get some gist of the story. Her appearance was of some one who has barely slept. Her skin has the pallor of one who lives at a sedentary pace, rarely taking advantage of a balmy day, either to go out walking or to sit beneath a tree in the open air. Her health, at the moment, however, was hardly my concern. I was trying to read her feelings from the tilt of her lowered head. She lifted to say she thought she might do the review in time, and we spoke of the substance of the book for several minutes. Then silence fell. She broke it to ask after Godwin's state. I replied that he still kept to the house, choosing to say so for consistency's sake, but bit my tongue, when I remembered that I had decided it was necessary that he immediately speak to her on our behalf. I thus added that, intending to take a walk after dinner, he would most probably be coming to take tea with her, if he felt sufficiently well. I had not dared face her, since we had begun speaking of Godwin, but now—full of sufficient courage to meet the sorrow I had caused—I turned and let my gaze be held by hers. I hoped she would be the first to speak. All that sounded was the sighing of her breath. I could not stand such stoical anguish. I rose to go to sit beside her, putting my hand on hers and, as I did so, felt her body stiffen against me, or against the force of her own feelings, for in another moment she was weeping in my arms. The pitch of her sobs reminded me of Fanny's staccato wails in infancy, when she would awake in darkness, a harsh, almost animal cry, which made me wrap my arms still tighter around the frail form in my arms to soothe her back to life. I wondered how I could talk rationally to her, even as she sat up, grew calmer, and daubed her eyes. I had come to swear her to secrecy, yet it seemed uncharitable to think of myself at such a moment. Thus I made a speech on the constancy of our sempiternal friendship which nothing could diminish—for I had sensed in the sound of her weeping some of the terror of fear of abandonment and wished to ease her mind that the union between Godwin and me did not change my feelings. I was yet her friend; I still loved her—I got back only the most mournful look from the face of an utterly desolate child. Finally I had to depart. I said I was home every morning with the exception of Wednesday and that she must come to take tea with me as soon as she possibly could, deciding that the best I could do, in the circumstances, was to postpone till next time all the many exhortations I had so carefully prepared in my way to her. I kissed her tenderly and left—without making the slightest dent in her sorrow.

I now write in a spare moment after dinner alone, and a hasty conference with Godwin, who immediately set off in his determined way to Hatton Gardens. I had only half a mind, as I read to Fanny, who was fully aware that I was elsewhere, and had a fit of weeping of her own. I finally had to shut the door upon her and be some time alone to make an effort to control my nervous state of irritation, for I had begun to see the consequences of my heedless act of revelation to just such a person as would suffer most by it. Godwin says Mary Hays is not vindictive, but he agrees, all the same, that she might fail to understand the importance of secrecy, believing as she does in utter frankness in human relations —in such a literal manner, that she allows so subtle shadings for discretion's sake. He quite thinks it within her character to assume that we must take the moral consequences of our passion, standing heroically against society's judgement like two tragic lovers upon the stage. To prevent being cast into such roles, Godwin has, very Mr. Francis-like, hurried over to reason with her. And I on tenter-hooks take to writing in my note-book to calm nerves jangling with the uneasiest suspense. The worst of it is that when Godwin comes to me, he will be unable to say a word to the point, obliged as he will be to make polite conversation with the Opies.

September 29, 1796

Opie was so young, when he married, that he had to lie about his age. The irony is that, since he'd been under-age, the marriage has never been valid, but if he should offer proof to that effect, to annul the union, he might be liable to be indicted for perjury, since to procure the marriage licence he'd had to *swear* he was of age. It is a quandary that sets Mrs. Bunn into titters of laughter. Though not ever married in a true legal sense, they must go to the greatest lengths of the law to obtain a divorce. I made a confession of my own, encouraged by the absurdity of their position: if Imlay and I had gone to the Hôtel de Ville to register our marriage, I would have been instantly executed. We, all three, burst into laughter. Any one eavesdropping might have formed an impression that we were the most heartless of libertines—yet, by all I believe in, I am convinced there is rectitude in those who are rigorously true to the dictates of their hearts. Opie's affection has been taken by a Miss Beetham, who is his pupil at the Royal Academy. When he sees her down one of the long corridors, his heart leaps like a young doe in the bracken. Miss Beetham will have 4,000*l*. independently, which Opie says he will not touch a farthing of, but will settle on her. He is quite comfortable, having for the last ten years got near 1,000*l*. a year.

Our destinies all seemed in such a curious balance of hope and despair as to make us the liveliest of companionable creatures, so that quite on impulse it occurred to me to pull from a drawer my little comedy and begin to read—to appreciative growls from Opie, sitting with both his legs straight out, his hands clasped behind his head, while pleasing laughter came from Mrs. Bunn, beside me on the sofa, her chin daintily poised on the back of one hand. The clownish aspect of my American hero's speeches made them laugh; they had to laugh, as well, at my English woman, when she addresses not the man before her, but rather some inner image of ideal goodness, which gives her language a hopelessness as comical as that drawn from the heart of Molière's "Misanthrope." A most Jacobin lady from time to time enters to tell of her travails—prison, loss of residence, her mother misplaced—a character based on Helen Maria Williams who, living through the convulsions taking place in the *République*, took delight in all its bloodiest actions, which she unswervingly justified in terms of revolutionary necessity, till she herself was arrested and flung into prison. Mr. Johnson had been particularly horrified at what he called my very indecent picture of her, which signifies, at the very least, that the character was recognisably drawn. As for Godwin, when he read my comedy, four months ago, he had not the slightest crinkle of laughter in his eyes, as he scolded me for rendering comic what he considers indescribably sacrosanct: a man's betrayal of the weaker sex. Richardson, he said, would never have made fun of Clarissa's struggle. His readers would have been appalled if he had, etc., etc. I was convinced by his reasoning at the time and hid away in the bottom of a drawer my poor little maligned play. But now the Opies, each in a different way, according to his and her sights, grew spirited before the dilemma of two lovers at constant cross-purposes. I was so gratified by their laughter that I began to read with a certain theatrical flair, pausing for emphasis, and in several subtle ways wringing every drop of bitter ridicule from the matter.

In the middle of it, Godwin entered. I had been so diverted, while reading aloud, laughing at droll effects only half remembered of two lovers locked in perplexity, that I had completely forgotten how anxiously I had been awaiting the outcome at Mary Hays'. He gave me a nod—it might have meant either that he had succeeded, or that matters stood in as serious a condition as I had imagined them. His usual bonhomie in company made him hide every indication of his mood. He brightened at seeing Opie, for whom he has the greatest admiration, and drew up a chair to sit beside Mrs. Bunn, who turned very prettily towards him, while my spirits yielded to the most anxious reflexions.

I needn't have worried. Godwin is masterful in the realm of rational discourse. For two hours he had been unable to bring up the subject of importance to us, while Mary Hays had made one of her lengthy, detailed, characteristic self-examinations, which she troubles ordinarily now to do only in letters, ever since Godwin bluntly informed her he had more pertinent matters to attend to when calling on her. He had allowed himself hardly a single observation, in order neither to complicate nor to prolong her discourse. When she exhausted herself, he had finally seen his chance, to tell her of our need for secrecy. She had leapt to anger at the notion that he should expect her to be duplicitous. They had cavilled over her definition of things for quite some time. He had argued for one's right to such privacy as allows the free expression of tender feelings to mature without the stunting hand of condemnation. He had entreated her to understand our adamant need for silence. And, at last, resigned to it, she had agreed. We were both—by the end of the day, a day of heart-rending suspense —utterly relieved.

M W T O W G

September 29, 1796

It is my turn, William, to be indisposed. Every dog has its day, you know, and as you like a moral in your heart, let me add, as one applicable to the present occasion, whatever you may think—that there is no end to our disappointments when we reckon our chickens too soon.

I shall be with you at five, to receive what you promised to give *en passant—mais, à notre retour, rien que philosophie. Mon cher ami, êtes-vous bien faché? Mon Bien-aimé!—moi aussi, cependant la semaine approach-ant,* do you understand me—

W G T O M W

Take your tea with me. If you do not like that, let me know.

Man

M W T O W G

I am under the necessity of dining out. Thus circumstanced, will you condescend to admit me in the evening at eight or nine?

Will you do me the favour to send Caleb Williams to Mr. Stoddard, No. 6 South Kow (opposite Chalton Street) Somers Town? I forgot it last night when I left you.

Adorable maîtresse. J'espère que vous êtes plus gai ce matin. Prenez garde à vous!

September 30, 1796

When there is not a good reason to prevent it I wish you to dine with me, or, I wish you, of a Saturday, to enable us to bear the privation of Sunday, with *philosophie*. Tomorrow is my turn, and I shall expect you. This arrangement renders it necessary to alter the previous plan for *ce soir*. What say you—may I come to your house, about eight—to philosophise? You once talked of giving me one of your keys, I then could admit myself without tying you down to an hour, which I cannot always punctually observe in the character of a woman, unless I tacked that of a wife to it.

If you go out, at two, you will, perhaps, call and tell me that you thought as kindly of me last night as I did of you; for I am glad to discover great powers of mind in you; even at my own expense. One reason, I believe, why I wish you to have a good opinion of me is a conviction that the strongest affection is the most involuntary—yet I should not like you to love, you could not tell what, though it be a French compliment of the first class, without my explanation of it. The being enamoured of some fugitive charm; that seeking somewhere, you find everywhere: yes; I would fain live in your heart and employ your imagination—am I not very reasonable?

You do not know how much I admired your self-government, last night, when your voice betrayed the struggle it cost you—I am glad that you force me to love you more and more, in spite of my fear of being pierced to the heart by everyone of whom I rest my mighty stock of affection. Your tenderness was considerate, as well as kind—Miss Hays entering, in the midst of the last sentence, I hastily laid my letter aside without finishing, and have lost the remain. I and it sunk in the quicksand of Love?

I have now only to say that I wished you to call by two because I go to the city around Finsbury Square.

If you send me no answer I shall expect you.

Friday

Sunday eve—

Reflexions on the Lives of Women

I entitle this blank page with a subject that has been, all day, labouring in my head, as I digest the matter of these last few days. Is it one's circumstance or one's character that determines what Hume has called identity? Would it not, for example, have been a matter of mere good luck for Mary Hays to have drawn in life a loving husband and domestic felicity? I cannot think her present situation foredestined, absolute, determined solely by character. The young man she was engaged to marry at seventeen need not have died—then the Miss Hays we intimately know would not have existed. We see her as reality has produced her, forgetting the infinite other possibilities that were hovering upon the ether eager to be born. Mrs. Christie, so brave in her particular solitary life, says the habit still prevails upon her of keeping some choice bit of experience in mind to tell Mr. Christie—that each time falls anew a blow of astonishment that he shall not be in the house when she opens the door, nor any where at all where she can reach him. I have gone to see her at Finsbury Square as often as I could, but have not yet had her here—I do not know why. I have lacked the courage to tell her, who nursed me when I no longer wished to live, how life has become once again agreeable. She sees me become vigorous, though the source of my health and happiness is some thing I have been unable to share with her, fearing my good fortune would, if exposed, leave me liable to the most cruelly barbed condemnation. Do I fear such from a dear friend who knew all my miseries? Yes, indeed. I fear that the tenderness which softens her features might vanish in a contortion of disgust, were I to tell her how, from throwing my life into the Thames, dragged out on a hook like some no-longer-living thing, coming back to consciousness with a groan of dismay that I had not finally done with life, I have been warmed back to life by Godwin's hands, warmed into a rapturous desire that thrills me to be alive. Yet it would be said, as it is said of widows, that they must pass a certain length of time in mourning, their recovery neither desirable nor seemly. So I must pretend with my good, old friend to days of duty and dull reward—and breathe not a word of Godwin.

Dining yesterday at home with him, I was forced to observe that this established familiarity is well worth preserving from worldly intrusion. Since we are seldom together Sunday—every odd Sunday taken by his sister, the even ones by Holcroft and their friends, long habits I have no reason to ask him to change—I had requested him to make Saturdays *en famille*. Perhaps I only imagine his easy delight in our company, but I think not. Fanny sat at the table on her box stool, inside of which she stores her playthings. She drank from the Toby mug, one of her dearest possessions, letting her glance rove from one to the other of us over its brim. Mary had roasted a fresh joint of mutton—6d. the pound!—and I had a bottle of claret. Any small sparrow who might have harboured away from the zephyrs on our window ledge, glimpsing the familial scene, would not have had the least troubling suspicion that the gentleman in spectacles, growing ruddy with wine, laughing at Fanny's table-talk, had once so notoriously defined the evils of cohabitation as inimical to true happiness, because opposed to the development of our best faculties. He was, however, not amused by my pointing it out. I suppose it was tactless of me. But his scowl vanished at some remark from Fanny, who was doing her best toward promoting philosophical dialogue. It gave me a rush of sweet pleasure to witness her diminutive charms. I had a view through a chink, so to speak, of the sort of woman she would grow to be . . . if, that is, one can have the least expectation of a woman growing, in England, at the present time, into a spirit not corseted by standards of unnatural decorum.

The artificial manners society demands of women, even in these times, was brought forcibly home to me on speaking the other evening to Mrs. Reveley. She has had a singular past. From her eighth year she grew up among the Turks—for her father, a sea-captain, dispatched her mother back to England, keeping the child. She recalls her unrestricted liberty; she would go wherever she liked, on horseback into the hills above the ancient city, or through the teeming market-place, with a servant for protection. There had been at that time no lodgings for foreigners; it was before the Empress Catherine had put into the country a horde of adventurous colonisers; and the few Europeans who had taken up residence were mainly diplomats and merchants, largely without families, a masculine society in which the child was an equal. It did not occur to her father, apparently, to restrict access to such knowledge and understanding as might be gained through conversation with his friends. By this lack of conventional bias against her as a female, she was spared any sense of inferiority. At fifteen she went to Rome to study painting with Angelica Kauffmann, who at once appreciated the girl's directness, which education had not destroyed. A young architect studying in Rome fell in love with her and brought her back to England as his wife. The change was, she said, equal to being cast into the darkest dungeon, such was the bigoted, ignorant, artificial code of conduct she confronted. For the first time in her life she knew what it was to suffer merely through being a woman. She found it an extraordinary experience. It had been her habit to be outspoken—now all intellectual honesty, interpreted as lack of gentility, had to be stifled . . . and, in fact, she was obliged, with as much difficulty as learning a foreign language, to curtail both curiosity and frankness for the sake of English convention. She had learned courtesy based on kindness, now she was asked to speak in a fawning manner which she despised, forced to an abject subservience unworthy of any free individual. Mr. Reveley's income of 140*l.* per annum, with two children, is hardly adequate for the genteel appearance required, so that life in England, as she knows it, is a subject to which she warms. I, for my part, like a child before a fable, listen in fascination to her tales of Turkey over tea.

I had gone to the city to visit Mrs. Christie, alone so much of the time these days, since she cannot entertain as she once used to, and I was to pass Godwin's later in the evening. When I did so, I found him chatting with Mrs. Reveley. I did not interrupt the course of their conversation, preferring to witness the spectacle of Mrs. Reveley parrying a rather dogmatic statement of Godwin's. With unexpected indolence, at the moment of disarming him, she yielded. I confess I sat up with a certain discernment at such skill and such mercy combined. She is charming and quite pretty, without any distinguishing characteristics, however, that might make one take note of her in a crowd. It is rather the play of her expressions, lively and full of humour, which sets her off from a dozen other handsome women. I was the first to leave. Convention constrains me into acting, not according to my desires, but to cloak my desires. Godwin accompanied me to the door, a swift look of disappointment in his eyes. His voice betrayed how hard it was for him to govern his feelings—and I felt a heart overflowing with love, as I picked my way over slippery cobbles in a night whose chill had no effect, so blazing had been his look.

M W T O W G

October 4, 1796

So I must write a line to sweeten your dinner—No; to give you a little salt for your mutton, rather; though your not partaking of a morsel, Mary was bringing me up, of this dinner as you were going out, prevented me from relishing it—

I should have liked to have dined with you to day, after finishing your essays—that my eyes, and lips, I do not exactly mean my voice, might have told you that they had raised you in my *esteem*. What a cold word! I would say love, if you will promise not to dispute about its propriety, when I want to express an increasing affection, founded on a more intimate acquaintance with your heart and understanding.

I shall cork up all my kindness—yet the fine volatile essence may fly off in my walk—you know not how much tenderness for you may escape in a voluptuous sigh, should the air, as is so often the case, give a pleasurable movement to the sensations, that have been clustering around my heart, as I read this morning—reminding myself, every now and then, that the writer *loved me*. Voluptuous is often expressive of a meaning I do not now intend to give. I would describe one of those moments, when the senses are exactly tuned by the rising tenderness of the heart, and according reason entices you to live in the present moment, regardless of the past or future—It is not rapture—It is a sublime tranquility. I have felt it in your arms—Hush! Let not the light see, I was going to say hear it—these confessions should only be uttered—you know where, when the curtains are up—and all the world shut out.

Ah me! What shall I do to day, I anticipate the unpleasing task of repressing kindness—and I am overflowing with the kindest sympathy—I wish I may find you at home when I carry this letter, to drop it in the box,—that I may drop a kiss with it into your heart, to be embalmed, till we meet, ~~love~~. Don't read the last word, I charge you.

MW TO WG

October 6, 1796

I was vext, last night, to hear the rain patter, while I was undressing myself—Did he get wet? poor fellow.

Will you give Mary the coat you mentioned, for her boy, if it be not inconvenient. And the corn plaster, for me, should it be at hand.

Are you very gay to day? Gay without an effort—that is best—Fanny won't let me alone!—Adieu!

WG TO MW

October 6, 1796

Non: je ne suis pas gai sans effort. The rain fell, but did not wet me; I wore a chastened skin.

If you would have your Latin books *cet après hier*—
Pray bring them here yourself.

Man

October 7, 1796

The weather has disarranged my plan to day—will you
come and spend the evening with me?—Let me see you,
if you please, at an early hour, and I will tell you why
you damped my spirits, last night, in spite of all my efforts—Reason may rule the conduct; but even philosophers, I find, cannot command the spirits—yet, we are so
happy some times, when we least know why. Can you
solve this problem?

I was endeavouring to discover, last night in bed, what
it is in me, of which you are afraid. I was hurt at perceiving that you were—but no more of this—mine is a
sick heart; and in a life like this the fortitude of patience
is the most difficult to acquire.

Au revoir

October 8, 1796

Godwin came in last night, while Opie was still with me. We had
been speaking of his divorce proceedings. Opie thinks I must make
a comedy out of it—he cannot see as tragedy a legal resolution of
what has already been thoroughly resolved: his wife, Mary Bunn,
living happily with Major Edwards, while he himself looks to his
own prospects of happiness with Miss Beetham. The means of
extricating himself from legal bondage are of proportions sufficiently farcical. I'd already heard how, last March, a friend was
sent down to Clifton, where the guilty couple were living as husband and wife, to advise the landlady that the lady was the wife of
another and the gentleman not her husband, thus to fulfill the
formalities required to bring an action in court against Major
Edwards for Trespass, Assault and Criminal Conversation—terms

which make Opie bark with laughter. After the first suit, it was necessary to bring a suit for libel, which, when won July last, gave Opie his freedom from bed and board. Now next month he petitions the House of Lords for a special bill to be passed to dissolve his marriage and enable him to marry again. What appears to me preposterously lacking in common sense, throughout this entire ordeal, is that Mary Bunn, Major Edwards and Opie are all dedicated to the same object on the friendliest basis; yet the law of the land demands a guilty party, going so far as to take testimony from a housemaid on the manner with which her mistress left the house, when she left for good, saying, it appears, that she was going out to dine with her father. These private slip-slop imbecilities, as Opie calls them, must be referred to a committee of the House of Parliament in a most debasing and public manner. Goldsmith might have made comedy out of it, Opie thinks. When the curtain is about to fall, two couples would be seen upon the stage, fondly joined, after one of each of them has survived the long and cumbrous procedures of divorce—while in the wings, Opie hastens to add, the Lords are counting out the money come to them through the affair. Godwin joining us as we were merrily improvising, our effects became broader and more absurd, which in the end left us in spirits.

Godwin has been impressed on reading "L'École des Femmes" by the different expectations habitual to men and women. I asked if he had not been outrageously amused by Arnolphe's marriage maxims for his prospective bride. Not at all amused, he replied; for every man, were he honest, would demand similar terms, if he dared. When Opie asked what maxims we spoke of, I rose to go to the bookshelves and find in its red Moroccan binding my copy of Molière's works, and turned to find the part in the play, where I read out loud bits of it in English—for Opie knows not a word of French.

Maxim Four

> Under her coife, when going out honourably
>   Her eyes must stifle their glance,
> For to well please her spouse
>   She ought to please nobody else.

Maxim Seven

Among her furnishing
She must have neither desk, paper, pen or ink;
By good custom, her husband will think
To write everything for her.

Opie begged me to read still others and I made out, as best I could in English—

Maxim Ten

Promenades
Or meals upon the grass
She never may:
For according to cautious thinkers
The husband
Will be the one to pay.

Godwin asked Opie if he did not agree that Arnolphe's "School for Wives," if not entirely practical, was yet a universal masculine ideal? Was there not in every man a bit of Arnolphe and his maxims? Opie agreed that unfortunately there was. And I rejoined that it was surely to *cure* such contagion, not to contribute to it, that had prompted Molière to write his play. I hunted and found the place where Arnolphe first asks Agnes to listen to him, to lift her head and turn her face. Is this then universal man speaking?

Votre sexe n'est là que pour la dépendance:
Du coté de la barbe est la toute-puissance.

Seeing there was little he might do to reconcile our positions, Opie made a hasty retreat, leaving Godwin and me in a thick cloud of sullen disagreement. Whenever he has a *démêlé* with Holcroft, or any other of his masculine friends, there is rarely as much emotion brought in as comes between us in a difference of opinion. His grievance against me is that I take personally every thing he says. Fear of wounding me often makes him fall silent. As an example, he had come to me this evening with the most joyous news, but should he now appear buoyantly to communicate it, he fears I might labour to twist it about to criticise him for being insensitive to my present ill feelings. He is equally afraid that, to please me, he will become one of those French gallants with not a single idea rattling inside his head except how to turn a phrase of flattery upon his mistress' eyebrow. I said I doubted if he risked playing such a pleasing role.

He had hurried to come to tell me, it turned out, as soon as he'd been free of engagements, that the King in a speech to Parliament had just announced having set on foot negotiations to restore peace to Europe. There is a spirit of excitement in the streets as news that war shall at last be ended is bruited about. I have now, this morning, read about it in the news paper, skimming the King's speech and the subsequent speeches of the Lords, before sending the paper to Godwin with Mary in her way to market. The war, indeed, has become such a fixture in our lives that the absence of it is almost unthinkable. Surely a great gulf separates parliamentary rhetoric from effective reality; in short, I remain unmoved by the King's intention to send an envoy to Paris with full power to treat for the object of peace. I cannot rise to the occasion as well as Godwin—who, in some way, is more naïve than I. Or is it that I am less quick to respond to impersonal news, my concerns restricted to the private realm, nearer joys looming larger than further ones? If such criticism is a just complaint, I must try to calculate improvement.

WG TO MW

October 10, 1796

Mr. Allen has been with me; Mr. Carlisle is coming. I believe his visit will be about three. I wish you did not dine at Mr. Johnson's; at least I wish you could be with me soon after dinner. I suppose they will spoil my dinner.

Do not be alarmed, my love. I am in the gayest health. I believe this boy pupil turns mole-hills into mountains.

Monday, eleven o'clock   William

October 13, 1796

Godwin keeps a journal. I asked him for what purpose; will he one day write his memoirs? He said he thinks not. It has simply become second nature, a methodical habit of life, to note how many pages he has written, what he is reading, whom he has called upon, what guests are present and some times the topic of conversation. I asked if I am part of his method. He says I am. April last he would write: "Imlay calls" or "Call on Imlay," but soon it had become *Wollstonecraft*, misspelled. Now I am W*t* as Holcroft is H*t*. I had to laugh. What, then, I asked, does he write these days of W*t*? Oh, that she comes to dine, or that he takes tea at her house, whatever the occasion. Nothing else? *That* he reserves to write in French: *chez moi, chez elle*—it means all the rest that transpires at such opportunities. Sunday last and Monday he could not resist adding the description *bonne*. For a long while I was lost in thought. Then I said that I supposed that, if he did not choose to write his own life, some one else, having in hand the journal, would take it upon himself to do so. Godwin considered his record of rolling weeks and months and years, that journal which sees through such a long vista of time—yet *sees* nothing. What could another possibly make of the abstractions, symbols, ciphers written there? Why, neither joy nor sorrow, pleasure nor pain. It would appear to yield its secrets no more than would a tablet of hieroglyphics whose significance remains impenetrable. I suggested that by small signs is our universe known, by bits of broken shell and weed upon a shore do we glimpse the manifold mysteries of the ocean's depth. So might his journal communicate the spirit of his life. This time it was he who, for a moment, was lost in reflexion.

October 16, 1796

We spent the evening over the essays, Godwin reading them aloud. Some times I am amused by notions of his which strike me as eccentric. One of these is his insistence that he does not write of things that he understands, but understands them *be-*

cause he has written of them. He shrugged off my laughter saying he is exposed to a thousand foolish and miserable mistakes. If we were to dive into the portfolios of men who have risen to the highest literary eminence, he believes we should meet with abundant matter for laughter. No man knows better than the man of talent that each stage is an improvement on the last, and it is perhaps only at the last stage of all that a philosopher will become what the vulgar supposed he already had been from the very moment of his birth.

Last night, unhappy over the slowness of his production, writing some days a page, some days nothing at all, unable to overrule his phlegmatic nature, I saw him make himself miserable recalling how Dr. Johnson in his usual dilatory way wrote, when he could bring himself to do so, in vigorous haste and gargantuan prolixity, finishing forty-eight printed octavio pages of the life of Savage at one sitting, and in a single day composing seventy lines of the poem "Vanity," yet putting not one of them on paper till they were completed in his head—a feat of memory that defies any mere ordinary mortal.

October 19, 1796

A wretched Wednesday. I walked about, soaking the hem of my garments, in a driving rain. A raw wind had blown down the sign of a tavern, which struck a poor woman selling shrimps and bloaters, the force of the blow cutting open the back of her skull, so that she lay flat upon what appeared to be a crimson cushion that some one had gently rested her head upon; it was, however, the thick clot of blood overflowing from her wound. I fear she may have bled to death before a physician could arrive on the scene. I was sickened by the sight of so much blood and by our human susceptibility. Our lives, which we consider safeguarded by all sorts of prudent observances, by the breaking of a link of chain upon which hangs a heavy piece of wood, slicing down like an executioner's axe, ends when we least expect it, even as we are in the process of anticipating the next meal that we relish in advance, or are rehearsing some witty anecdote to recount, or wonder if we are loved as faithfully as we love the person dear to us—every thing fond ended by a casual condemnation of fate, frivolously. Poor soul! I still see in the mind's eye the way the toe of one shoe turned one way, the other in the opposite direction, with a kind of waywardness quite comical. There is some thing unjustifiably cruel in ending one's time upon the earth without any warning. I would wish to know when my time to depart has come, as I told William. For what cause? he asked. I did not know, nor do I know now. Perhaps only to be conscious, for a single brief illuminating moment, of the whole of my life which, while living it, has never composed itself long enough to let me have a good look at it.

MW TO WG

October 26, 1796

I think, as an *amende honorable*, you ought to read my answer to Mr. Burke.

Fanny wishes to ask man's pardon—she won't cry any more.

Are you burnt up alive?

MW TO WG

October 27, 1796

Mrs. Cotton comes tomorrow, should it prove fine, or Saturday. She talks of a few days. *Mon Dieu!* Heaven and Earth!

Tuesday, November 1, 1796

What days! I have barely had a chance to sit still, none at all to carry on the causes of philosophy for, as a friend of Dr. Johnson's once said to excuse himself for neglecting its pursuit, cheerfulness keeps breaking in. Mrs. Cotton came on Saturday, so late in the day that, though Godwin had gone to the trouble of getting a box for "Fortune's Fool," she was too thoroughly exhausted from the coach ride; indeed, she appeared a martyred figure, tossed about for tormenting hours, her usually benevolent glance, framed in drifts of loosened hair, wild, distracted and unstable. It did not, therefore, seem unkind to leave her to refresh herself while I went to Covent Garden.

We were five in the box: Godwin and I; Francis Twiss, who more and more each day resembles the knight of the dark countenance; Mrs. Inchbald, who gave me one of her narrowest smiles, so narrow it barely passed through the crack, a flat wafer of a greeting, as it were; and one of Godwin's acolytes, who chattered so gaily in my ear that I could scarcely refrain from warning him that to Godwin *cheerfulness breaking in* would serve as no excuse. Mrs. Cotton's empty chair was lifted from the box above our heads with shouts of encouragement and sallies from the stalls. While we waited for the play to begin, Twiss told us one of the most malicious anecdotes I have ever heard—on the subject of Lord Derby's passionate attachment to Miss Farren—while his prying fingers stripped an orange bought from one of the women sellers down below. He paints over life a bitter coating of malice. I laugh with a laughter that catches in my throat, and am left with a tinge of melancholy from the nastiness he imputes to human behaviour. During rehearsals he skirts Elsinor or Rome or Burnham Wood, a creature accommodated to crisis, his features lighting into a ludicrous mask of comedy for sociable occasions, when in that shrill, piping voice of his—which caused him to fail in all efforts to join the Kembles as an actor on the stage—he trills tales of such malice and mockery that one wonders at his bilious burden of self-loathing.

Next day Mrs. Cotton, recovered from her journey, flew away at her nephew's invitation to dine at Vauxhall. I saw her off in a coach in her little trim country bonnet, her voluminous skirts showing beneath a dark, heavy worsted cape, while I kept a weather-eye out for clouds that blocked all but bits of remote and intermittent blue, on which Mrs. Cotton based her happy expectations. I would have wished to accompany her—on the brightest June day—in one of those wherries so slight and slender they look like nutshells as they float down the Thames to the piping of French horns. Two shillings provide entrance through a wicket into a magical world amidst enormous elms and sycamores, down promenades of a thousand feet of fading vistas, to pleasure domes, pavilions open to the view, or to Druid Ruins favoured by lovers. I would at last sit dear, tired, dazzled Mrs. Cotton within a supper-box, perhaps the very one where Dr. Johnson used to dine with Mrs. Thrale. At six, while we would still be sitting over glasses of wine, the orchestra would strike up a sad song, softening our hearts with sighs for all young shepherds by love sore oppressed. At nine we should wonder before a waterworks, ingeniously devised by a curtain and some mechanism which deceives one into imagining he stands beneath a roaring waterfall: trees blow down in a wind, thatches are ripped off rooftops of small dwellings that still cling like a bird's aerie; I am told troops of soldiers have been seen to march across a swaying bridge, in a monstrous moving picture of the kind that it is not easy to persuade oneself is not nature herself. If it should rain, Mrs. Cotton's music would be enjoyed from inside the Rotunda with its surrounding gods and goddesses under an umbrella-roof in the form of a single fluted pink shell. Each time I have visited—Fuseli having liked to walk down the straight walks with a companion to listen uninterruptedly—I have demanded a moment to myself to pay respects to a statue which used to stand in the centre of a semicircular pavilion shaded by trees. Fuseli would be annoyed by the expression of reverence on my face, my eyes misting over at that greatest musician of any age, sculpted from marble in the guise of Orpheus. I still recollect how my heart fell when, one day, going all the way across the South Walk to reach the range of pavilions before which the figure stood in rain or hoar-frost, winter or summer, I discovered in its place only a small clump of dark green box—Handel having found asylum from the weather in a supper-room newly added to the Rotunda, when the Gothic orchestra was erected—all manner of enlargements and improvements for ever engaging the attentions of hundreds of architects, gardeners, and every sort of artisan.

What seemed in store for me that Sunday, while Mrs. Cotton for whom I had left myself free enjoyed Vauxhall, and Godwin dined at Holcroft's, was to be abandoned and solitary. Unable to disguise my aimlessness when he called, I was surprised to learn that he was on his way to Wimbledon, and that nothing would do but I join him. After changing my garments I returned to the parlour to see his eyes lift from the pages of his book with a shine of admiration that was pleasing to my vanity. Stepping out, my arm through his, we must have appeared quite an ordinary pair.

However vehemently we protest against *la vie bourgeoise*, upholding our right to keep to independent ways, both of us equally
vehement, although not always simultaneously so, whenever we
do slip into the ordinary domestic mold, it has all the peril of in-
dulging in creature comforts, such as warm rooms and good meals,
which satisfy in moderation, though sate when too frequent. I
could not help casting a sidelong glance at Godwin with his utterly
satisfied air, as we set off for Lincoln Inn Fields to gather one of
the young faithful, from there to proceed by coach to Wimbledon where Horne Tooke has retired from politics to cultivate his
garden.

Godwin thinks it the most presumptuous arrogance on Tooke's
part to have run against Fox, who this past June defeated him
in the elections at Westminster; but Tooke is so persistent in
wrong-headed reasoning that, although he lost the election, he
celebrated the *triumph* of having convinced three thousand un-
suborned voluntary voters to support principle—Principle against
Interest—which signifies, he said, that the people, at length coming to their senses, are to be trifled with no longer. It is certainly
some thing in our national character that has us for ever grasping
victory from the jaws of defeat: Tooke's celebration at the Crown
and Anchor but one example of the devious art, as is our insistence
on commemorating the naval victory of June the First, when
Commander Howe was able to wound several French sail of the
line guarding a convoy of grain: every one conveniently neglects
to recall that *the grain got safely through*. There is some eccentric strain in the British character that claims victory on the basis
of smaller incidental gains, but then I suppose it is a sanguine sort
of valour to see it so.

We were eight of us at Horne Tooke's table: Godwin; his disciple Montagu, a young law student who wears the dewiest smile,
somewhat like a child attending the counsel of his elders, all the
while that he seems to treasure his own private reveries; another
law student; a free-thinking Catholic priest by the name of
Beauvieux, or Bonville it might have been, I never did precisely
catch the name; a gentleman active in the London Corresponding
Society; a parson from Bristol who sat beside me; and I—the solitary woman. Tooke sits at the head of his table as if on a throne.
His narrow, feral features put one in mind of the many busts and

engravings one has seen of Voltaire; I wonder now if it is not a resemblance which he practises before his looking-glass. His speech has a finicky precision, which makes one look for innuendo or witticism where some times none is to be found. We were gathered over innumerable courses of fish and fowl and beef and a variety of fruit tarts from fruit picked from the orchards behind the house—each dish honoured by a respectful intermission, in which one's digestion was able to recover and the discourse to grow more animated. At Johnson's table Horne Tooke once admitted that his difficulty was never in bringing out words, but in stopping them. The little parson on my right appeared spellbound. Godwin held his lips pursed, ready to respond by laughter at any general sign of mirth, or by disagreement, as the case might be. He is ill at ease in Horne Tooke's presence; yet is scarcely in disagreement on the subject of desiring the downfall of Pitt's government. Tooke drew an analogy to the manner in which horse-dealers try their animals by binding them to trees. Some of the horses will draw with spirit and vigour for a little while but, when they find the tree does not follow, will lie down and no amount of lashing will make them draw again. Other horses will drag and pull and, though the tree refuses to follow, still they will drag and pull until the horse-dealer is satisfied with the *bottom* of the horse. "Gentlemen," Tooke said solemnly, "*we* are tied to a tree, to a tree of corruption which is enormous. I say, Gentlemen, pull again, pull again, and it will totter; and again, I say, pull once more and it will tumble." I have known Tooke commended as a conversationalist equal to Burke, yet it strikes me as a style that issues from the mind of a mere lawyer—lawyer and grammarian are what he is! I felt rising in me the spirit of contradiction; yet, not wanting to displease Godwin by one of my masculine rodomontades, I kept it under. There is, to my sense of things, a coldness and pettiness in Tooke's manner. In Parliament he had seemed, they said, to represent no one but himself, unable to understand that others did not come into the House of Commons with the sole purpose of breaking a lance with him, but to get through the business of the day. With Tooke it was all political sparring to no practical effect; he might almost have been on stage for the way he would significantly smile into empty corners and take his snuff with a gentlemanly, negligent air.

Still, whatever my feelings, I decided to hold my tongue till Godwin, Montagu and I had made the long trip back to Judd Place and had fallen into various seats and sofas in my parlour. I had to go upstairs to change my clothing once again, my skirt having picked up all manner of filth in the streets. When I re-entered the room, Godwin was lecturing Montagu. He brings him every where; it is a peripatetic sort of education they are engaged in. He was speaking, when I rejoined them, of the sorry state of Horne Tooke's talents and of what he had been. Two long trials—and a term of imprisonment on the first indictment—though they have not weakened his resolve against tyranny, have broken his health and strengthened certain faults in his character. Montagu appears quite young with his rosy, round, angelic face, too young to have remembered that earlier conviction of Tooke for treason when, as head of the Constitutional Society, he had sent Ben Franklin money for the widows and children of those inhumanly murdered by the King's troops at Lexington. The money was not sent in secret, but with a defiant flourish. Soon afterwards he was arrested, tried, convicted and imprisoned.

Godwin's description of prison in "Caleb Williams" comes largely from what Holcroft later told him of his experience in Newgate, when awaiting trial; and from nightmares which Godwin had at the time, when he knew he ran the risk of publishing "Political Justice"—the question of whether or not to indict him having been debated at length in the Privy Council. He would awake to stare for hours into the darkness of his own bedchamber, having escaped the figment of his dreams, dreams of imprisonment so recurrent and vivid that for a long time he had sought comfort in imagining how he would endure such a fate, should it come to him.

Tooke, during his sentence, had been permitted visits from friends, and even the privilege of dining out with them once a week at the Dog and Duck. That did not, Godwin patiently explained, take away from his moral courage. It considerably adds to his stature, in his estimation, that he continued his studies under such circumstances. I have ever been disinclined towards philological fine points, so that, while Godwin discoursed on the subject of Tooke's celebrated study written during that year of confinement—some thing to do with the use of *that*—I occupied myself pulling a thread in my skirt, resuming interest only when Godwin began to speak of Holcroft.

When a Scotsman had previously been tried for sedition at Edinburgh, Godwin had written him that, when he stood up to establish in court the lawfulness of having convened with others for the purpose of petitioning for parliamentary reform, he represented *all of us*. Certainly Holcroft, who was one of us, represented our deepest sentiments; his crime a belief in equality and justice, beliefs upheld in the highest doctrinaire spirit. It seems absurd that such a man should have been arrested for high treason (for it was high treason, not sedition, which the Chief-Justice declared against these men) and that he now is forced to carry the stigma for sins neither committed nor proven. When Godwin, as he was telling Montagu, heard of his friend's arrest, he closed himself into his study, with Marshal to take dictation; speed was absolutely necessary if what he intended was to be effective; in two days he had composed an answer to Chief-Justice Eyre's charges. The country's return to reason—to perceiving, I mean, that men earnestly met over consideration of the health of the republic are innocent of any intention of regicidal design—was largely due to Godwin's account. Our countrymen tend to believe that the State must have clear evidence of treasonable conspiracy, or else they would not act. But Godwin had shown how unfounded were the charges. His glance grew spirited at the memory—though no one at the time had known he was the author, for the personal danger such a signature would have entailed. Montagu was listening the way Fanny does to heroic fables of the past, unblinkingly, when Godwin began to shake his head and smile, remembering how, months later, he had been dining in a fairly numerous company at the house of a friend, when Horne Tooke had begun to chafe him for the truth of the report that he was the true author of the "Cursory Sketches on Chief-Justice Eyre's Charge to the Grand Jury." Only then did Godwin admit to having written the pamphlet. Tooke commandingly bade him approach—which had required walking down the length of the table, wondering as he did so what was in store for him. Tooke grasped his hand, saying that he could do no more than kiss the hand that had saved his life. In telling the tale, Godwin appeared rapturous, on his features an expression of guileless pleasure at being praised by a man whom he had for years admired. I had heard the tale. All that was strange to me, in this recounting of it, was that, fresh from the fount of dining at Tooke's country retreat, fresh from having feasted on Tooke's various expressions of saturninity, I saw some thing more in the scene. On his face which nestled against Godwin's hand I saw, beneath a mask of flattery, a concealed sneer—Godwin the butt of some secret, malevolent glee.

Only Mrs. Cotton's entrance, I do believe, withheld my asperity. We made a lively company over the tea and cold baked meats, Mrs. Cotton, hectic and happy at the end of her excursion, singing a lightsome song she had heard at Vauxhall and committed to memory. I say we were a lively company; I ought to have recorded that we were lively, all four, till Godwin, resting his cheek on his hand, smiling with the sweetest benignity, began after supper to doze. He can fall asleep in the midst of the most spirited discussion, equally oblivious for some twenty minutes to the chime of teaspoons or a team of horses in the street; he wakes, rejoining the conversation as though never for a moment absent. This time, it so happened, he returned to life with an absurdly incongruous pleasantry that had us all in fits of laughter, Mrs. Cotton actually laughing till she wept, wiping her eyes on the corner of her napkin, Godwin irresistibly impelled to join the general merriment.

We took Mrs. C., the following evening, to "Hamlet," played by Kemble. And what a Hamlet he is! From the moment he appeared with his dejected air and comfortless countenance, I was captivated. Godwin did not approve of the manner in which he took Ophelia's fan and gallanted it, although he soon turned it to use, speaking to her, his eyes scrutinising the dark soul of his uncle, all the while that he artfully shaded his observation. I thought it was cleverly done; too cleverly, Godwin thought. He has seen Kemble's performance of Hamlet many times and believes it is a newly added artifice. How I trembled when, in the graveyard, on lifting Yorick's skull, Kemble seemed neither to move, nor to breathe—and I am sure I did not either, for fear of disturbing him. He stood stock still in an ink-black feathered cap, a dark cloak bordered by sable, all in black, as dark as the night behind him—black tunic, breeches, stockings, pumps—all black save for a frill of white lawn around his neck, one foot on the raised earth of Ophelia's grave. Against his thigh rested the skull which he could no longer bear to look upon, his gaze bent far into the distance. What nobility and calm upon his features! "What a piece of work is man!"

November 3, 1796

Opie has been here. He wandered about my parlour in an excess of vigour and joy. Mrs. Cotton, who was pulling on her gloves in her way out to attend Mass at St. Paul's in Covent Garden, thought him quite mad, I could see, keeping her eyes on him uneasily till she had edged out the door. Poor Opie can scarcely believe that all his agony is coming to a conclusion; nor could he resist, once sitting beside me, reporting the rumour that is abroad, which he heard yesterday on visiting the studio of Farrington. It is being said that Opie, when he will obtain his divorce, is going to be married *to me!!* How do you like that? he asked. I replied that I supposed I would like it well enough, if I might know when we were to be married and where we were to live, when we were. He smiled with that brightness of a smile of his which breaks through the stolidity of his intelligent regard, saying that all that had prevented Farrington from rejoicing at our forthcoming marriage was puzzlement at how he could marry me, since I was already married to an American. Opie told him that, had he such intents, it would present no obstacle, since I had lived under Imlay's protection at Paris to avoid prison, but had not married him. Opie knows my principles on this subject: there is nothing for which I need feel ashamed, yet it is seemlier that a friend should spread the truth, rather than I proclaim it. I find it increasingly odd, however, that certain persons prefer to adhere to the belief that I am married, though they have heard I am not. I refer to such as Mrs. Inchbald, for one. Perhaps the notion of a true and legal marriage serves her purpose, which may be to put an irremediable obstacle between me and Godwin, had I any intention of marrying him, which I have not. I relish my freedom. I was perfectly content with Opie's reply to Farrington, troubled as I am by a deception which I want to have done with. The blows rained so thickly when I returned to England last November that my judgement was impaired. I lied to some, not to others, which makes for confusion, especially since I tend to forget my lies, and remember only the truth. I returned to England under the impression that Imlay and I were to live together, only to have him inform me that he had been previously married, proposing then that I live under the same roof with him and his wife, for whom he said his affections had grown cold—a young woman, it transpired, whom he had known only some few months and who was his mistress, not his wife. I learned the truth from the cook. So much was I affected by his usage, by one lie piled upon another like Pelion on Ossa, that a year ago—a year that seems an epoch!—I hired a small boat and rowed along the Thames to Putney, having only learned that summer in Norway how to navigate, drew up to mount some steps from the river in the rain, walking about so that my skirts should become sufficiently drenched to be heavy, not buoyant, and flung myself into the dark waters. Certainly that attempt to end my life is common knowledge. I had not meant here to revive such distressful memories, only to opine that *my scandals*, in Johnson's words, are general knowledge.

Fortunately I have been able to speak freely with friends to relieve some of my bitterness; as Opie has been able, in the atmosphere of confidence between us, to confess a tumult of feelings for "that tulip of a girl," his pupil, Miss Beetham. He now spoke with anxiety lest he apprehend renewed difficulties in gaining permission from her father, a man, he hears, who is fiercely conventional and might withhold consent to the marriage after the notoriety of the divorce. To day's *Times* prints a notification of a second reading of Opie's Divorce Bill, thus nothing is secret, nor sacred. We got down to the business of reckoning who might make the most impressive intermediary; we turned various possibilities over and over to look for blemishes, as one does with pieces of fruit at the fruit-stalls, agreeing finally on Farrington himself, an eminently respectable member of the Royal Academy, the same age as Miss Beetham's father, who might the more easily therefore approach him on Opie's behalf.

I had divined that divorce was an extrication both laborious and costly, but only through Opie's determined action for his freedom have I learned how much marriage is a Gordian knot. The Ecclesiastical Courts would have given Opie a separation from Mrs. Bunn, but to neither afterwards the right to remarry. To obtain a divorce *a vinculo matrimonii* it was necessary to have testimony that Mrs. Bunn was guiltily living with Major Edwards; then to bring action against him in the Court of King's Bench, an action which resulted in an assessment of 150*l.* damages besides the costs of the suit. Opie next had to sue for libel in the Consistory Court of the Bishop of London, which he won when Edwards allowed judgement to go against him by default. Last month he petitioned the House of Lords for leave to bring in a bill to dissolve his marriage and to enable him to marry again. Lord Walsingham presented the bill. Opie was present this morning on another reading, there being by this time an amount of paper presented to the Lords, Opie said, that would have started fires in the chimney-piece in his studio throughout the bitterest winter. He clenches his teeth to endure still a third reading of his bill, at which point, if not defended, it goes from the Lords to the Commons and from there to the King, whose Royal Assent will finally make Opie free.

Northcote said, the day we dined at Clifford's Inn, that Opie should no more be married than should a stick of wood. When I asked why he made such a judgement, he said that any man who spends from half past eight in the morning till half past four in the afternoon in his studio, ceasing work then only because the light has vanished, who has interest in nothing that is not connected with painting, that man, he said, should live alone—as he himself does, his household overseen by a young niece. I did not, of course, repeat Northcote's comment, but asked Opie, in earnest, if a painter ought to have a wife and, if so, what sort of woman would best suit him. Another painter, Opie said with no hesitation. I smiled. Sir Joshua had never married, I recalled. Opie says he fell in love, however, with each young lady who came to sit to him. It is better to marry than to burn, said Opie. And it is better to marry late, when one's judgement is formed. Fuseli married his model, who sews and cooks, but neither reads nor writes—I sighed for a man who systematically tyrannises younger women, whether they write or no. I asked Opie whether he thought genius required some special matrimonial circumstance. He has a way of staring at one with no change of expression, almost as if he has not gathered the meaning of what is being said, and then in a flat voice and with biting certitude will reply in a few pointed words.

He wants, he says, a woman who, were she a man, he would yet like. When I grew thoughtful, he asked what was on my mind. In truth, I'd been thinking still once more what a pity it is that our hearts, Opie's and mine, are differently occupied, for, if they had been free, I wager we might have intrigued one another, and fulfilled the prophecy of rumour.

M W T O W G

November 3, 1796

If you are not *all alive* at your essays I will come to you in the course of half an hour—Say the word—for I shall come to you, or read Swift.

You have almost captivated Mrs. C—Opie called this morning—But you are the man—Till we meet joy be with thee—Then—what then?

Thursday morning   Mary

November 4, 1796

On entering Lawrence's new lodgings on Greek Street in Piccadilly, yesterday afternoon, I was at first startled by innumerable plaster casts, so closely assembled against one wall that they seemed to be fleeing some general holocaust, arms and legs thrust every which way from torsos of wrestlers or cupids, gladiators and horses, as well as chimeras and river-gods, not to speak of several figures of Christ and those of Jupiter. These bone-white replicas infused me so profoundly with a sensation of infernal chaos that I began to form a notion about their influence on Lawrence. He was not there in the studio. One of his pupils had let us in—Godwin, Mary Hays and I—and went to fetch Lawrence who was visiting upstairs with his father, who lives with him. Another boy of perhaps fourteen years of age was working on a canvas. Lawrence does only the heads. There was, last summer, an amusing result to the practice. In July Mrs. Inchbald sat to Lawrence for a redchalk drawing, which she had hoped to be engraved in stipple by the news papers when the reviews of "A Simple Story" appeared. Lawrence did the head and, as is his practice, gave one of his young apprentices the task of filling in the rest. Presuming knowledge from the common run of experience, the boy sketched in the shoulders and a full, rounded bosom—whereas Mrs. Inchbald is remarkable for having no bosom at all! Fuseli recounted the story at Johnson's, between snorts of laughter telling how infuriated Mrs. Inchbald had become; every painter in London is relating the tale with relish. Godwin sat to Lawrence less than a year ago. I have seen the pencil sketch, with its bit of brightness of blue chalk for the eyes, and pinkness for the lips. But I do not care for it very much. It is not a good likeness; it misses some thing powerful and obstinate in the face and emphasises, to the sacrifice of all else, its visionary idealism. I have heard that Lawrence, arriving one morning in court in time to get a seat among the spectators during the trials, busied his pencil on a sketch of Godwin and Holcroft sitting together, immediately after Holcroft's acquittal, Godwin drawn in one of his characteristic gestures of rubbing one eye behind his glasses, which he often does when he has been intently straining his attention. In a sketch done of me, when Johnson wanted a portrait to use in that ill-fated edition of my translation of Lavater—Holcroft's translation appearing first—he made me out to be such a docile pink-and-white milkmaid of a creature that I could not help making a grimace at the sight of it, at which Lawrence, constantly concerned as he is with the opinion of others, could not bring himself to speak to me for more than a year. Fuseli thought him a fool to carry on so and, seeing him one day in the corridor of Somerset House, lectured him on the subject to the effect that a painter must be superior to criticism; I was then able to express how much I regretted having injured his feelings, for I have always liked Lawrence, and find myself frequently defending him, most recently to Godwin, who is irritated by his affectations. It is for Lawrence's habit of living above his means that Godwin takes him to task, predicting that such reckless spending will land him some day under a rain of lawsuits. But Lawrence only looks penitent, and continues on his path. He is the rage amidst women of fashion who desire their portraits painted and who must, at all costs, sit to the painter in extraordinary to the King. I have heard a malicious report that, taking half-pay before he consents to do a portrait, he then goes on taking other commissions, never finishing what he promises, pocketing half-pay every where. Such reports, which are becoming more frequent every day, have not, however, put out the brightness of his meteoric rise to fame.

Lawrence has said, in moments when he and Godwin have walked together discussing every thing under the sun, that, once he can see his way clear of debt, he will give up portraiture to devote himself exclusively to historical subjects; but I cannot see how he will ever be able to give up taking commissions, when his prices are fixed at 40 guineas for a head-and-shoulders, 80 for a half-length and 160 for a full-length, particularly when he is addicted to borrowing against tomorrow, as he has been doing for countless years, though he is only twenty-six years of age, I believe. Whatever agreement he and Godwin reach upon their walks, Lawrence inevitably returns to letting things go the way they have been going—with a tragic inevitability to it, it seems to me. Resolutions taken at moments of repentance are powerless to change the course of our lives, which some times appears to me to be almost mechanically sprung from forces indifferent to our will.

I had been standing for some time beside a mahogany sideboard covered by glass. A porphyry slab for grinding colours sat beneath a shelf that held in glass jars a rainbow of powdered pigments. The apprentices must keep things straight, I thought to myself, for all was remarkably tidy in contrast to the cultivated disorder that Fuseli used to say signified his genius—what others saw as disorder was his own personal sense of order. I felt a surge of nostalgia for those bygone days when I had been welcome in his studio. There is a grief far more bitter than that of remembering some one loved no longer living; it is grief for one still living whom one loves no longer.

At the far end of the studio Mary Hays was sitting upon Lawrence's Florentine sitter's chair, her head thrown back, her wrists broken upon the arms of the chair, Godwin a pace or two away, indifferent to her posturings, studying a painting. What fools we women are the way we flash out bright signals of love, which, when disregarded, we flash out again in renewed desperation. Mary Hays was, I fear, not too unlike myself when I would creep into some corner of Fuseli's studio, following his every movement with worshipful eyes.

I was relieved of my train of thought by Lawrence's show of

amiability which rushes up these days in both our hearts at the sight of one another. He seemed so radiant at seeing me that I could not understand how any one could impugn his character, so magnificent is his carriage, so sleek and handsome—Sheridan told him he would have been the finest actor on the stage, should he have wished such a career. We had last seen each other at Mrs. Siddons', whom he has known since his boyhood at Bath, when he drew her likeness with small, chubby fingers that were barely able to grasp the chalk. Lawrence was taken aback to see Mary Hays all limp upon his sitter's chair. I watched with amusement to see how quickly he recovered from surprise, radiating his smile upon her. We had come to take a look at the Rembrandt. Lawrence—who said he could barely remove his eyes from it and would get no work done at all if he left it uncovered—bid one of the boys to pull aside the brown velvet curtain.

When my eyes grew accustomed to the golden light shining from within the painting, I saw before me an unclothed woman seated upon a bench, such as I might see in the baths here in London, when a door to one of the stalls stands ajar. The woman, in fact, seemed so ordinary a figure that, anticipation having been whetted by the painting's reputed beauty, I felt immediate disappointment. I could hear, with the annoying persistence of an insect winging around one's ears, the contemptuous phrasing of Fuseli on the subject of *that Dutchman's* common touch; but I wished to experience the painting with no intrusion of received ideas and made a movement of impatience which successfully drove off my devil. The more I stared and studied the seated woman, the more ordinary she appeared to be—until I sensed the beauty that emanates from ordinary creatures. How much we have been corrupted by gods and goddesses, by the sporting Cupids, Pans and nymphs, that entire panoply of a world of imagination, our taste so formed by huge heroic creatures, that we become uneasy before a painting of a mere woman, whose servant pares her toe-nails. It might have been Ruth Barlow sitting there, some thing about the roundness of the breasts, the heaviness of the belly, reminding me of the friend with whom I used to breakfast after our early morning bath.

Lawrence then brought out a portfolio of his matchless collection of drawings by Michel Angelo Buonarroti, holding up to

Mary Wollstonecraft. Engraving after a portrait by John Opie painted 1797. (By courtesy of the Trustees of the British Museum)

William Godwin. Engraving after a portrait by James Northcote. (National Portrait Gallery, London)

William Godwin (right) and Thomas Holcroft (left).
Drawing by Thomas Lawrence made at the "treason trials"
of 1794. (Collection Kenneth Garlick)

Henry Fuseli. Self-portrait. (National Portrait Gallery, London)

Joseph Johnson. Engraving after a portrait by Moses Haughton. (By courtesy of the Trustees of the British Museum)

Sarah Siddons. Portrait by Thomas Lawrence. (The Tate Gallery, London)

Mary Robinson. Portrait by George Dance. (National
Portrait Gallery, London)

Elizabeth Inchbald. Portrait by George Dance. (National Portrait Gallery, London)

Amelia Alderson. Portrait by John Opie. (National Portrait Gallery, London)

John Opie. Self-portrait. (Royal Academy of Arts, London)

Thomas Holcroft. Portrait by John Opie. (National Portrait Gallery, London)

Thomas Lawrence. Self-portrait. (From Croft Castle, a property of the National Trust)

William Hazlitt. Portrait by William Bewick. (National Portrait Gallery, London)

Samuel Coleridge. Portrait by Peter Vandyke. (National Portrait Gallery, London)

Robert Southey. Drawing by Henry Eldridge. (National Portrait Gallery, London)

The Journal of William Godwin, August–September 1797.
(Journal page from *Shelley and His Circle, 1773–1822*.
Copyright © 1961 by The Carl and Lily Pforzheimer
Foundation, Inc. Reproduced by permission.)

Mr Godwin
Wedgwood Esq,
Etruria
Staffordshire.

128

Tuesday, June 6th

It was so kind and considerate in you to write
sooner than I expected that I cannot help hoping
you won't be disappointed at not receiving a greeting
from me on your arrival at Etruria. If your
heart was in your mouth, as I felt, just now at the
sight of your hand, you may kiss or shake hands
with the letter; and imagine with what affection
it was written — If not — stand off profane one!
I was not quite well the day after you left me. but
it is past, and I am well and tranquil, excepting the
disturbance produced by Master William's joy, who took
it in his head to frisk a little at being informed
of your remembrance. I begin to love this little
creature, and to anticipate his birth as a fresh twist to
a knot, which I do not wish to untie — Men are
spoilt by frankness, I believe yet I must tell you
that I love you better than I supposed I did when I
promised to love you for ever — and I will add what

Letter from Mary Wollstonecraft to William Godwin dated
June 6, 1797. (From Lord Abinger's Boscombe Mss.)

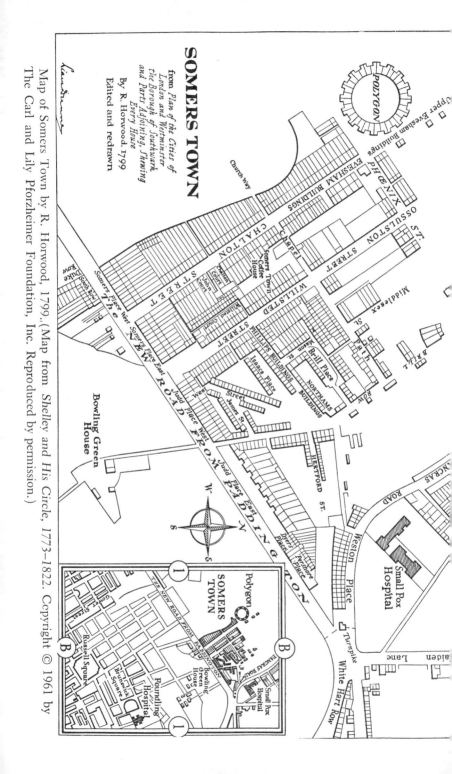

Map of Somers Town by R. Horwood, 1799.,(Map from Shelley and His Circle, 1773–1822. Copyright © 1961 by The Carl and Lily Pforzheimer Foundation, Inc. Reproduced by permission.)

shock us a sketch of the artist and a friend dissecting a corpse, which lies on a table, arms hanging, a lighted candle fixed in the cavity between the ribs to light them at their work, one measuring with a pair of callipers, the other with a triangular rule. Mary Hays turned aside, but I looked long and fast. I then held a sheet of paper with some poetry in the artist's own hand. I was yet absorbed in what could be thus communicated of the divine spirit of the artist, when the door was flung open and into the studio came Horne Tooke, who broke our reverential silence with a sharp staccato tap of the heels of his boots.

Looking more than ever like Voltaire, he dipped the pointed beak of his nose into the wooden rack where Lawrence had placed for our perusal studies for the anatomy of a horse very strikingly drawn on the reverse side of the sonnet. Tea had been brought by the fire side, the spell laid upon us by the world of Buonarroti intruded upon by Horne Tooke's indignation at news he had heard on the street.

Drury Lane has withdrawn "Venice Preserved." I had never seen Mrs. Siddons in the role of Belvedira, but I hear she played it with a delicate glow of conjugal affection. It is a rather tame theatrical plot in the style of the last century; yet last year it set off a train of explosions, when it was revived, resulting in the Lord Chancellor banning it for sentiments which might have incited seditious disaffection. Godwin pointed out to all of us that the purpose of the play is to expose the uselessness of rebellion against tyranny —quite the opposite of the Lord Chancellor's fears. Tooke wonders how it can serve the purpose of the government to have some fool stand and cheer at a denunciation of the Venetian Senate— in words which Mary Hays happened to know by heart:

> To see our Senators
> Cheat the deluded People with a show
> Of Liberty which yet they ne'er must taste of.

I remarked that it could only be one of Pitt's hired villains who at such words would throw a red cockade into the air. Mary Hays became quite voluble in disagreement, making a speech full of republican fervor, her face having taken on a mottled look like a peach in the extravagance of her passion. Godwin could not tell, he told me later, whether she was in favour of at once storming Drury Lane, the Lord Chancellor's office or the *Morning Chronicle*, her *sansculotte* sentiments embarrassing him, so curiously far did she carry them, without any rational guiding principle; in just such a way he disapproves of the illustrator Blake who took to appearing in the streets, some years ago, in the red cockade, which Godwin felt was carrying things too far, with no other result than to make himself conspicuous.

Pursuing her polemical course, Mary Hays did not at once notice Horne Tooke. Her eyes brushed past him and she turned back to see his figure jiggling up and down in his seat, as though he were sitting a horse. She looked, in fascination. Some how by now she was out of her chair, although I don't recall her having risen, standing in an attitude of confusion and disarray, some few locks of her colourless hair drifting about her brow and upon her long neck which lifts from the collars of her dresses like a thin stem from a vase. My instincts were aroused. Hooke was eying her. The two of them stared at each other. I suppose one of us might have intruded between them, but none of us did. Tooke began begging, most humbly, for definitions of one word, then another, in order to break down the meaning of some phrase uttered in the heat of her righteousness. I can't recall quite the sequence of the questions posed. But she answered in a hectic spirit of elucidating a favourite Jacobin proposition. In this case, since she might assume that she and Tooke were of like mind, she took no precautions, put off guard, I should imagine, by the bonhomie of his smile. She did not perhaps remember that in his trial he had said that his friends might, if they pleased, go as far as *Slough*—he should go no further than *Honnslow*; but it was no reason he should not keep them company so far as their roads were the same. Mary Hays was one of those who went further than he cared to go. She stammered, contradicting herself like a schoolchild. I could stand this cruel chafing no longer. I rose and took her by the arm, so that she might feel somewhat steadied by my touch, affecting to catch the stray wisps of her hair about the nape of her neck, as if we were preparing to leave. But I had not counted on her own single-minded desire to gain approval from this juggler of words. She unhinged her arm from mine to face her tormentor, who was sitting back in a small French chair, pretending to be drawn back into the argument quite against his will. I looked at Godwin, who was half asleep in the heat from the chimney-piece. I turned then to Lawrence, who had one leg crossed over the other, his head resting on both hands stretched behind him. I wanted to stop Horne Tooke's sport. I wanted to make him deal with *me*, if need be, to let off this tantalised mouse whom he had got into a corner. And so, only half aware of what I was saying, but choosing all the same from some sound instinct, I offered that I might perhaps excite his laughter by dropping a hint, which I had meant some future time to pursue with him: I wondered what he might say to the thought that women ought to have elected representatives, instead of being arbitrarily governed, and having no share in the deliberations of government. He rose gloriously to my provocation—this time not only getting off at Honnslow, but taking to his heels with a look of fright. He had cast a panicked glance at Mary Hays, then at me, must have calculated that together we presented too formidable a force, and ran as fast as his two legs could carry him. So this is the man about whom Godwin speaks in admiration! One who is preparing for Parliament a petition which is to be a history of the abuses of the English Constitution and an eulogy on innovation. And yet I have made him cower and rush for cover to the safety of Honnslow, that half-way sanctuary along a road that reaches to an ideal place, where equality is as natural as the air one breathes, privilege—even masculine privilege—unknown. The idea of women gaining representation is one which makes most men weak. My belief in such a principle is proof my enemies give of my eccentricity. But it served to stop Tooke's eternal flow of words, and for that I'm grateful.

M W   T O   W G

November 10, 1796

I send you your household linen—I am not sure that I did not feel a sensation of pleasure at thus acting the part of a wife, though you have so little respect for the character. There is such a magic in affection that I have been more gratified by your clasping your hands round my arm, in company, than I could have been by all the admiration in the world, though I am a woman—and to mount a step higher in the scale of vanity an author.

I shall call toward one o'clock not to deprive the world of your bright thoughts, this exhilarating day.

Thursday   Mary

November 13, 1796

If the felicity of last night has had the same effect on your health as on my countenance, you have no cause to lament your failure of resolution: for I have seldom seen so much of live fire rousing about my features as this morning when recollections—very dear, called forth the blush of pleasure, as I adjusted my hair.

Send me word that all is safe—and that we are to hear no more of the bad word; though, since I have seen Mr. Allen, I should not lay so much stress on it. The place is to be taken to day. There seems then some thing like a certainty of freedom next week—are you sorry?

Return me a line—and I pray thee put this note under lock and key—and unless you love me *very much* do not read it again.

Sunday morning

Send me Mrs. Robinson's Poems

I have sent one volume of Mrs. Robinson's Poems, and at this instant I can not find the other. I hope it is of no moment.

What can I say? What can I write with Marguerite perched in a corner by my side? I know not. I am in health: I do not lament my failure of resolution: I wish I had been a spectator of the Bonfire you speak of: I *shall* rejoice in our freedom.

Send me, the next time anybody comes, my bottle of ink: you can fill an inkstand. Fill it as high, as your image at this moment fills my mind.

Sunday

Sunday, November 13

For two weeks Godwin and I have had to meet most circumspectly, Mrs. Cotton having been here the entire length of time. Thank Heaven! she has taken her place on the post-chaise for early tomorrow. As dear a creature as she is, a friend from bygone days whom I yet treasure, I miss my privacy—and have missed Godwin, although I have *seen* him every day. Last night, after we returned together from an engagement, I lingered at his lodgings, much to our mutual benefit. Now, Sunday, with Mrs. Cotton going to dine with the family of her nephew, and Godwin off to Holcroft's in a company of masculine society, I pull from hiding those poor pages of "Maria" which I have barely been able to glance at these past weeks; I have been so busy reading others' works, and writing summaries of them, that my eyes gloss over my own pages with the same nonchalance. How shall I be so many *different* people in one? How do others manage it? When shall I be left in peace to be *uninterruptedly* occupied with my book—though, if truth were told, would I want to be?

M W   T O   W G

November 18, 1796

How do you do this morning—are you alive? It is not *wise* to be cold during such a domesticating season. I mean then to dismiss all my frigid airs before I draw near your door, this evening, and should you, in your way from Dr. Carlisle's *think* of inquiring for the fourth act of Mrs. Inc's comedy—why it would be a pretty mark of attention—and—*entre nous little* marks of attention are incumbent on you at present—But—don't mistake me— I do not wish to put you on your mettle. No; I only want to rescue a play, of some kind or other, to rouse my torpid spirits, *chez vous.*

Friday morning   Mary

Yes, I am alive. Perhaps I am better. I am glad to hear
how enchanting and divine you will appear this evening
—You spoil little attentions by anticipating them.
Friday

MW TO WG

November 19, 1796

I wish you would take my ye for a ye; and my nay for a
nay. It torments me to be obliged to guess at, or guard
against, false interpretations—and, while I am wishing,
I will add another—that you could distinguish between
jest and earnest, to express myself elegantly. To give you
a criterion, I never play with edged-tools, for (I believe)
when I am really hurt or angry I am dreadfully serious.
Still allow me a little more tether than is necessary for
the purpose of feeding, to keep soul and body together
—Let me, I pray thee! have a sort of *comparative* freedom, as you are a profound grammarian, to run round,
as good, better, best;—cheerful, gay, playful; nay even
frolicsome, once a year—or so, when the whim seizes me
of slipping out of bounds. Send me a *bill of rights*—to
this purpose, under your hand and seal with a *Bulletin*
of health.

How I have an inclination to be saucy and tell you that
I kissed Fanny, not with less kindness, because she put
me in mind of you this morning, when she came crooning
up the stairs to tell me that she did not cry when her face
was washed—I leave you to make the application—

Johnson has sent to inform me that he dines out tomorrow; probably with your party.

I was going to close my note without telling you to
what particular circumstance the first sentence alludes.
I thought of not sending Marguerite to day, because I
really felt with respect to her as you imagined I did in
the other case the day before yesterday; but Mary had

business for me another way, and I hate to disguise any feelings when writing or conversing with you, *cher ami*.

Voilà! my resolution—

Saturday morning

W G T O M W

I can send you a bill of rights and a bill of health: the former *carte blanche*; the latter, much better (as I think.) But to fulfill the terms of your note, you must send me a bill of understanding. How can I distinguish always between your jest and earnest, to know when your satire means too much and when it means nothing? But I will try.

I have somebody with me, so can write no more.

Sunday, November 20, 1796

All my writing paraphernalia is disposed about the counterpane, as I write and read in bed, between seizures from a severe catarrh. It is so cold outside that I can see nothing for the frost on the window-panes, the clip-clop of horses' hooves resounding upon iced cobble-stones. Fanny has been whimpering that she can neither go outside to play on the Green, nor come into bed with me —taking such strictures as punishment, where none is meant. I querulously explain that I should infect her were she to crawl in bed beside me. Marguerite brought me a mug of heated white wine with pepper, cinnamon and aromatic spices, so that for a few moments, at least, I could breathe more comfortably. But why am I writing of such things? I meant by writing to *clear* my mind, not compound its irritability.

I am irritated this morning both by Godwin and by Amelia Alderson—by Godwin for attending Carlisle's course of lectures in anatomy at the Royal Academy, where upon Reynolds' recommendation Carlisle was admitted as a student—to learn to cut up cadavers, I dare say, and to use human ribs for candle-holders. He has written an essay on the connexion between anatomy and the fine arts which Godwin presses me to read. I do not understand why he is going daily—as it seems to me, though he insists it is only every second or third day throughout this month—to present himself with Montagu at five in the afternoon in the great lecture hall at the Royal Academy. Nor do I see why he would choose to spend time on Montagu, who is for ever about these days. It rubs me the wrong way. I see in it the same sort of wallowing in worship of riches which made me so stiffly formal when I was brought to make obeisance to the famous Mrs. Robinson. Basil Montagu is the natural son of Lord Sandwich by an actress. He was left motherless at eight years of age when his mother, leaving Covent Garden after a performance, was shot to death by a man in a fit of jealousy. Having had an allowance settled on him by his father, he is now studying for the bar. Godwin's deference seems almost some times an infatuation. When presenting his young friend, he rolls the name of *Montagu* upon his tongue as if he sucked a sweet. We have been over this ground innumerable times, but leave it always as we found it, he for ever denying his allegiance to riches, while I grow almost strident in my criticism.

While I am making complaints on this order, I may add that Amelia Alderson writes that "a richish oldish bachelor" among her friends in Norwich, having heard of my financial distress and being long an admirer of my work, has wanted to convey through her, as evidence of his esteem, an anonymous gift of five guineas. She thought it a tribute; Godwin did, too—I alone scorn the suggestion. I value my independence and, yes, even my difficulties, too highly to consider patronage. The offer put me in mind of a marriage proposal made me once by some superficial puppy who, seeing I was working for my livelihood, thought I would prefer to prostitute my person for a maintenance. Godwin says I am too sharp on these matters. Does he know that I am in an agony to calculate how to keep things going? The small stipend gained from work on the *Analytical* does not support my household. And I do not seem to have the peace of mind to sit uninterruptedly to a long solid work. No matter, no matter; such a day as to day is no time to analyse the dilemma.

For the last week Godwin has been rereading my "Rights of Woman." It seems to him not improbable that it will be read as long as the English language endures. He says that I have performed more substantial service for the cause of my sex than all the other writers, male or female, that ever felt themselves animated by the contemplation of their oppressed and injured state. I am overjoyed by all he said. Last night, he began to speak of the direction I ought now to take—for he is not unaware that I am in a period of incertitude. I would like, for the money involved, to write such a Gothic romance as Mrs. Radcliffe's or Mr. Walpole's. On the other hand, I have little patience with novels, and no longer even read them unless I have to: they falsify human experience, putting above all else the causes of sensibility, and create such circumstances that some times, reading them, I have to laugh out loud. If only my life would assume some settled state, and my debts be paid, I might sit down to a work of philosophy and write, this time, of the laws of marriage, for I have not yet said all I might say on the subject of men and women.

But when in all my world of living have I known peaceful, uninterrupted periods of time, unbroken by anxieties? Certainly I can say I know more happiness to day than formerly, surrounded as I am by Fanny and Godwin. But when Godwin remarked, the other day, on Marguerite's prettiness, my happiness grew clouded with fear. She is pretty and pert, with her saucy dark eyes and lilting laugh; but *his saying so* set me to wondering if he might have taken a fancy to her—a wonder that lasted for hours, with stabs of pain in the abdomen as if, having ingested poison, I could not rid myself of its effect. In this case, I was merely borrowing fear. Yet three days ago I paced my study over Mrs. Inchbald, who, of all of them, is, I suppose, the nearest I have to a rival. Kept to the house with the first signs of this contagion that makes my head so hot and my thoughts so pessimistic, I could not help worrying over a rival who needs him constantly for counsel. He has seen her on Monday—Tuesday *he* had the fever—Wednesday, Thursday and Friday! This state of affairs torments me. With such ardent conversation between them, could not an *accident* occur? —for such is Godwin's way of phrasing our first August tryst. Could such not happen between them, as it happened between us, more easily now that he is so well schooled? I wrung my hands, as I thought of them together. Nothing is in a settled state, nor ever will be; my amorous soul lifted up, blown away and dropped down in sudden airlessness, as the will of the wind disposes. Dear me, let me throw these sad pages to one side and take a fresh, blank page to write upon.

MW TO WG

I do not think myself worse to day—yet, from the appearance of the weather, must determine not to go to the play tonight. The heavy clouds promise snow, and I have suffered so much that I have learned prudence.

What will you do with yourself *mon cher ami*—is there any probability of my seeing you to day? or, will you confine all your load of love in your own bosom and keep yourself warm?

Adieu   Mary

MW TO WG

I am decidedly better to day, but I have suffered so much that I must be careful. I think I may venture to go with you to the play tomorrow, and then I will renew my acquaintance with your kennel, for which, by the bye, I have *some* kindness.

I do not intend to be out late yet, as I shall be attended, I must go home, and I cannot well go out again immediately, now I am considered as indisposed and probably I should only come to cough with you—you may look up at my window for a sign, if you please; but I had almost rather you should spend the evening *comme autrefois*, because I do not like—may I say? to disappoint you—

Our *sober* evening was very delicious—I do not believe you love me better than you imagined you should—as for me—judge for yourself—

Fanny will scarcely let me write she is so affectionate, because I breakfasted in bed. I am not well—for holding down my head makes it ache—yet I begin to hope—

MW TO WG

The references were, in general, just. I have inserted the few words left out or mistaken. There were a few other observations on the first and second essay.

My pen will not allow me to add any thing kind. This is a day for friends to be together—

MW TO WG

November 23, 1796

My cough is still *very* troublesome—so that, I believe, it will be most prudent to stay at home tonight—I am sorry I kept you with me last night—and insist on your going without me this evening. I own, for I like to tell the truth, I was a little displeased with you for mentioning, when I was seriously indisposed, your inclination to go—and was angry with myself for not permitting you to follow your inclination—I am now quite well enough to amuse myself—and will dine with you some day next week, to day it would fatigue me, for my head aches with coughing.

Thursday

MW TO WG

Half after two

I mean to call with this note, just to say that finding myself better, and the day clearing up, I might have been tempted to accompany you this evening had you thought of *tempting* me—

MW TO WG

November 28, 1796

You tell me that I spoil little attentions, by anticipation, yet to have attention, I find, that it is necessary to demand it. My faults are very inveterate—for I *did* expect you last night—But *never mind it* you coming would not have been worth any thing, if it must be requested.

I have just written to Mrs. In to say that I cannot go to the play. I insist on my not preventing you from going

this evening to see Milwood. I am not such a child as I thought myself.
Monday morning

November 30, 1796

Holcroft makes me laugh. He can turn Fanny's tears to sunshine by rattling at her at such a rate that, though she has little idea of the meaning of the sounds he makes, the lilt of his voice enchants her. I, too, some times listen less to the meaning than to the melody; no one speaks faster, nor rants so resonantly. His father had been a hawker, having turned from one thing to another: a vendor of rags, a hardwareman, a dealer in buckles and buttons and pewter spoons, at one time hawking Staffordshire pottery throughout the north of England; his mother going about the streets with pins, needles, tape and garters on her arms, while Holcroft, barely able to stand, trotted after her. Before he was ten years of age, he was accustomed to walk as much as thirty miles in a day; or with luck might slip upon the back of some worn-out, weathered Rozinante for a few dusty miles. Poverty and homelessness had prepared him for the hardships of a life as a strolling player. Godwin's mind, being too tranquil, stands in need of the stimulus and excitement he gets from his friend, a friendship that has endured ten years. Yet the vehemence of their arguments amazes me; as a woman bred to consideration of the feelings of others, I stand in awe of certain masculine brutalities that pass under the name of various virtuous intentions.

The last occasion for wounded feelings occurred when Holcroft showed Godwin some thing he had written, getting back his manuscript with some written remarks which pained him. Whenever Godwin brings some thing of his to read, it is with minute rules to be observed, rules which he, when the case is turned, utterly disregards. One of these is not to find fault in such an absolute and wholesale style as might at once kill ardour and damp all future progress. Yet Godwin came at Holcroft with a sledge-hammer—telling him his play could not survive five nights or, if it did, that every body would say it is the least of his plays, contemptible and damned. Godwin defends himself, saying he had only thought it his duty to speak his thoughts plainly, avoiding any triumphant banter which Holcroft uses in similar circumstances. Holcroft says he doesn't banter, only endeavours to shed a light over errors, the way a link-boy holds high a torch. Godwin admits to being cast down by rude, unqualified assault, whereas Holcroft, he had thought, was made of iron. So should he be, Holcroft agrees, early life having hardened him in suffrance, so that he usually can shake off obloquy the way a lion shakes the dewdrops from his mane; yet in this last argument of theirs he had lain abed for hours ruminating on Godwin's conduct.

Opie says that, when judging character, I do not sufficiently study the modelling of the face, whereby most private habits of mind reveal themselves. He sees in Holcroft's face an openness of regard somewhat like a child's reverential attention. His youthful features were beautifully and sparingly modelled with a sparkling gaze and a full sensual mouth, straight nose and firm jaw; now, at fifty, there is more fixity in the expression of the eyes and, from the endurance of much physical pain, there are deeply incised furrows between the eyebrows, which give his regard a quality both reflective and compassionate. He is, I own, one of the kindest of men. Opie is right, one need only glance into his face to feel oneself becoming more cheerful under the benevolence of his gaze.

These thoughts of Holcroft have to do with last night's fiasco. It was to be the first performance of "The Force of Ridicule," which no one, with the exception of a few of his friends, knew was Holcroft's. Not to raise a prejudicial storm of denunciation against him, because of his part in the treason trials, we had advised him to leave his name off the play. Godwin had secured a box for me, Mrs. Inchbald, and his friends Ritson, Taylor and Woodhouse, Godwin and I arriving together by half past five for fear of being detained by the weather. With the prevalence of ice in the streets, some of the hackneys have refused to take their horses from the stables, so numerous have been the accidents on slippery streets. I myself have seen a coal waggon with six pairs of horses try to mount a hill, ascending several feet only to slip back again; at last, being unable either to make his horses draw their load to the crest of the hill, and equally unable to turn them around in the narrow street, the cartman had to unyoke each of his six horses in turn, leaving the load of coal for a multitude of small boys, already pressed around the waggon, to stuff as much as they could carry into their shirt fronts. The frost has been so severe these past ten days that entire branches of elms across the way, heavy with a coating of ice, have snapped and now like a bone-yard of antlered animals litter the Bowling Green. No one dares walk across it for fear of being executed by a falling branch. Godwin consequently came to call for me earlier than usual, a provision which would allow us to proceed on foot to Drury Lane, failing our finding a coach. Scarcely speaking for the stab of pain each inhalation cost us, we walked in the very middle of the streets unharmed, for nothing passed us by, not a single carriage, until we approached Bedford Square where there appeared to be a large reception taking place in one of the houses, which was lit from top to bottom, its façade alive in the flickering flame of torches that illuminated whiskers of ice over the iron railings.

We needn't have arrived at the theatre as early as we did, for we were to sit in our box expectantly, with freezing hands and feet, till full seven-fifteen when, at our stamping feet and enraged shouts, Mr. Palmer appeared on the stage to beg our forgiveness for the tardiness of the curtain. Much to our general disappointment, he then announced that we could either have our money back or hear Mrs. Siddons in another piece, instead of the new play, since Miss Farrens was too indisposed to come to the theatre. Mr. Palmer, twisting one hand inside the other, was drowned out by a cry of protest. In the end half the audience got up and left. Mrs. Inchbald, who takes all things in stride, whispered into Godwin's ear that he should accompany her home for supper, which in a hasty, almost furtive manner, which revealed his confusion, he agreed to do, while I gave every semblance of indifference. Before we had left the theatre, Holcroft succeeded in threading his way through the crowd to tell us that Miss Farrens, who has not been paid for weeks, had given the prompter a letter for the managers earlier in the day, expressing a refusal to go through her role in the evening, unless the managers performed their pecuniary part of her engagement. Though gravely affected in consequence of her behaviour, he staunchly defends her right to refuse to play her role until she has been paid. Mrs. Inchbald did not agree; as a daughter of a manager of a theatre company, in which years ago she and Holcroft had been players, her sympathy still lies with the managers. I think it did not occur to her that her taking their part did little to assuage Holcroft's disappointment. I asked if he would like to have supper at my fire side; but he and the managers were immediately to meet to decide on a future course of action. Godwin appeared so crest-fallen at the postponement, that poor Holcroft felt bound to make light of his own catastrophe.

December 6, 1796

I am not well, to day, yet I scarcely know what to com-plain of, excepting extreme lowness of spirits. I felt it creeping over me last night; but I will strive against it in-stead of talking of it—I hate this torpor of mind and senses.
Tuesday morning

December 7, 1796

I want to scold you for not having secured me a better place, because it is a mortification to me to be where I can neither see nor hear. We were thrust into a corner in the third row, quite as bad as the gallery—I had trou-ble enough with my companion without this circum-stance; but I am determined to return to my former habits, and go by myself and shift for myself—an amuse-ment loses its name when thus conducted.

If you will call on me this morning, and allow me to spend my spite—I will admit you after the play to night. You and Mrs. I. were at your ease enjoying yourselves—while poor I! I was a fool not to ask Opie to go with me—had I been alone I should not have minded it—But enough for the present—
Wednesday morning

December 8, 1796

The news papers this morning are unanimous. The play is a fail-ure. One shall never know if it could have captured the imagination of the audience, had Miss Farrens appeared with more composure: so agitated was she that she was unable to respond to the speech addressed to her upon her entrance. Six times did Mr. Barrymore make his bow and recite his opening discourse, and six times did Miss Farrens continue in silence, till there was a confused mixture of applause and cries of *Off! Off!* The application of a smelling bottle proved no relief. After attempting a feverish time to deliver the author's words, she was led off the stage. One of the managers appeared to beg pardon, both for the disappointment of Tuesday last and for the commencement of this evening, an apology received with approbation. I could see only by leaning over precipitously, so near was the box to the stage, my seat in the third row of chairs; in all this discourse I had viewed only the top of the manager's head since, having come down stage, he was hidden by the two giants seated before me. I could, in fact, see only one side of the stage at any time, any thing transpiring on the other being concealed from view; so that during the commotion I had been able to see only Mr. Barrymore, delivering his lines in the direction of a mysterious silence.

Throughout the course of the action the audience expressed its discontent, some times with far more witticism than from on stage. By the third act the performers were compelled to withdraw. Mr. Palmer appeared again, requesting permission of the audience only to go through the play to the end. If then it did not meet with our approval, he promised it would not be acted again. And so once more the actors came out, and once again tried to drum up interest in the laboured efforts of the playwright. The only thing that met with any sparkle of interest was Miss Farrens' dress in the very last act. It was of white muslin under a white sarsenet scarf-cloak, her slippers of white satin embroidered with silver: when she entered, the costume sent a gasp of pleasure throughout the theatre. But so bored were we all, some conversing more loudly than the actors, which made it impossible for others of us to hear what was being said on stage, that the curtain was finally dropped before the end. Thus, said this morning's *Times*, the comedy has experienced the force of ridicule which it announced. Mr. Palmer appeared for the last time to assure the audience that the play would be withdrawn in compliance with the general opinion. It is known by now that it is by Holcroft. I simply do not agree with those of his friends who assert that the play failed because of his political denomination; it failed because it was a weak play, whose entire substance could be found in the first act—the audience rightly seeing no reason for staying on. Poor Holcroft! I feel for him. It must be such a day, to day, as to make him wish he were not alive. But Godwin assures us that his friend's mind is tranquil. It makes me think I must be made of different stuff, so differently should I feel, had the play been mine.

M W T O W G

December 12, 1796

I increased my cold yesterday, or rather cough, yesterday. The dress of women seems to be invented to render them dependent, in more senses than one. Had not Miss B promised to call for me, even Mrs. Siddons would not have tempted me out to day, though I want winding up. I do not know how you make authorship and dissipation agree, my thoughts are some times turned adrift.

I will take care of the two news papers, which contain the debates, if you will let me have them again, with this day's—

M W T O W G

December 13, 1796

I thought, after you left me last night, that it was a *pity* we were obliged to part just then. I was even vext with myself for staying to supper with Mrs. R. But there is a manner of leaving a person free to follow their own will, that looks so like indifference. I do not like it. Your *tone* would have decided me. But to tell you the truth, I thought by your voice and manner, that you wished to remain in society—and pride made me wish to gratify you.

I mean to be with you, as soon as I can, this evening. I thought of calling in my way, at three o'clock—say shall you be at home; but do not stay at home on that account unless you intend it, though I do not intend to *peck* you.

Tuesday morning

WG TO MW

December 13, 1796

I like the note before me better than six preceding ones. I own I had the premeditated malice of making you part with me last night unwillingly. I feared Cupid had taken his final farewell.

Call on me at three as you propose, unless you see me first in Judd Place.

MW TO WG

December 18, 1796

I do not know whether you have sufficient philosophy to read this debate without indignation. I could not and I love Mr. Fox, for feeling and expressing it in so forcible and so manly a manner—This is what I call humanity— I will own to you that I am hurt when humanity and cruelty are beheld with indifference, as speculative points —I could say more, but of this, however, I am certain that true eloquence is only to be produced by the embodying of virtue and vice.

Shall I see you before you go to dinner, I do not mean to stir out to day. If you intend to call, say when, because I do not wish you to come the moment of dinner, when you do not dine with me.

December 18, 1796, Sunday—

For a long time, this morning, I have been unable to put from my mind the suffering of Mme. La Fayette at the hands of the Austrians. The report of her entreaties to the Emperor, printed in yesterday's *Times*, has been a source of horror: her voluntarily entering prison with her two daughters to share her husband's fate so stabs my heart that I stand unnerved before whatever had been my purpose. According to witnesses, the one person the late Queen of France could not forgive was the General of the National Guard, La Fayette. Her Austrian relatives are fully resolved to continue her revenge. Burke, who once could not bear to hear a word of disrespect to the memory of the unfortunate Queen, must have a mind strangely perverted to be the voice now raised in justification of the barbarous treatment calculated to humiliate a noble and loyal creature, whom the Revolution has equally made a victim.

When Godwin attended the session of the House Wednesday last, there was controversy on the subject of a loan to Austria of public money, which had been transmitted without the knowledge of Parliament. Fox rose with a dark scowl of contained rage, his cheeks quivering as he delivered a speech against Ministers so reckless as to dare clandestinely to send out of the country near a million of money—the purpose of such secrecy to render voting of any appropriation henceforth ridiculous and nugatory. It was equal to smuggling money from the kingdom. Surely our Austrian ally would fight no less valiantly, understanding that their needs are paid for by Parliament, rather than in secrecy by the Minister.

Meanwhile, La Fayette languishes in prison, and his wife is refused permission ever to return to him, should she be obliged to seek medical attention in Vienna, refused no doubt from the fear that she might try to reach the Emperor, who is surrounded by those who wish to keep him ignorant of injustices executed in his name. The motion to ask His Majesty to intercede was voted upon —and failed to pass.

Young men, these calamitous days, come in droves to Godwin's study, sitting about in such a spirit of adulation that some times I strike the wrong note merely by walking in all naturally, instead of in a subdued, reverential and mortuary mood. Some of them who speak of life purely from philosophical principle, lacking all living knowledge, make me feel unwholesomely old; yet others, their fierceness of ideals untarnished by years of vain effort, exalt me. We move, Godwin and I, like pastors amidst a flock. Dyson and Dibbin, inseparable friends, had come to call the other day. Dibbin was sitting listening with his head thrown back, an open look of amusement on his face; while Dyson, standing, told us of an incident that had befallen him earlier at the bookseller Debrett's, where he goes to peruse the papers and catch up on gossip. Godwin has known him since, as a boy, he would visit young Cooper. He has an insouciant manner, helping himself, I noticed, to a second glass of wine without formalities, Godwin appearing less tutorial, more impassive, in his presence than with the others—for Dyson is some one, he has said to me, from whom he feels he may always learn, having a mind that is, though too volatile, uncommonly endowed. I find appealing the intensity of his opinions and the little laugh which follows, as if he feels called upon to soften the intransigeance of his intellect. I found him looking at me with curiosity. I confess I examined him—to determine, if I could, how some one so young might be, according to his own admission, one of Godwin's few principal oral instructors which includes the Reverend Joseph Fawcet, Holcroft and now Dyson. Such a recommendation may have led me, merely from a spirit of contradiction, to find fault with him; but such was not the case—I fell under his spell, pondering his facile, lively train of thought. I asked him to come to tea next day, with an end in view of speaking about myself and my work. It seemed, when the time came, an inspired idea to let a perfectly unknown young man carry my M.S. off under his arm. I acted on impulse. Now waiting for him to come to tell me his opinion, I cannot put down another word for apprehension. Since I cannot write, I shall improve my mind—

Sidney	Addison
Hooker	Swift
Shakespear	Shaftesbury
Raleigh	Bolingbroke
Knowles	Middleton
Milton	Sherlock
Clarendon	Locke
Temple	Fielding
Tilotson	Smollet
Smat	

M W TO W G

December 20, 1796

I send you the work which Mr. Dyson says is "so dear to curiosity." He sent it home this morning, he tells me, does he tell lies? that lameness prevented his bringing it himself. Fanny says, perhaps man come to day—I am glad there is no perhaps in the case—as to other perhaps —they must rest in the womb of time.

Send me some ink.

M W T O W G

December 23, 1796

Was not yesterday a very pleasant evening!

There was a tenderness in your manner, as you seemed to be opening your heart, that rendered you very dear to me.

There are other pleasures in the world, you perceive, beside those known to your philosophy.

Friday morning

Of myself I am still at a loss what to say.—

M W T O W G

Wednesday, December 28, 1796

I am not well to day. A lowness of spirits, which I cannot conquer, leaves me at the mercy of my imagination, and only painful recollections and expectations assail me. Should it freeze to night, I believe, I had better have a coach—I would give, more than I ought, not to go—I dare say you are out of patience with me?

Send one bottle of wine no more, because your stock is almost out.

M W T O W G

December 30, 1796

Unless it rains I mean to dine with Johnson to day; and will be with you in the evening; but shall not tie myself to the hour of tea . . .

I spent a pleasant day yesterday; only with Opie and Peter.

Friday morning

December 31, 1796

I shall dine with Johnson; but expect to be at home between seven and eight.

If you were to get the constant Couple and bring it with you to read this evening—would it not be pleasant?

Looking over some of your essays, this morning, reminds me that the one I most earnestly wished you to alter, from the most perfect conviction, was that on Public and Private Education—I wanted you to recommend *Day* Schools, it would obviate the evil, of being left with servants, and enable children to converse with children without clashing with the exercise of domestic affections, the foundation of virtue.

Saturday, December 31, 1796

You treated me last night with extreme unkindness: the more so because it was calm, melancholy, equable unkindness. You wished we had never met, you wished you could cancel all that has passed between us. Is this— ask your own heart,—Is this compatible with the passion of love? Or, is it not the language of frigid, unalterable indifference?

You wished all the kind things you had ever written me destroyed.

December 31, 1796

This does not appear to me just the moment to have written such a note as I have been perusing.

I am, however, prepared for any thing. I can abide by the consequence of my own conduct, and do not wish to involve any one in my difficulties.

Saturday morning

January 1, 1797—Sunday morning

I have brought Johnson the outstanding reviews for January—for two days making rounds to various abodes to sweep from table-tops, the ink still drying, reviews put off till the last moment. Johnson and I, reading, correcting, consulting over them, sat in a corner of his office. I had glanced up to see him holding the pages to his eyes, lips rounded as his breath whistled in and out, with a rapidity that might have led one to think he had been running up and down the stairs, though for a full hour he had been sitting in his familiar, disproportionately large, dark brown velvet chair which always seems to dwarf him, making him look particularly frail, wizened and ill. At one point he had twice to pose a question, till I gave a start, so torporous with misery had I become.

Dear Heavens, how happy I had been the day before! I had passed the entire day with Opie and Peter Pindar, who never ceased telling anecdotes as we walked first to Christies' for a look at the paintings, and then went to his place at Tavistock Row, Covent Garden, to take tea. Opie has been in a peculiarly light-hearted mood these days, since his divorce. He has dared declare his hopes to Miss Beetham, the two of them now secretly engaged. His smiling equipoise could be read in all the lineaments of his body, as he lay tumbled by spent laughter on a sofa in Peter's disordered room, through whose single window—the rest having been bricked up to save paying tax—a little light fell. Peter was reading us his new lampoon. Opie who has known him for years and years says that, though considered a profligate reviler of his sovereign, he is constantly surprised his work provokes such opinion, having nothing more in mind, it seems, than to make verse profitable. Three years ago he sold his copyrights for an annuity of 250*l.* and could live very well on that. But he is ever in litigation. Opie considers him to have a tradesman's mercenary heart.

Peter had blubbered up his lips to splutter out his Hanoverian accent in imitation of the Royal Court. Meaning to say *Welcome*, he says:

> Well! in a come—King George to town,
> With doust and zweat as netmeg brown,
>   The hosses all in smoke;

> Huzzein, trumpetin, and dringin,
> Red colours vleeing, roaring, zingin,
> So mad seem'd all the voke.

We laughed at Peter swelling his cheeks, plumping his lips, spitting, snorting, sneezing. To please the Royal chops, he has them prepare a feast of

> Vish, vlesh, and vowl and vruit

at which bassoonish melody of *zounds* Opie clapped both hands to his abdomen, as if stricken by green sickness. Godwin thinks—thinks he rightly?—that Peter is our modern Pope, though, I notice, he keeps neither Pope nor Peter on his bedside table, but rather a prettily bound volume of Donne and another of Ben Jonson. All day, during hours of unexamined cheerfulness, I had been at ease, exchanging wit in masculine company—a woman with *thinking powers*, not one dominated by her female organs. Yet a King is always a King, a woman always a woman: his authority, her sex, ever standing between them and the world.

Gloomy were my thoughts, next day, at Johnson's, when I stayed to dine with him and a few of his friends. Fuseli was there, a nephew of Johnson's from Liverpool as well as several others. I sat dully amidst the company, the odour of brown gravy, following the joint of mutton, assailing me. Were Fuseli or Johnson or Johnson's nephew or the nephew's wife, or the doctor who had observed diseases of the Army in Jamaica and written of the means of preserving the health of Europeans in that climate, to suspect the truth! The thought made me rise in panic, excuse myself and hasten to leave. Johnson accompanied me to the stairs, thinking I was overcome by fatigue from our long labour. I grasped his hand as though I were taking leave of him for a long time to come, my intensity as surprising to me as it seemed to him, though he merely nodded in his fashion and clasped the rounded newel post as he watched me retreat down the flight of stairs.

When Godwin came to me last night, I had worked myself into a fever. I had put aside the pages of his essays, and sat at an angle to the fire which crackled like a disturbing presence between us so that, for a moment, I had been oblivious of any other sound.

So sorrowful a sensation had swept over me that I could not move for its heaviness. I heard Godwin sigh and stir, and I thought he would have liked more cheerful company. He shifted in his chair making the rush seat creak, and asked what reflexion could have so robbed him of my company. Unspoken incertitudes had been for weeks harassing me. While still I could suspect them to be merely idle fears, I had tried to put anxiety from my mind, knowing that, with no effort on my part, things must of themselves, in time, come clear. *Time!* that terror of women's lives. We live to a tide no man knows. I said—speaking at last—that what we had now for weeks suspected, feared and put aside, depending on the ripeness of time to tell the truth of the matter, could now no longer remain unrecognised—that the fluxes, though often delayed by mental anguish, some times by unusual physical exertion, or by climactic changes, cannot long go unrelieved, but that there is one single overwhelming and unavoidable cause of such abeyance. I had determined to force to rational discourse consequences which must be drawn from the fact that, for an entire month, I had futilely awaited my menses and waited in vain. He who had quieted my fears now winced at the prospect that will destroy for ever the even course of his life. It was only a mere flinch of apprehension that had crossed his features, yet it hurled me into a gulf of despair. I said—in a voice from the tomb—that I wished I had never met him, wished I had pursued my solitary walk to the grave, wished that I could undo what I had done or perish in a lightning bolt, leaving not a cinder upon this earth. I know not what I said, for whatever it was was spoken in a moment of such distraction of the spirit that it was as if the ghosts of past terrors had assembled to wail a dirge of dire prediction and dismay. Frigid, unalterable indifference? Calm, equable unkindness? This attributed unkindness of mine . . . what is there to say, but that such reasoning left me in despair.

I scarcely heard Godwin saying that I was never again to express a sense of solitary responsibility for difficulties in which he fully shared. If there was to be a child, it was to be his child as well as mine. How had I ever imagined him so base as to allow me to consider that he would not wish to involve himself in consequences which, though unanticipated, had become, as he had allowed himself to accept the certitude, a blissful prospect. I smiled wanly, convinced of his good nature, but not of his ability to transcend insuperable obstacles. Were he to become my husband, the law of the land demands that he assume my debts.

I have borrowed every where. I must owe Johnson more than sixty pounds, a sum that the sale of my books barely diminishes. It is impossible for me to know what further bills, which Imlay did not pay, will suddenly be sent to my door. As for my father, who inherited *ten thousand pounds*—which might have been made use of for his independence and for ours—he has been, his whole life, a master of Quixotic schemes that have reduced the family to penury. It is all spent. Edward, the eldest son, who earns a decent livelihood as attorney at law, has wiped his hands of us. He has done little for his sisters, and will do nothing for his own father. I have been sending a quarterly sum—often enough having to borrow it from Johnson to do so, money which, though cast down a bottomless pit, was yet necessary to my peace of mind. I had assumed, in those days when first I came to London, the burden of both my sisters, and one or another of my younger brothers, as they drifted in from the country, all characteristically aimless where it concerned making a living. Often I would write far into the night, barely sleeping, keeping myself alive on a diet devoid of animal flesh, wearing my old beaver hat till it was scuffed to the very leather, all in order to provide for creatures whose great common resemblance seems to be that they are unable to provide for themselves. I now have such an urgent need of money that I wish I might collect from the past every penny spent in useless aid of those who, in the end, resent my refusal to continue to bear their burdens. Godwin is considering asking his friend Thomas Wedgwood for a loan. The thought of borrowing, however, does violence to his nature, so that he wishes, first of all, to pursue a plan to go to Robinson to ask him to bring out a new edition of "Political Justice." He can count on revenue from the essays, which he has every expectation of finishing before the end of the month. My condition will remain secret for a little longer yet; in the meanwhile we might pursue a practical course of preparing for the eventuality. For the lease of a house where we may live together, we shall have to wait till the end of this quarter—till Lady's Day.

I *ought* to have been consoled, but I was not. There is a difficulty to which, alas! there is no solution. How could I hope, following Opie's example, to free myself from an unhappy marriage by divorce, *when I have never been married?* I have been known as *Mrs. Imlay,* for convenience's sake, a convenience that now turns onerous. When it becomes known that *Mrs. Imlay* will marry, I shall become the world's laughing-stock. It moves my gall that I shall be made to seem to lie, when I tell the truth, admitting that I *had* been lying. It sounds a play on words, though I feel no wit, only a dull, dead sense of dread at what is to become of me.

I must now dress to go out into weather as wet as it has been cold—a cold, in fact, of such severity during all of December, that when a sergeant relieved a soldier who had been standing guard all night, he found him frozen to death in the sentry-box. The sun has been fitfully appearing, melting the ice, so that one cannot walk any where but a team of horses clatters by, dashing one's skirts with a filthy flood. Instead of passing New Year's Day at Holcroft's, as we have planned, I long to curl up with a book at home. The night before last it was pleasant to read aloud, the two of us, from "The Constant Couple," forgetting our dilemma in Sir Harry Wildair's. A lady of jilting temper has to say of him that of all the lovers she ever had, he had been her greatest plague, for she could never make him *uneasy;* I understand her meaning— uneasiness often a sign of feeling.

M W   T O   W G

January 1, 1797

The weather is so unfavourable that I find I must have a coach, or stay at home. I was splashed up to my knees yesterday, and to sit several hours in that state is intolerable.

Will you then come to me, as soon as you can; for Mary, after leaving this with you, goes on for a coach.

I am not well—I have a fever of my spirits that has tormented me these two night's past. You do not, I think make sufficient allowance for the peculiarity of my situation. But women are born to suffer.

I cannot bear that you should do violence to your feelings, by writing to Mr. Wedgewood. No; you shall not write—I will think of some way of extricating myself.

You must have patience with me, for I am sick at heart
—Dissatisfied with every body and every thing.

My depression of spirits is certainly increased by in-
disposition.

Sunday morning

MW TO WG

January 5, 1797

I was very glad that you were not with me last night,
for I could not rouse myself—To say the truth, I was
unwell—and out of spirits. I am better to day.

I shall take a walk before dinner, and expect to see you
this evening, *chez moi*, about eight, if you have no objection.

Thursday morning

MW TO WG

January 12, 1797

I am better this morning. But it snows, so incessantly;
that I do not know how I shall be able to keep my appointment this evening. What say you? But you have no
petticoats to dangle in the snow. Poor Women how they
are beset with plagues—within—and without.

Thursday morning

MW TO WG

January 13, 1797

I believe I ought to beg your pardon for talking at you,
last night, though it was in sheer simplicity of heart—
and I have been asking myself why it so happened. Faith
and Sooth, it's because there was nobody else worth at-
tacking, or who could converse—I had wearied me before
you entered. But, be assured, when I find a man that has
any thing in him, I shall let my every day dish alone.

I send you the Emma for Mrs. Inchbald supposing you
have not altered your mind.

Bring Holcroft's remarks with you and Ben Johnson.
Friday morning

January 13, 1797

It was a passing fancy that made me, leaving the Polygon, last
night, cast a lingering look at the crescent. It occurred to me that
it might be well to look for lodgings in this handsome new building which stands in open fields five minutes on foot from our present corner of Somers Town. It has a peculiarity of making me
think myself once again in France; for, having been built by a
M. Leroux at the northwesternmost edge of London, its fairly
cheap lodgings have attracted a number of emigrants. Tea last
night was at the Abbé Carron's, whom Godwin has decided to
cultivate as a source of all things revolutionary. The essays nearly
done, he is at pains to seek some monumental subject for his next
book. He thinks to find it in the manner in which social inequities
lead to a violent struggle for justice, the very struggle inevitably
yielding to the horrors of tyranny that so marked Robespierre's
reign. I warn him he will hardly satisfy curiosity, nor learn the
truth, from either impoverished French aristocrats or embittered
émigrés such as Carron, home-sick for the dear countryside of
France and the cathedral school he quitted so reluctantly. The
French who live among us would all, it seems to me, fly back to
their native land, were they enabled; they put down no roots, but
like air ferns seem yet to thrive; I am fascinated at how their national habits persist: French merchants opening shops of every
sort, so that the very streets begin to take on the character of a
French quarter. The blockade having made wines scarce, cham-
pagne unobtainable, Godwin considers himself fortunate that
through the Abbé he has been able to lay in a very good supply
of claret.

I had hoped, when opening "Hubert de Sevrac," Mrs. Robinson's new novel, to read of the precarious lives of those in exile
who, having committed themselves to the Monarchy, or to the
conservative forces of the Revolution, had to flee for their lives
and now with England and France at war are forced to remain.
Peace had seemed imminent when, some months ago, Lord

Malmsbury went to Paris to negotiate with the Ministers, but he has just been dismissed, returning chagrined. Mrs. Robinson's novel might have opened uninstructed hearts to the suffering of the exiles among us. What should have been an absorbing story is unfortunately flawed—her sentences confused, entangled, half-expressed and false. That such a subject should fall to the hands of one who writes too rapidly to mature any invention seems a pity. Writing a book is no easy task—yet Mrs. Robinson dashes off her 950 pages in the time it takes me to go from Somers Town to St. Paul's Church-yard. I could hardly give it a generous review in the *Analytical*. I was able, however, to praise her volume of sonnets which trace Sappho's ungovernable passion for Phaon—expressed with tenderness and harmony not unworthy of the theme, as well as a means once again of evoking echoes of her past amours with the Prince of Wales—*Prince of Whales*, as Peter calls him, for he adores her and hates her Hanoverian Prince.

We writers who write of the works of other writers, especially those of personal acquaintance, run the risk of overpraising what is not praiseworthy. Godwin's flattery, to my way of thinking, only encourages Mrs. Robinson's slipshod literary style. With Mary Hays I have often been a cranky critic. I have yet written her an admiring review for the January issue. I was pleased to do so. It is a novel which, though she may not have been aware of it in the writing, displays a moral which declares that sensibility, if it be the parent of our most refined enjoyments, may also give birth to the keenest anguish and deepest distress. If fault I find, it is that there are too many sulphureous flashes of lightning illuminating lovers standing in trembling apprehension. I wonder if reading and reviewing has not hardened my heart to characters so circumstanced. Yet, in general, I rejoiced in reading the two volumes completed, pleased that I could sincerely write well of them, believing as I do that literary friendship, although it must never corrupt one's principles, puts on one the happy obligation of publicly praising what one might have criticised in private.

Godwin thinks what I want is flattery, but it is not so, though I find it puzzling that he should flatter Mrs. Inchbald and Mrs. Robinson and Miss Alderson, and be so severe with me. Yesterday he finished my "Rights of Woman"; to day he has begun to read what he insists on calling Wollstonecraft versus Burke. He intends reading every thing in a studious manner, in order that he may counsel me how to direct my energies where I might best gain from them—writing as if our lives depend on it, as indeed they do! We want money. We must have money with which to pay my debts; to move to larger quarters; and to keep the lodgings on Chalton Street, or elsewhere, so that Godwin may continue to have the privacy to study and to write, and meet with friends without the distractions inevitable in a household of small children. Working for Johnson deters me from my true vocation. I am wasting my vitality trekking all over London for some dull topical tract. Godwin could only remark that I owe Johnson . . . my sharp, bitter laugh stopped him in the midst of his phrase. *I owe Johnson!* says every thing. I am indentured to him as much as any poor creature who goes to the new world, working his passage, once there. I am dependent on him in order to repay my passage from governess in Ireland to literary drudge—though once I thrilled at the notion that I was thereby gaining independence. No wonder I am ill at ease with my former friend; no wonder I cannot bring him my present writing, nor discuss my circumstance. It was the measure of my feelings of defeat that has brought Godwin to the point of offering to help me determine which way now to turn—whether, as Johnson seems to think, to devote myself to mere works of the imagination or, as I begin to think, to tilt not at ghosts and Gothic castles but at those real, solid, visible injustices in society. Only in one book have I joined heart and head, writing from a wholeness of spirit I had never before known—returning from my willingness to die in the Thames with nothing more either to lose or to fear from life. It was, Godwin once said, a book that would make any man fall in love with me. But enough of the subject—except to add that I promised to show him my "Wrongs of Woman" as soon as I can rewrite pages still illegible, so many times have I crossed out words and tucked in others, so that the entirety resembles nothing as much as a ball of twine a cat has rolled about the floor.

A woman such as Mrs. Barbauld, who was handsomely gowned in grey silk at Carron's last night, must glide unerringly through life; her look tranquil, her clear eyes set on lofty purposes; her writing profitable and reputation unblemished. She and her husband live in the village of Hampstead, where they have a very pretty little house, where I once went with Johnson on a Sunday. I have always admired her "Hymns for Children" and the "Early Lessons." Yet I find her, in truth, a disputatious sort of person. She has a habit of listening to one with the raised eyebrows of some one apt to contradict as soon as the speaker has finished, her lips flattened in the way of country-women who do not wish to be taken in, the nostrils flared as though at a bad odour. At Johnson's dinners, where she often reigns, speaking in her irreproachably schooled accent, her thoughts like good children carefully drilled, I had always found myself, by contrast, passionate and erratic. Her eyes look me over with a look that says I simply won't do. Generally this so discountenances me I fall silent. But last night I enjoyed a brisk argument and talked so boldly that she froze in her good grey gown into mute, malodorous disdain. Perchance it has some thing to do with their *baldness,* I said to Godwin in our way home—that I should raise the scorn of *both* Mrs. Inchbald and Mrs. Barbauld.

M W   T O   W G

January 15, 1797

I have only a moment to tell you that I cannot call this morning, and I do not know whether I shall be able to go to Mr. J's tho' I should be sorry to fail. If the weather be tolerable, or I catch a coach I shall go, and therefore cannot say when—but probably before the hour you set out, normally. I am not quite so well to day, owing to my very uncomfortable walk, last night. I was very glad I did not promise to call on you for I was obliged to undress immediately, on my return. To morrow, I suppose, is out of the reach of fate. Yours truly,

Sunday   Mary

M W   T O   W G

January 21, 1797

I forgot to invite you to dine with me this present Saturday the 21st of January. Still I shall expect you at half past four—so no more at present from yours &c—

Saturday morning—   Mary

MW TO WG

January 24, 1797

I am still an invalid—still have the inelegant complaint, which no novelist has yet ventured to mention as one of the consequences of sentimental distress. If prudence permit I shall take a walk this morning, and, perhaps, call on you, going or returning; but do not stay at home a moment for me. Should I continue unwell, I believe I had better spend the evening alone; but you shall hear of me, or see me, in the course of the day.

MW TO WG

January 27, 1797

I am not well this morning—It is very tormenting to be thus, neither sick nor well; especially as you scarcely imagine me indisposed.

Women are certainly great fools; but nature made them so. I have not time or paper, else, I could draw an inference, not very illustrative of your chance-medley system—But I spare the moth-like opinion, there is room enough in the world &c.

January 28, 1797

A cousin of Helen Maria Williams', whom I used to frequent at Paris, posed me a seemingly innocent question last night. The question, which silenced the room, was: When had my American husband and I been married, and had there been no difficulties for foreigners marrying in France? As it was generally known, at Paris during the time, that Helen Maria Williams lived under the protection of John Hurford Stone, who had deserted his wife for her, so it was common knowledge that I had sought protection in the same manner *at the advice of Miss Williams*. The four of us, for a short period, formed a friendship largely based on common circumstances. I have never admired her style of writing, nor her breathless enthusiasm. "My political creed," she used to say, "is an affair of the heart." Not a single portentous event of those days was lost on her: even imprisonment an experience she could convert to profit, in the writing of it, making herself an imperilled heroine, although her gaol was but a convent and the term of imprisonment brief. What *thinking powers* she may have had were drowned in warm treacle on her smiling lips. Some resemblance in the pink-cheeked, young woman sitting before me last night brought back the memory of Miss Williams in her parlour in the Rue de Bac, where we all used to gather in the evening. It was there I saw Imlay again, having met him first in London at the Christies'. To be put into the position now of being forced to answer, in an oppressively theatrical silence, when it was that he and I had been married inflamed me. I don't know what possessed me to say, in an off-hand manner, that my American husband and I had *not* been married on French soil, no more than had Miss Williams and Mr. Stone; that the French had passed the Law of Suspects decree in September of '93, making the marriage of two Englishwomen, such as we were, not only difficult but impossible. I had spoken with no indication of pique and then had turned to carry on my conversation with a pleasant young man, who was unable to restrain a small smile which seemed almost congratulatory. It confirmed my suspicion that, in the guise of an innocent question, the little plot had been commonly prepared. I had glimpsed the consternation of the young lady who had been put up to the business and the confusion of spirits of the woman of the house, whose notion it must have been.

Despite being indisposed, some portion of the day, every day, I have been continuously working. A week ago I gave Godwin fifty-six pages—I have more but only in rough order—and the same evening told him I was considering showing them to Johnson to obtain his promise to print the book. Godwin says he finds it gratifying that I am writing more slowly, allowing my powers fully to expand. I am such a strange animal that if he criticises my work, I sink into misery, whereas if he praises it, I worry lest he may have enkennelled me with the others of the fair sex, to whom mere flattery is due. That was Saturday; Sunday Godwin and I were invited to Mrs. Robinson's in a small gathering that included Mrs.

Inchbald, who had admired "Emma" and wished to say so to its author. I had to wait till Monday to take my pages, bound in blue ribband, to lay on Johnson's desk, indicating that my hopes for the new offspring, these "Wrongs," might prove as profitable as had the "Rights." Johnson smiled, untying the knot, leaning over the title page, while my heart beat as much as any untried author. Wednesday, the day I ordinarily spend at Johnson's, I woke with a sense of some thing pleasant in store for me, before being fully awake enough to remember it was my day to go to St. Paul's Church-yard. Johnson's time had been wholly taken with troublesome errors concerning the printing of Paine's letter to Washington, a copy of which I managed to slip away for Godwin; thus he asked me to come to see him yesterday. I had worn out the brightness of the interview by anticipation. Besides, I was not well. I could read Johnson's face as he bade me sit down. I know him so thoroughly that I can surmise his thoughts, even beneath a kindly mask meant to conceal them. Before he had uttered a word, I knew he was about to do his best to spare my feelings. He does not think the M.S. sufficiently well ordered to be able to say whether or not he will engage to print it. He can see what I am aiming at, but is not convinced by it, and does not find it terrifying to see the heroine shut up in a madhouse, since there is no factual detail to substantiate my claim. I had found inspiration from Amelia Alderson's description of once having befriended a poor soul in an asylum, and from my sister Bess' experience, my point being that the law supports a husband in any conflict with his wife, her sanity often judged a matter of compliance to his will. Johnson found no fault with my reasoning—only repeated, shaking his head, that his imagination had not been captured by my performance.

MW TO WG

January 28, 1797

I was glad that you were not with me last night, for the foolish woman of the house laid a trap to plague me. I have, however, I believe, put an end to this nonsense, so enough of that subject.

A variety of things assail my spirits at present and some

of my endeavours to throw off, or rather to extricate myself, by failing, have only given an edge to my vexation.

I shall expect you this evening.

Saturday

MW TO WG

February 3, 1797

Mrs. Inchbald was gone into the City to dinner, so I
had to measure back my steps.

To day I find myself better; and, as the weather is fine,
mean to call on Dr. Fordyce. I shall leave home about
two o'clock. I tell you so, lest you should call after that
hour. I do not think of visiting you, in my way, because
I seem inclined to be industrious. I behold I feel affectionate to you in proportion as I am in spirits; still I must
not dally with you, when I can do anything else—there is
a civil speech for you to chew—

Friday morning

MW TO WG

February 4, 1797

When I promised to visit you, this morning, you forgot
that you had previously mentioned your intention of calling on Fuseli. Only say what you mean to do; and
whether my visit is to be to day or to morrow.

I shall probably invite the Frenchman, to drink a glass
of wine; if you say you shall not come to night—

Saturday morning

February 6, 1797

Mondays are visitors' day at Bedlam. Johnson, Godwin and I presented ourselves, this morning, at the gate. I had not known that
Bethlehem Hospital, erected in the sixteenth century, had been
built on the plan of the Royal Palace of the Tuileries; nor, as Johnson recounted, that Louis XIV took such offence upon the occa-

sion that he ordered offices to be built upon the plan of St. James's. A well-dressed assemblage had gathered for the sake of the sort of spectacle people go to find at Ranleagh or Vauxhall; our threesome must have seemed without any more definite purpose than the usual entertainment. When the gate was flung wide, and we had traversed the court-yard, a female keeper unlocked a door with a key that clanked among numerous others, all buckled upon a ring that hung from her waist; she led us across a hall, opening large double doors of oak that had some sort of ornamental carving above them on which was *not* written, though appropriately it might have been: "Abandon hope all ye who enter here."

The doors led into one of the main galleries from which, even before we had a glimpse inside, there came to us the voluble babble of voices. We entered a gallery of some hundred feet or more in length, in which the inhabitants of the place were walking about, seated, or slumped upon the floor; some stood by the long barred windows gazing out into the branches of the bare trees against the leaden skies. Johnson supporting my arm on one side, Godwin on the other, I strolled upon uneven tiling with lowered eyes, for, though it might seem false delicacy, it appears to me that even madmen have rights that ought to be held inviolable.

By this time the visitors were ambling down the corridor in groups of twos and threes, so that, by the time I lifted my eyes, I was unsure which of those that milled about had come through the gates with us. Godwin had observed he should like to see Margaret Nicholson, who has been for ten years within these walls. He looked about among the faces of the women, but was not sure that he could recognise her. He determined to ask one of the keepers if she was there, at which he fell behind. I asked Johnson if she were not the same woman who, in the act of presenting a petition to the King, had thrust a knife towards his breast, which he had only just avoided by quickly drawing back. At the time of the incident, I had been impressed by the words which the news papers had represented the King to have said: "I am not hurt; take care of the poor woman; do not hurt her." Upon examination, she had been able to utter nothing but that the Crown was rightfully *hers*—a poor creature, alone in the world, who had lived by taking in plain work, given to talking to herself, thriving on that dangerous illusion which had been her sole comfort in a world of dreariness. I would have liked to grasp her hand in an expression of sympathy—not sympathy, to be sure, for an action which might have had terrifying and odious consequences, but for a life that once had been so restricted that even Bedlam may have been of benefit.

Johnson and I had marched the length of the gallery, and had turned and were walking back again, when a decently dressed woman approached us with a delightful smile to ask if Lord Ackley were with us. A nod from Johnson in the negative made her rush off to inquire similarly of others; whether she was actually expecting a visit from one so grand, or if her question was merely to exalt a notion of her own rank and consequence, we never did have a chance to determine. My nerves were afflicted by the wailing of an unhappy creature whose despair chilled my heart, a prey, we were to learn later, to the guilt of imagining she had murdered both her father and mother. Her constant plaint dinned into our ears as we made our slow progress up the corridor and half-way back again: "What will be done, oh, oh, what will be done?"—a woeful plaint which must have burdened the others, whose melancholy sentiments it could only have echoed. When Godwin rejoined us, it was to say that the woman who had tried to murder the King was being kept apart from the others. He pointed out the mother of four, who had severed her infant's head from its body—but I could not look upon her, so pitiable did she seem, sitting with her hands upon her lap, staring before her in utter resignation and hopelessness. The keeper had told Godwin that she avowed that the Devil had directed her to do the deed. We formed a circle, with other visitors, around a woman in her forties, who had contracted a most singular persuasion that was described to us by a gentleman, who takes a fancy to visiting the hospital whenever some young relative of his comes to London, thinking such visits instructive. It may seem cruel to make of those who are mad a public spectacle—yet physicians maintain that the company of visitors, ordinary conversation, noise, even the taunts and jibes, invigorate the inmates and are, by being an example of reality, more conducive to leading them back to sanity than would be the continual languor of isolation. We were informed that the woman within our curious circle, fancying herself to be a man, is particularly attached to the matron, whom she calls her beauty; otherwise, she is orderly, quiet and harmless. She was saluting us in the manner of a footman, almost appearing amused by her own performance, as though she did not take it in earnest. Indeed, I had a sense of theatre in the gallery—it is difficult to believe that the inmates cannot relinquish at will behaviour so very inconvenient. My interest in a fictional personage, shut into Bedlam not because she is mad, but because her husband wishes to be rid of her, led me to search among these creatures for likely examples; except for the elderly woman who had asked if Lord Ackley was with us, their peculiarity of character was unmistakable, a peculiarity not voluntarily chosen, nor apparently to be cast off at will. Some element of life—such as the solitude of sewing all the lighted hours of the day in a room the size of a closet—had so debilitated the constitution of these poor women, that their minds had been destroyed. It frightened me that we are not to be brought back to our wits once we lose them.

There remained the visit to the cells, which Godwin had arranged with the young woman who had let us into the gallery. I was able to query her then on some things that I had prepared to ask. She amply satisfied me on the subject of the inmates' food: their breakfast of gruel with milk and two ounces of bread—I have had no time during the day to transcribe such information, and wish not to let the details slip from memory—for dinner rice-pudding and bread. Table beer is served. Knives and forks of bone, wooden trenchers, and bowls for the beer and the gruel, are supplied. I studied the strongly marked features of the keeper as she spoke. She brought out her words in a rough, surly manner, not from ill feeling, but rather from not knowing how to ingratiate herself. I asked about her duties. She told me she was one of three gallery maids on the woman's side. They open the doors of the cells that patients may come out, at six in summer and seven in winter; for those inclined to be mopish she must make them quit their cells to lock the door, that they may not return to their beds. Her other duties are to change the straw whenever damp or dirty, the linen and sheets before ten on a Tuesday; to see that the feet of every patient in chains be well rubbed and covered with flannel, night and morning, in winter; to see that all patients be washed Monday, Wednesday and Friday. There are fires to be lighted . . . and more work, she said with a sullen, hostile stare, than such as us could ever imagine. I asked softly when she was free to go out. One Sunday out of three, one evening each week. Poor soul! Her eyes were puffy and complexion yellow. She made an ominous clanking sound that came from her ring of keys as she preceded us down a corridor leading to the deserted cells, which we had persuaded her to show us—for, as Godwin has explained, in writing of prison he had been able to give even the exact dimension of the quarters in which Caleb unremittingly passed his days and nights, such factual information having given a great semblance of reality to his theme. Johnson had kindly thought to bring with him a small *cloisonné* egg, inside of which, behind its perforated hinged door, was a sponge saturated with patchouli. I now held this beneath my nostrils, the stench that had arisen from the cells overwhelming me, an animal odour intensified by the fear and anguish which must be endured in those brutish, dark dungeons. We had stepped on a damp stone floor and now peered, in the little light which pierced through tiny windows high in the walls, into quarters in which the inhabitants were literally buried alive. Upon the walls I made out iron rings by which one is manacled. Such an imprisonment of vext spirits was heart-rendingly pathetic!

Sitting here to night with the lamp turned high, casually strewn books upon my long deal table, keeping me company, the morning seems some far-fetched dream. My imagination goes into a whirl of wonderment that such a Fate lies some where beneath us, should we but stumble on our way in life and fall. What stays in mind with particular force is a look in the eyes of the gallery maid, who seemed the model of my Jemima, the haunted, exhausted look of her dark eyes as I put my questions—I am stung with re-morse that it did not occur to me to question her concerning her past, for I should like to know what sort of life compelled her to seek such a situation. Were there no less mean possibilities? Did she, too, sit in some room alone, or cramped beside several others, doing plain-work all the day, sewing till her fingers ached, her eyes teared, her legs grew numb from sitting—and for how many pence a day? Or had she been one of those poor wretches one sees through the open doors of a washing-place, some steamy vision of hell in which one glimpses women lifting heavy vats to pour boiling water into a basin, or kneeling in back-breaking labour upon stone floors. It shames me to sit so comfortably musing upon such things. The inclination of my mind is to turn away from this unrelieved brutality—but both Godwin and Johnson chide me that I must write of such things plainly, if I am to write of them at all.

February 10, 1797

Mary is scrubbing the stairs, so that Fanny is prevented from going up to fetch her monkey. I sit her upon my lap to dry her tears and wipe her nose, holding her tight against my breast, as I whisper into her ear that Aunt Everina is coming all the way from Ireland across the seas. Did she remember the ship that rolled over the waves when we came to England from France? She says she does and falls into a doze. Nothing will do for her to day. When I lift her down, she grows once again fretful. Now while I write at my table, she is playing with some marbles Lucas gave her. I don't know what has put me more out of sorts, Fanny's crankiness or my apprehension about Everina's visit.

I cannot help associate her arrival with those times when she had no where else to go and fell into my lodgings like a sack of grain, that melancholy inertness of hers the single characteristic I find most debilitating. I have not seen her in six whole years. Surely she will understand that my life now is vastly different from when we last saw one another: I have a child of my own to take care of (little does she know, nor will I confide to her, that another is on its way). And she shall surely be able to deduce by the number of times we are in Godwin's company that he is a significant presence. She is expected in her new position at the Wedgwoods' in less than a month. I cannot imagine why I grow uneasy, unless it be that my lot is so much happier than hers. It has always put her into a grudging frame of mind, as if life's bounty were a pie to be evenly apportioned. I have *earned* my independence, not sat idly by querulously complaining. But enough of that! I shall try to keep an even temper, though I fear her presence will re-animate scenes from the past and cast on these walls shadows of family ghosts. But to dwell on subjects less mournful . . .

I had a notion yesterday that either Godwin had entrusted to Holcroft our intentions, which he says he has not, or that Holcroft has divined them. On New Year's Day, when we passed to drink a glass of wine with him and his family, I observed him listening sharply to Godwin's discussion of marriage and of children. I had glimpsed a quizzical look on the features of Miss Holcroft, who has only recently married a cousin, I believe, or a nephew of Horne Tooke's; perhaps she thought to draw an inference to herself, for it is difficult, I know, for young people to suppose that those much older than themselves might also have passions and act on them. Holcroft with a benevolent look upon his face was studying me, or so I imagined, for it was that period during which I was suffering a raw agitation of the spirit, not knowing into what abyss my heedless actions would hurl me. Yesterday when we went, Godwin, Holcroft and I, to see "Marriage-à-la-mode," the discussion begun on New Year's Day was pursued, Holcroft very witty on the subject—though never cynical, for he is never that—behaving towards me with a nicety which made me imagine he has perceived our plans. Recently widowed, he speaks of domestic life as the ordinary, desirable state of man and says he would like to marry again. I believe, though no one will clarify the matter, that Mrs. Inchbald turned him down. She is supposed to be secretly in love with a Dr. Warren, for whose sake she furtively gulps down rhubarb pills in some sort of ritual of love. I have not heard the rumour from Godwin, who imagines she is in love with *him*. It was Twiss who brought me that morsel. For a number of years, Holcroft has disputed Godwin's inclination to remain unwed; it must come with some thing like surprise to hear him now expatiate, as he did after "Marriage-à-la-mode," how the couple in the play might have improved their life together by several small adjustments. It was then I fancied that Holcroft gave me a smiling glance.

February 13, 1797

Everina has gone out; Fanny is at market with Marguerite; Mary has given off banging saucepans in the scullery, Lucas apparently has worn himself out chasing Puss on hands and knees up and down the stairs. And I come to my table to gather my thoughts.

Everina so amused me, the first night she came, telling tales of her life in Ireland, that I was convinced she had learned to bear with resolution and patience life's unavoidable evils. She painted a picture of Ireland with the broad strokes of Swift, that Irishman who roared his indignation at his countrymen. The servants, she says, were savages—drunkards, liars and thieves—the house a pigsty, devoid of comfort or convenience, ever filled with people, three or four beds to a room. Often there was no water, since the servants were obliged to go two miles for it. On her first Sunday she set out for church with the family at eight in the morning, a distance of nine Irish miles over roads so bad that the gentlemen and ladies were forced to alight and walk the bad steps, though there were four able beasts to draw the coach. One of the husbands rode beside the coachman, the other by the postilion, keeping their good humour the whole day long—for the trip to church ended at *seven in the evening*, which no one considered extraordinary.

Once comely, her fine light hair disposed around full ruddy cheeks, Everina would race after me through the green, open fields of Beverly, carried away by some childish enthusiasm, raising a voice high and piping with excitement. Has that child dissolved into the listless woman who sits before me embroidering, some times without uttering a word? One cannot fail to read in her body which droops from the shoulders, and in the hang-dog slope of her neck, as she bends over her needle, a spirit of cultivated disappointment. She has always lived in dreams, never being any where at all but that elsewhere seemed to be where the resolution of all her hopes might lie. I can, at this point, merely plan some small pleasure which might distract her from an overwhelming sense of life's unfairness.

Sunday evening, when Godwin came to take tea with us, she made hardly a move save for twitching a handkerchief beneath her nose—for she had caught a cold in the coach—expressing no more curiosity for this man whom every one in London gives himself the trouble to meet, and thinks the effort worth while, than if he were a stick of furniture. Godwin went to some lengths to entertain her with stories of that proliferating clan of Wedgwood sons. It had seemed to us such a happy combination of chance that she had found a position as governess in England with the Allen sisters, who are married to the two older sons of Josiah Wedgwood, and whom she has known since our childhood in

Wales, where Father failed to make his fortune as a farmer twenty years ago. As for Godwin's connexion with the family, he had once planned with Thomas Wedgwood a common household that might suit both the narrow economic circumstances of a philosopher's life, as well as by equal economy allow his young friend to contribute to the common good, a philanthropic tendency which raises my hopes that, should we be desperate, it is not far-fetched to think that Godwin's request for a loan would be generously received. Smiling over his conclusion to a story, not generally published, about the business of the potteries, Godwin's look pried into Everina's. But in her bag of tricks she had not a single smile. The handkerchief was drawn from sleeve to nose, her only sign of liveliness. I had indeed been precipitate in thinking she had made any conciliation with what she called "the bad steps" along the road, which all of us meet with and some of us traverse with patience and good humour. What infuriates me is that she makes so little effort to appear agreeable, as though to say that Fate has singled her out for suffering, which she must dutifully endure to the end of the chapter. It is the old story! I am weary of it! But a little patience. "A little patience, and all will be over," as my poor mother used to say.

Everina throws her long shadow over my child as she reasons from her great height. I lifted to observe them yesterday, and saw Fanny's eyes shine with tears. I forget now what had been the cause of the scene. Fanny said she was sorry, but Everina, rattling on in shrill anger, failed to hear her, so fixed in her critical track that nothing and no one could dislodge her; she went on harassing the child from some undelivered spite. There had been no end to her impatient harangues of our pupils at the school; several of them, growing ill from fear and frustration, had to be sent home. A child told that she has done wrong will try to make things right —but Everina would never allow placation. Such vexation serves no purpose. I took Fanny upstairs at once to separate her from Everina, in the way I once would interfere to spare our pupils at the school. It saddened me, as I soothed my child, to think that, should some thing happen to me and I no longer be there to look after my darling, I could not trust her to the care of either of my sisters.

It has been such an implacable part of my existence to assume parental care for both Everina and Bess that I cannot remember a time, even when in pinafores, that I did not take them both by the hand to direct them. It became, I think, an obligation upon me, as soon as I understood that Mother could not manage the children: she was too frail, too unsure of her powers of judgement, continuously driven into a state of terror by the violence of Father's conduct; when he was absent, she timidly put off any activity which needed decisiveness; yet when he entered the house, she cowered submissively, fearful of his moods, slavishly endeavouring to please him and, in the course of things, sweeping us out of his way. At such times, I would take to reading to my sisters in our little room, keeping them silent and secure, for I was old enough to be aware of dangers from which I hoped both to save them and which I meant them to ignore, as if I alone might bear the burden of a recognition of the evils which were upon us. I begin to divine that one's position in the family determines significant elements in one's character. That I was the first girl, the next to oldest child, next in line after my elder brother Edward, has coloured my life with a profound sense of responsibility, making me a mediator between two factions who, I came to understand, did not have a common language between them: I attribute any verbal facility of mine to having been a diplomatic courier between the nursery and despotic authority, given as I was to flying back and forth from one to the other with messages which needed softening or elaboration.

What I cannot abide is how often some thing is said by Everina with the sole purpose of eliciting my approval, the absence of which—should I lapse into reflexion and fail to produce the proper oval sounds of encouragement—causes her to wilt upon the stalk. It occurs to me that it is precisely this weakness which wears me out, equally, in my dealings with Mary Hays: she, too, hangs heavy for a look or a sound of approval, as if I were under the obligation of assuming the throaty capacity of an entire rookery of doves. Indeed, Mary Hays seems to have inherited several aspects of what I feel for my sisters, even to the scorn I bear them. I dare say we would never have grown so close, she and I, had it not been for her requiring relief, which animated me into a familiar role of usefulness, persistently pursued beyond the very limits of patience. One wishes to be useful—is thoroughly engaged in helping another—then, once it is taken for granted, suffers a recoil from duty, which brings to mind Rousseau's experience with a beggar who, at first pleasurably anticipated, became an exacting burden. This sense of onerous responsibility came back to me, last September, when Godwin and I trespassed upon a garden in its wild and ruined state to peer into broken, cobwebbed windows of an uninhabited house in Barking, some eight miles from London, where the family lived when I was six. We moved from place to place unceasingly—another cause for the children insecurely having huddled together—till, when I was seven, we settled at Beverly, in Yorkshire, which seemed to have suited my father's restless temperament till my fifteenth year. On that excursion to my old childhood home, dimly remembered and hunted out, I recalled, as we sat in the sunshine, my own early characteristic determined goodness, which I thought might win me love; that it failed to do so never deterred me from my insistent practice, which was a matter of faith, not logic.

I would have doggedly kept the school, one way or another, if living in close quarters with Everina and Bess had not been so alive with unhappiness and ill humour. Godwin once thought such disagreeableness the natural condition of cohabitation, yet I do not think it is any more natural than that gloom and grime and disorder is natural to the interior of a house; a bit of industry and opening of windows to the fresh air is all it takes to scour dreary rooms of their sullenness. And I believe all that is called to make relations agreeable is good will and delicacy. Perhaps some stubborn element from our many dislocations in early youth implacably hounded my sisters and me, following at our heels to the very doorway of the school. There was also the fact that a disproportionate share of the work fell to me—or was it my quickness and self-assurance that made Everina and Bess so childishly inadequate?

An extraordinary misinterpretation of the past slipped through Everina's guard, as we spoke of one thing and another last night. It was on the subject of my having tried to secure poor Bess a position as governess to a family in France, when first I went abroad. Some thing was said of how I'd let her down—*let her down?* when what had put a halt to my exertions was the passing of the Sir John Scots Bill, which would penalise all those who quit England for France after the spring of '93. It was history that dashed her hopes! Yet my two dear girls, between them, have kept alive a memory of my faithlessness. For a restrained moment, sitting opposite Everina, I had trouble regulating my breath, seeing suddenly how constant effort to promote my sisters' interest had been a mere conceit of self-sacrifice, which at times has made me live like a drudge and dress no better than a servant. Did I not send Everina to France to learn the language the better to qualify as a governess?—although she complained throughout about the French, whose habits assailed her delicacy as much as any Irish household. Did I not arrange that Bess be a parlour-boarder in a school where later she might earn her living by teaching there? And did I not raise the money for James, when he came back from sea, to go to Woolwich for instruction, so that he might earn the rank of lieutenant in the Royal Navy? And Charles!—in whose future I reposed so many diverse hopes—does he, too, forget how I slaved to fit him out for going to America, how I kept at Barlow to make provisions, and even wrote books upon which rests, for the sake of some spurious authenticity, the name of Captain Imlay, a name I borrowed as a writer before I borrowed it as a wife? Where *is* Charles? And why will he not write? I had not, in truth, expected gratitude for what was undertaken from a sense of duty, but I had, prey to some small illusion, hoped for love. Charles with his handsome features, marred by a pout of superiority upon his lips characteristic from the earliest childhood, has put the distance of the rolling sea between us, declaring good riddance to the entire family. So much for all those exertions, belittled or cancelled by convenient memory!

When my thoughts turn to remembrances of my father, or to stories told by Everina, who visited him a year ago, it is as if my mind entered a different dimension than common, every-day reality, plunging into those horrors which reside on the sleeping side of reason. He lives in shambles, in disgrace, in dreams of bliss sucked from a bottle of gin, till all the misery and muddle of his life is bathed over in the rosiest glow. There is no hope. There has not, for years, been the slightest thread of hope whereby he might redeem himself. He is the deepest thorn in my side. A resolution taken years ago to see him no more might in all conscience seem cruel and unfilial, were it not that I solemnly took upon my shoulders, at the time, an obligation to see that he shall never lack for funds. On the sole condition that I shall not have to see him, and that he never write, I have put at his disposal a sum upon which he might live. At the beginning of last year I wrote Charles, begging him to contribute to lessen my burden, since I now had a child of my own to support. I have heard not a word, nor has Johnson, who also wrote to Philadelphia describing the urgency of my request. Johnson is disgusted by his unmanliness. I know, however—not that it exculpates him—how Charles suffered from the whimsical tyranny of a father, who would one moment hug him to his breast as his darling boy and, the next moment, upon no provocation, beat him relentlessly with a strap, the fingers of one hand like a cleft stick about his slender neck to hold him down —such changing winds to make one's sails, now luffing empty and now overblown, send a small skiff vanishing over the horizon. I do not blame Charles for his unstable nature, yet I had hoped . . . oh, for some thing kind. Yet does the ghost of a father no longer visible, but still prowling the corridors of fevered memory, poison us all, casting over our every encounter a sickly hue. Everina and I speak of him in whispers—as if mere resonance might evoke his presence. His boots still sound with terrific menace overhead. Even in writing of him, I feel my heart race. What did he desire? Where was the pleasure in terrifying a household of children and a poor woman who died, some say, of fright—a poor, weary, patient creature, who was, when death came, the same age as I am now. Everina said that, when she saw him, he did not recognise her, calling her Mary, berating her—or me!—for having disobediently quit the house. From his incoherent railing against my having hurt my leg tripping over coils of rope on the wharf, it came to Everina, paralysing her, impaling her upon the spot, she said, that he had in mind that we were yet in Beverly—from where we had the habit of running all the way to Hull to play on the docks. His mind has toppled like the walls of an old barn left to rot in wind and rain, trees and grasses growing out of its interior where wild owls nest. He can hardly speak but that he rambles, doomed to the infernal disorder of all still taking place, nothing ever laid to rest. For me he is always in mind, standing there, his arms outstretched like Hamlet's father's ghost upon the battlements, vapourish, emaciated, the flesh of his face gouged out. He wrings my heart. He no longer makes my lips turn blue from holding my breath in prayer for our very life. He wrings my heart, in truth. Yet I have done with him.

MW TO WG

February 13, 1797

I intended to have called on you this morning, but for the rain, to beg your pardon, as Fanny says, for damping your spirits last night. Everina only said that she was so oppressed by her cold that she could not sit up any longer, but she hoped you would not think her uncivil, especially as she found herself unable to join in the conversation. So you shall seal my pardon when we meet. Monday morning

MW TO WG

February 14, 1797

Unless the weather prove very tempestuous, my sister would like to go to the play this evening. Will you come to early tea.

I intended to have called on you this morning—we were shopping and I am weary.

MW TO WG

February 15, 1797

I have been prevented by various little things from calling on you this morning—you must excuse this seeming neglect—do not say unkindness. I write now lest I should not find you at home, to say that Everina will pass to morrow with Miss Constable and that I will dine with you—if you please.

MW TO WG

February 17, 1797

Did I not see you friend Godwin, at the theatre last

night? I thought I met a smile, but you went out without looking round.

We expect you at half past four.

If you have any business in the city, perhaps you will leave a letter for me, at Johnson's, as it is not perfectly convenient to send Mary. But do not put yourself out of your way. I will try to contrive to do it *myself*, should you have had an intention of directing your steps in another.

MW TO WG

February 20, 1797

You will not forget that we are to dine at four. I wish to be exact, because I have promised to let Mary go and assist her brother, this afternoon. I have been tormented all this morning by Puss, who has had four or five fits. I could not perceive what occasioned them, and took care that she should not be terrified. But she flew up my chimney, and was so wild, that I thought it right to have her drowned. Express concern to Lucas—Fanny imagines that she was sick—and ran away.

MW TO WG

February 21, 1797

My sister talks of going to Miss Constable's to morrow or next day, I shall not then expect you this evening—I would call on you this morning, but I cannot say when—and I suppose you will dine at Johnson's. The evenings with her silent, I find very wearisome and embarrassing. It was what you said in the morning that determined her not to go to the play. Well, a little patience.

I am going out with Montagu to day, and shall be glad by a new train of thoughts to drive my present out of my head.

Tuesday

February 22, 1797

Everina's cold is still so bad that, unless pique urges
her, she will not go out to day. For to morrow, I think, I
may venture to promise. I will call if possible, this morning—I know I must come before half after one, but if you
hear nothing more from me you had better come to my
house this evening.

Will you send the second volume of Caleb and pray
lend me a bit of indian-rubber. I have lost mine.

Should you be obliged to quit home before the hour I
have mentioned—say—

Monday, February 27, 1797

There is panic in the City this Monday morning. The banks have
withdrawn from circulation all specie. It means—but Heaven
knows the ultimate portents of such an unprecedented measure!
From my window I see people gather about the fishmonger, into
whose large, red hand they count out their precious pence. What
will become of us?—oh, oh, what will be done? as the poor woman
in Bedlam wailed, expressing the fear in the hearts of all. Godwin
will shortly pass. He has certainly woken up in an anticipatory
mood, for it is publication day for the essays and, though nothing
ever happens on publication day, to be sure, it is a day of fidgets
for us all. I have sent Marguerite with the paper, upon which I
wrote the summons *Please come at once*. I only regret he may
read into the desperate imperative all manner of personal disaster,
rather than realise that the summons is connected to the news
about the banks.

Godwin has just been here with Holcroft, who seemed quite
pale, when he entered, affected by the public disorder I surmised,
only to learn that he and Godwin have had another of their literary disturbances, this one over a new play Holcroft is in the
midst of writing and which he had been reading Godwin. When

the two friends crossed the sill, I pounced on them with such a phrenzy that they seated me gently and tried to calm my nerves—for since sending Marguerite, I'd spun fancies so excessive that I was panic-stricken. If there is to be no cash in all of England, what is one to do? How are we to buy bread and meat? How will Johnson pay me the money he has promised for weeks and postponed paying from negligence. I had emptied my reticule, spilling out four pounds five which rolled over the table-top and came to a resounding clatter under eyes that blurred with tears. How, tomorrow or the next day, am I to pay the greengrocer and every one else? And how on earth shall we manage to carry out plans to make a nest for the babe in my womb? In the presence of Holcroft I could voice only a portion of my fears.

The government has directed that the banks issue only paper notes. Our national debt has made such a course of action necessary. The bank having advanced eleven million to the government, has found its cash unequal to the heavy demands upon it, and must break with its public creditors. It is an ill-calculated remedy which Godwin thinks will not stave off national bankruptcy. Holcroft wondered what Fox, as head of the opposition, will have to say of the matter when Parliament meets. Godwin does not doubt that the measure is a legalisation of fraud. When laws are made to counteract fixed moral principles, they only tend to accelerate the evil they meant to have remedied. If a great quantity of banknotes should now be issued, it would be impossible to keep up paper credit. There is one simple solution: *The government should pay its debt to the bank.*

What shall we do if the merchants of London refuse the notes? Oh, said Holcroft, they will not do that. They will meet with the Mayor to day or tomorrow, to consider a resolution to promote the universal circulation of bank-notes, will give them every currency rather than refuse them, to express undying faith in the Bank of England, at the same time that they praise themselves for their own show of patriotism. Tomorrow we shall get used to paying in paper—next year, if the government so wills it, in pumpkin seed.

True, my nerves have been rubbed raw by the propinquity of Everina, much of our mutual past spent reeling from one pecuniary calamity to the next—money, or the lack of it, remaining a source of great terror to us. And the quickness of life beneath my breast beats time unfailingly. Godwin has made some money, yet it seems like digging at the mountain of my debts with Fanny's toy shovel. All this being so oppressively in mind, I was grateful when Holcroft leapt up, saying he was late. I accompanied him to the door where he lowered upon me his kindly smile, lifting his hat from the hall table as he said he looked forward with pleasure to seeing me on Saturday. For the first performance of Mrs. Inchbald's new comedy, Godwin has secured a box. I nodded, my thoughts elsewhere, and then, when it was too late, regretted having failed to collect myself in time to have made some response.

To my chagrin Everina had come into the parlour during my absence, and had made herself comfortable, so that I was obliged to talk over her head, as it were, in order to communicate to Godwin. I said that I hoped he would be writing Thomas Wedgwood to day. I noticed, with relief, that he gathered my meaning—and was sure that Everina had not. It is a coincidence that her fate, as well as mine, depends on members of that famed family. Godwin and I have often spoken of this loan as our final resort; he had nodded in understanding. Then, with a sweetness that reduced my nervous state to one almost of ease, he gave a copy of his essays to Everina, having written in it very prettily.

We are, one moment, the poorest of common creatures, the next seraphically winged. Thus were we—or fancied we were—the other evening, when we went to sup at Mrs. Robinson's. Everina had given herself pains to look her best for the occasion, growing cross with me for flinging on my every-day turban, which I removed to rummage about for some thing more elegant. It was to *the* Mrs. Robinson's we were going, as Everina put it, high-strung with excitement, keen to keep a sharp eye out so that she can make a full report in her letter to Bess, and to tell it in detail to the Allens—or the Wedgwoods as they are now—when she joins them next week. Mrs. Robinson's great white dog sniffed at our footwear and, satisfied in his dog's manner of judgement that our intentions to his mistress were harmless, let us pass through a doorway to reception rooms where those younger ghosts of Mrs. Robinson hover over every conference carried on below, as though augurs or idols. I'd warned Everina, remembering my own confusion the first time I'd paid a call, not to expect a figure of high fashion, neither powdered, patched nor painted, the Perdita of the past having fallen on evil days. She ever reclines on a pink satin sofa with a light shawl disposed over her crippled legs—lame Sappho, as Peter has called her. The dog creeps disconsolately to her side, poising its chin on a seat cushion of the sofa, or with a long-drawn worrisome sigh sliding full-length to the carpet, the fur, which her daughter claims to brush each morning, as thick as ermine on royal robes.

Mrs. Robinson says that of all the painters she ever sat to, it was to Sir Joshua she posed with the greatest pleasure, his conversation diverting her from the misery of sitting still. She believes that part of a painter's necessary faculties has to be the capacity to entertain, to provoke one out of the closeted sense of solitude into social vivacity. Gainsborough had not the faculty. In consequence, her portraits by him flaunt a pretty dress, luxuriant trees, but a morose expression, the lids heavy from sleep; she could hear nothing but grunts from behind the easel, which hid him from view, except in those rare instances when he would peer to one side of the canvas and quickly dodge back again, leaving her to her own devices, senselessly bored. She had enjoyed the flow of bright conversation from Sir Joshua, who had never ceased entertaining her, and of Zoffany when he had painted her as Rosalind. I observed that, although she also spoke of George Dance and of Romney, she did not mention Stroëhling. It was not something I felt free to ask her, but rumour has it, and I should have liked to hear whether or not the circumstance was true, that she once sat to Stroëhling for a full-length portrait in a state of undress. So Fuseli told me.

Godwin is forty-one this week. It is high time, he says, before he loses teeth and hair, and becomes more than ever cramped by rheumatism, that he have his portrait done. The day before he'd been at Northcote's; he had drawn up a little stool to sit in such a position that he might watch him paint a naval captain, posing in full regalia on the platform. He found himself blurting out to them how timid he has always been of looking-glasses, how he shies away from them whenever he confronts one in a stranger's parlour, in a familiar house making it a rule to avoid sitting where he might be forced to meet his own reflexion, for he is thrown into consternation by the length of his nose. When his expression is

animated, the defect may pass unnoticed; but in repose, the nose
has such generous proportions that even the most flattering and
facile of painters could not make it more modest. Northcote, however, rhapsodized upon this prominent, this ponderous, this noble
nose of Godwin's. If he would ever paint him, he should sit to him
in profile. I think Godwin was endeavouring to entertain Mrs.
Robinson as she lay in pain beneath her shawl. He gave her a quick,
boyish glance, as she rose to the occasion to remind him that forty
was the age at which the Greeks believed a man *flourished*, as they
would call it—meaning he had reached the height of his power.
He must not let the moment pass, but must immortalise his aspect, so that in a hundred, two hundred, years hence one might
still be able to trace the living features of the greatest philosopher
of his age.

February 28, 1797

Godwin has brought me his letter to Wedgwood. He asks for fifty
pounds. The prose is so tied in knots, that even I, privy to the
sense of the matter, have some trouble deciphering its meaning.
What lies at the heart of the trouble is Godwin's discomfort at the
inconsistency between his written doctrines and his present conduct—having once written of marriage as an unnatural constraint
to one's fullest development. He says he has not changed his mind
in believing that marriage *as commonly practised* is wrong. He
adheres to that opinion. It is our mutual desire to live after the
ceremony in much the same manner as we live now. It has been
my contention that we must navigate our bark into the safety of
a harbour in readiness for the full blast of a public storm. How
shall it be, I wonder, once the news is bruited about that "Political
Justice" and "The Rights of Woman" *have wed???*

March 4, 1797

What an enchanting evening we passed together, last night, in
Godwin's study—to celebrate his birthday. I teased him that he
must rush to have his portrait done, before growing uxoriously
stout. He extracted from a portfolio the sketch by Kearsley, made

two years ago, which I held tenderly under the lamp—a face freshly scrubbed, his hair newly combed, chin lowered into a starched, white ruff as his gaze turns upwards from dark liquid eyes. I am slow to see he wants to make me a gift of it, yet quick to show my pleasure. I had found in one of the small shops behind Oxford Street a porcelain inkstand with a lion and a unicorn upholding a royal blue inkpot. He cups it in his hands, holding it a moment with pleasure, before putting it upon his table. I'd found it hidden behind cups and candlesticks in a dusty, crowded cabinet in the rear of the shop, and managed to get it for sixpence —because of a chip in the lion's tail.

I also brought him Isaac D'Israeli's satire, as he cannot avoid hearing of it on his own, since he is the butt of it. I read the book all day yesterday and decided, as it is in my power to review it or to give it out for review, that no one would be more suitable to estimate its worth than Godwin—thus to take his revenge, if he will. In this novel, which is entitled "Vaurien: or, Sketches of the Times," a Mr. Subtile comes from a parsonage in the country to London, where he is immediately surrounded by all the spirited youth of the age, like Socrates in his stoa. From youth alone he expects a warm reception to speculative notions that for ten long years he has been nurturing in his imagination. Such a concentration has given him the gloomy habit of methodizing all of life into a system, himself having become a cold-blooded metaphysician, sombrous and sublime. In uninterrupted cogitation he paces the streets with firm step and elevated countenance—gazing at the heavens, or is it rather at the pendulous shop signs?—keeping step with his friend Mr. Reverberator, the perfectibilitarian, who surely is Holcroft. Well, it is cruel, but also hilarious.

M W T O W G

Monday, March 6, 1797

Everina goes by the mail, this evening. I shall go with her to the coach and call at Johnson's in my way home. I will be with you about nine, or had you not better *try*, if you can, to while away this evening. Those to come are our own. I suppose you will call this morning to say adieu! to Everina. Do not be hard, for a child is born.

March 6, 1797

There was a high wind yesterday, sufficiently savage to tear one to bits or to try to, tugging and nagging at us. It needed only that to add to Everina's nervous state amidst her many parcels—for besides portmanteau and hat-box, she had a package of macaroons which the younger Allen sister dotes on, and was taking a pair of perroquets as a present for the children. Several times the wind nearly bore off the cage, covered in an old calico curtain of mine from Store Street which I had come up with at the last moment. We made a pretty sight on the street, with the screams of the two birds, and the wind, and Everina in a state of nerves over what she might have left behind and what lay all unknown before her. I kissed her on both cheeks, she clung to me, and I saw the last of her, squeezed inside the coach beside a very fat gentleman, the cage on her lap, the birds silent, dead of fright perhaps. I waved as the coach ground off, waving with a show of gaiety which collapsed of itself when the coach, top-heavy, groaning, waddling from side to side as it was drawn down the street and around the corner by a team of four stalwarts, disappeared from view.

I called at Johnson's, as I had promised, and was rewarded by seeing Dr. Fordyce flapping his coat-tails before the fire. The last time we had seen one another was a month ago, when I had visited his consulting room in the Strand where, examining me, he had found me in a state of radiant good health. He had been delighted when I told him how easily I had delivered my first child, with so little of the weakening effects that keep women in England abed for a month that I had dressed, on the eighth day, to accompany Imlay in the streets of Havre. Dr. Fordyce has assured me that I may obtain the services of a midwife, when the time comes, though here in England it is not the general custom, physicians—men!—being thought more trustworthy to bring forth life. It is only the poor here who resort to midwives, or those of the upper classes whose false modesty determines such a choice. Fordyce is a thoroughly charming man. I thought so, years ago, when I first met him as he was preparing for publication a treatise on digestion, he and Johnson—the one from Aberdeen, the other from Liverpool—speaking a common language which has bound them in close friendship ever since. I once passed a particularly pleasant evening at the Fordyces', impressed by the erudition and unconventionality of his two daughters, one of whom had talked very astutely on the subject of the rights of woman. Dr. Fordyce, who has never ascribed to the inferiority of women, says that his daughters received many of the same advantages he would have given his two sons, both of whom died young. I did not stay long at Johnson's, staying only to chat with Dr. Fordyce and to listen to the Reverend Mac-Intosh—what a conspiracy of Scotsmen I've fallen into! I wished to hasten home to see Godwin who, earlier, had accompanied Mrs. Inchbald to a performance of her "Wives," and who later was to sup with some one to whom he wished to air his notions about the banking crisis, for he intends writing on the subject. I had wanted to see him, as I was saying, but it was not to be, since he was unable to free himself till late in the evening, and I did not wait up for him, blowing out the lamp by ten o'clock to sleep the sleep of the just.

It is so peaceful this morning. I· take up this book to resume my pleasant practice. Godwin has already passed to wish me good morning and to assure himself that he may count on my company this evening. I was able to let him have in proof a nine-page review of his essays that will appear this month in the *Analytical*, which he rolled into a baton to take off with him. He shall not be disappointed.

I've had no chance to dissect Mrs. Inchbald's "Wives as they were; Maids as they are," which we saw on Saturday. *She* did not attend the performance—provoked, I hear, by a remark made on her reading of the play in the Green-Room at Covent Garden, which decided her to stay away till the fate of the play was determined by the public. A flurry of attention rose when Mrs. Robinson was carried aloft into our box, the object of every eye, for she has not been sufficiently well this past winter to appear publicly. I observed that, though fully conscious of the conversation behind lifted fans which her entrance caused, she remains aloof, as if we alone at close range were all that interests her, every thing beyond blurred into generality. Lawrence fawns over her to make himself conspicuous, for he has the most common avidity for attention. Dear kind Holcroft earnestly conversed with Everina to try to put her at ease. When she is uncertain, her hands grow icy-cold, which I was reminded of when I happened to rest my hand a moment upon hers, as I spoke across her to Holcroft. She is conscious of living a negligible life which could be of interest to no one; putting, I think, undue emphasis on celebrity, the result is that, though she finds herself in the presence of the very persons she most wants to see, such circumstances paralyse her with a sense of her own inadequacy. I believe she will, in making an account of the evening, give it a flow of gaiety it lacked for her in the living of it; for I could perceive her taking full inventory of Mrs. Robinson's studied simplicity in a lustrous ivory gown, which manifested her high bosom in a manner that fascinated young Lawrence, he himself dressed in all the colours of a cockatoo.

Although I had not attended the reading of the play, Godwin had passed me parts of the M.S. so that I was acquainted with the general outline. It is one of those farces where all the characters rush about to make the audience laugh, the animation on stage seeming a great machinery producing only sniggers. Her subject might have been of extreme interest, *might have been*, I say with regret, for she threw to the winds of mere dalliance any discrimination of the difference between a dutiful wife, representing passive obedience, and the modern independent maid. I regret a chance missed for accuracy of observation of present-day manners. Yet perhaps she had some thing else in mind. I think she did. It is my view that her annuities and charities influence her to do again what profitably was done before. For each performance of a play she stands to earn 33*l*. 6*s*. 8*d*. The play shall have worldly success, I'm sure, the published version selling out. Even yesterday Mrs. Inchbald was busy cutting. Godwin said she sat beside him in the darkened theatre, scribbling notes to remind herself, to day, of what must still be done, the play falling short of her high standard of perfection; yet I feel, for all her industry, that she dissipates her talent in a taste for eccentric and whimsical originality. It is the same characteristic that puts me off *in her*: where one desires seriousness, she grows capricious, flirting rather than warming to a full embrace.

Whoever happened to have been in the theatre last night will never forget the rousing applause which burst out during the epilogue at an allusion to the glorious victory gained by Sir John

Jervis over the Spanish Fleet. "Hearts of Oak" and "Rule Britannia" were shouted for. We stood and sang with swelling hearts, Mrs. Robinson insisted on standing with every one else, supported between Godwin and Lawrence. There was hardly a dry eye amongst us, our hearts warmed in universal benevolence. That morning a letter from Sir John Jervis had reported his brilliant and decisive victory over the Spanish Fleet off Cape St. Vincent, on February 14th last, his mere fifteen sail having pursued, attacked and conquered an enemy which amounted to nearly double our number. Parliament has moved to ask His Majesty to confer some signal mark of his royal favour on the Admiral for the important services he has rendered his country—it has even been suggested that he should be called *El Salvador del Mundo*, this being the name of one of the captured ships. Again this morning the papers are full of gratitude, as well as relief over dangers narrowly averted, for it is believed that the junction of the French and Spanish fleets was designed to effect an invasion and conquest of Britain. It is being said that the French Directory has, for a considerable time past, delayed an exchange of prisoners, and has recently contrived to pour into the country a set of men trained as secret agents, who in the hour of invasion might proceed to open the public prisons, and thus form a bandit auxiliary for the purpose of preventing any opposition to the landing of their troops. They also hoped to strengthen their forces by the accession of the seditious in the north of Ireland. The French Fleet had been cruising off Bantry Bay, where the Irish Coast had been left in a defenceless state. Now, deprived of the co-operation of the Spaniards, these same ships will be compelled to remain for a long time inactive in the port of Brest.

I cannot avoid wondering how much this general exultation keeps us from sorrowing over more mundane consequences of the war. I refer to the price of butcher's meat which Parliament—less sensitive to matters which ordinary people have been speaking of for months!—has noted at last. The House Committee lays blame for the high price of meat on the jobbers who go about the country buying cattle, which they sell again to others, some times several times over, before the same beast is brought to Smithfield Market, an enormous deal of money added to the price by this trade. The carcass butcher must then raise his price upon the cutting butcher. There are laws against these practices, but they seldom seem to be put into execution, few persons willing to undertake the trouble and expense of prosecution. I, myself, do not believe an enquiry in good faith which does not even make passing mention of abuses of the victualler's supplying of our troops. The country's economy seems to me corrupted throughout by engaging in war for so long a period of time. There is talk of putting into circulation during the present exigency copper coinage. It was a business, they are saying, that ought to have been done long ago—by this time waggon-loads of copper money ought to be coming up to London, to put into our pockets one-pence, two-pence and three-pence pieces, a solution to the want of specie to pay the fractional parts of demands which cannot be paid in notes. The banks have even issued dollars at 4s. 6d., resorting in the emergency to foreign specie. And every day a list of bankrupts—coal-merchants, tanners, potters, upholsterers, innkeepers—common people who, in the long chain of creditors, are the first weak link that breaks.

MW TO WG

March 11, 1797

I must dine to day with Mrs. Christie, and mean to return as early as I can; they seldom dine before five.

Should you call, and find only books, have a little patience, and I shall be with you.

Do not give Fanny a cake to day. I am afraid she stayed too long with you yesterday.
Saturday morning

You are to dine with me on Monday, remember, the salt beef awaits your pleasure—

MW TO WG

March 17, 1797

And so you goose you lost your supper—and deserve to lose it for not desiring Mary to give you some beef.

There is a good boy write me a review of Vaurien. I remember there is an absurd attack on a methodist

Preacher, because he denied the Eternity of future punishments.

Friday morning

I should be glad to have the Italian were it possible, this week, because I promised to let Johnson have it this week.

March 22, 1797

I have just received a letter, without a date, that leaves me totally at a loss to guess what Everina means when she speaks of a parcel to be sent to York Street, which street I have never heard of before! She has left nothing behind but some powder. I wish she would not bother me with trifling cares, when my own are so numerous. The general scarcity of money makes all the tradesmen send in their bills, and I have had some sent to me which I could scarcely avoid paying. The mantua-maker called so often for Everina's bill of three pounds four, and seemed in such distress to pay her own rent, that I was obliged to let her have it, though it was all the money I had. I am continually getting myself into scrapes of this kind. Out of some money I shall get in a day or two from Johnson, I must send a guinea to Everina, or at least some part of the money I still owe her. My pecuniary distress arises only from myself, I know—from my not having had the power of employing my mind and fancy when my soul was on the rack. I can no longer be obliged to let my father have all my money. Charles' silence, in answer to my request respecting a provision for him, makes me very uneasy. I had also hoped that Imlay would have paid at least the first half year's interest of the bond for Fanny. A year, however, is nearly elapsed and I hear nothing of it, and have had bills sent to me which, I take for granted, he *forgot* to pay. Had he been punctual in paying them, I should have, after the first of the year, put by the interest for Fanny. What part of all of this will the fifty pounds from Thomas Wedgwood pay? And how can we, now that we have it, ask for more?

Everina's description of the females of her happy family makes me hug myself in the solitude of my own fire side. It fatigues me to hear of the dozen novels they devour in a week—a party destitute of sentiment, fancy or feeling; taste, to say the least, is out of the question. She asks for food for thought, such as in Mrs. Radcliffe's "Italian," which I cannot let her have till it is reviewed. Johnson would not like to have two sets soiled; but I shall warn her to read it in her own chamber, not to lose the picturesque images with which it abounds, and shall send her Mrs. Robinson's work to read in the drawing-room. I must see if she cannot prevail on the family to do some thing for poor Lucas, whom I can no longer keep, since Mary has been unwell, and it is yet another mouth to feed. I have been trying to get him into a school, but should I succeed it cannot be before the end of the year. It would be well for him to be in the potteries. I am sure he would make a good engraver were he properly taught.

Amelia Alderson is back in London, with reports that the banks at Norwich have stopped payment in specie, and not a guinea is to be had in exchange for bank-notes on any of the public roads. Godwin is to see her tomorrow at Holcroft's. I hope to see her soon *in private.* For I have a world of confidence to impart, a multitude of events having taken place since she was last in London. It was in August that her father took ill and sent for her. I have some times thought it was well that she then vanished from the scene since, had I given her a step-by-step account of the course of things, I tend to think I would not have had the courage to have persevered. I can imagine the gambol we might have made of certain instances; even in her absence I seemed, at times, to hear her clear voice cautioning me against a man who, though celebrated, kind, a loyal friend, could never be trained to the more difficult role of lover. Will she not be astonished at how far things have progressed in that direction! Will she not be forced to admit that love itself is a tutor? Perhaps I shall ask Godwin to invite her to dine here Tuesday with Holcroft—for that is a company which would give me particular pleasure, and be a celebration of sorts, though neither Miss Alderson nor Holcroft will have a clue to divine the cause.

WG TO MW

I will call on you and it will not then be too late to determine. I may possibly dine at Robinson's the bookseller, and not see you but seven or eight o'clock.

I will have the honour to dine with you—you ask me whether I think I can get four orders. I answer with becoming gravity I do not know, but I do not think the thing impossible.—How do you do?

I must write, though it will not be long till four. I shall however reserve all I have to say. No, *je ne veux pas être faché quant au passé.*

Au revoir.

March 30, 1797

This morning is like any other—no mark, no distinguishing sign, nothing to signal momentous events save for Marguerite's smile which softens her face, whenever her eyes alight on me, only that and a scrap of paper folded under some spare keys in the middle drawer of a commode in my bedchamber.

I thought it would be a nicety yesterday to have Marguerite accompany us to church, since her exertions, these many months, running between Godwin and me, contributed to tightening the bond; also, there seemed more symmetry to have her beside me, given that Godwin had asked his companion Marshal to be with us as a witness. We were due in the church at eleven o'clock. The day was fortunately dry, windless, with some meager sunlight shining into my room when I awoke, having awoken with a presentiment of some thing pleasant in store. I lay abed, prey to stirrings of nostalgia, remembering how as a mere girl I had imagined my wedding day—things never occurring as one dreams them in innocent fancy; it is well, I might add, they do not. I had always supposed I would be married in the village church. No matter how often the features of the man I married was to change, what remained constant was a dream of ascending those broad, steep steps of St. John's, whose unique pride it is that it holds the ashes of King Athelstan who, after victory over the Danes, a thousand years ago, ruled that no one would henceforth pay toll or custom in any port or town in England, to which immunity the inhabitants of Beverly even now owe their flourishing trade and riches. As children we committed to memory the dictum which swelled us with a sense of superiority over the rest of the world:

Als free make I thee
As heart can wish, or egh can see.

I could hear my small high voice as it chanted these words which are written at the upper end of the body of the church on an ancient tablet. The words flashed into mind as I lay abed, listless from the heaviness in my womb. I then had to scoff at such sentimental reminiscences. We marry, Godwin and I, to have done with it, nothing more. We marry because we dare *not* marry and leave unprotected from society's scorn our small babe. We marry not from free choice, but because one cannot flaunt custom *a second time*. We marry to prove that even the institution of marriage, as conventionally practised in England, need not be a deterrent to a determined man and woman, who wish to live independently, in the manner we have been living for months. *All free as heart can wish* truly marks our intentions, Godwin's and mine, so it is not merely a haphazard memory, it seems, that surprised me in my bed, but the very heart of the matter.

Marguerite went to fetch the coach into which Marshal guided us with gentle nips at our heels; for any other purpose, save the singular one for which we hastened, Godwin and I would have walked the small distance to Old St. Pancras. We arrived during a christening, which—had I had Godwin's ear alone—would have led me to remark that, had we waited to marry, we might have made an economy, on the principle of two birds with one stone. I felt a spirit of facetiousness it was hard to keep under—but felt I must, in the light of Marshal's gravity and the nervous rapture of Marguerite, who had gone quite pale, I observed, as though she, not I, was the lamb prepared for slaughter. Marshal, officious to the last, the proper papers in his coat-tails, wore a distinct air of fatuous self-importance. Godwin and I stood about, not much occupied by the business of this marrying of ours which—I can only speak for myself—seemed merely an unnecessary distraction from the more serious pursuits. While waiting for the christening party to abdicate the place, I sensed that, had Marguerite and Marshal *not* been there, Godwin and I would have had to conduct ourselves more pertinently; that they, in some manner, acted for us, freeing us, so that we might idly look about at the long stained-glass windows, as if mere spectators of the scene. Marguerite, bride-like, once or twice clasped my hand for comfort. And Marshal, a shadow of Godwin on ordinary days, extraordinarily grave, looked cross when Godwin yawned.

After the ceremony I had to fly, for it was Wednesday, and I was obliged to leave Godwin to dine alone, after which he took a stroll to the bookseller Debrett's where he encountered several friends, the talk universally about the economy. At night I came to him and stayed *all night*, one of the luxuries of wifedom. To night he comes to me. And in a week we shall remove to our mutual home in the Polygon, where we have taken more room than in my narrow little house on Judd Street. M. Leroux, the builder, called on Godwin yesterday for payment of the first quarter of the rent. So it is settled.

MW TO WG

March 31, 1797

I return you the volumes—will you get me the rest? I have not, perhaps, given as careful a reading as some of the sentiments deserve.

Pray, send me, by Mary, for the luncheon, a part of the supper you announced to me last night—as I am to be a partaker of your worldly goods—you know!
Friday

WG TO MW

I will do as you please. Shall I come to consult you; or will you call on me?

MW TO WG

April 4, 1797

I am certainly not at my ease to day—yet I am better
—Will you send Mr. Marshal to me and I take it for
granted that you mean, and can conveniently get me my
spectacles, before you go to dinner—or I will send Mary.
Tuesday morning

WG TO MW

I dine at two: if I were to call on Mr. Marshal before
dinner, it would devour the whole remainder of my little
morning. Yet I want to say to him a few certain words. I
wonder how this can be contrived? Can you lend me one
of your half dozen servants for this purpose? Can she deliver the inclosed, and wait for an answer? And can the
answer, so procured, be permitted to lie on your table till
I call in the evening?

April 7, 1797

I have just rested on the window-sill, leaning out to look down
upon costermongers crying their wares to gather a crowd, my mind
on so long a reach of revery that my arm was pins and needles
when I finally lifted and latched the window. There is spring in
the air—and an elated sense of new beginnings. Fanny has rushed
about all morning exploring the rooms. The bedchamber she is
to share with Marguerite overlooks the quiet backs in which I spy
a pair of handsome twin mulberry trees that in summer shall throw
a broad-leaved shade over paths radiating from a little fountain
at the very centre of the garden. My own bedchamber is wider
than at Judd Street; the parlour, as well, is more spacious, which
makes ludicrously out of proportion my poor painted canvas floor-
covering. The chimney-piece is ample and draws well. For the last
three days, household effects have been packed in cases to be carried by donkey-cart around the corner, down Chalton Street past
Godwin's quarters, to the Polygon, where every thing must then

be unpacked and put in place. Marguerite maddeningly sings the same tune under her breath these days, some thing about *le bonheur* and *un ciel bleu*, all delight at finding a family of Parisians next door and, I think, she rather fancies the Landlord, who has been about this morning to show us how things work. There is still considerable disorder, packing-cases lying about, though we were all able to spend the night, last night, and to have, this morning, some bread and butter and tea—*without* sugar, however, since the sugar-loaf nippers was not to be seen. I've asked Godwin, to day, to find his dinner elsewhere till we can put every thing away. He has kept his quarters in Chalton Street, but will inquire in the Upper Evesham Buildings across the way, for if he removed there, which M. Leroux thinks it possible to arrange at a not unreasonable rent, it would be a matter of merely crossing the street, rather than a five-minute walk in inclement weather. Also I might more easily fetch him, when I need him, although he has expressed a desire not to be unnecessarily disturbed at his work—a masculine prerogative I seem unable equally to claim.

Having now stolen a moment's quietude, I once again read over Holcroft's letter, relishing his bold, self-assured hand and words that, had I been apprehensive of his true feelings for me, relieve my every doubt. "From my very heart and soul," he writes, "I give you joy. *I think you the most extraordinary married pair in existence.* May your happiness be as pure as I firmly persuade myself it must be. I hope and expect to see you both, and very soon." Then—dear, kind friend!—he hesitantly adds he cannot, can he, be mistaken concerning the woman, it *is* Mrs. W.?—for in his letter Godwin, taking me for granted, failed to mention me by name. How like him to wind up his courage to make a clean breast of things, and leave out what he most wanted to communicate.

Holcroft has cheerfully applied himself to my problem with Lucas. He could understand my inquietude at negligently apprenticing the boy, when one hears constantly of boys being beaten in a most inhuman manner and not even allowed sufficient food. There was a case only this winter in St. Martins-in-the-Fields of an apprentice, bound by a charity for a term of ten years to a cordwainer, who beat the boy with a truncheon, striking such a violent blow on the side of his head that he was obliged to seek the assistance of a surgeon. The court found sufficient cause to order the fifty shillings paid by the parish refunded, and the boy was sent to a workhouse—an experience sufficient to uproot for ever any tender trust in the benevolence of the world he might have cherished. Holcroft listened with his brow all wrinkled up; brightening, he exclaimed that nothing would suit the boy better than to become a stable-boy. There is nothing so certain in life to strengthen character as the business of a jockey. He recounted his own early memories as a small fry. I had to smile at the ecstatic look upon his face. He explained how his life formerly had been spent in every want and weariness, so that happy had been those times when he had had enough to eat. In the stable one was always warmly clothed, even gorgeously. The boys were in health; they had the company of other boys. They were borne over hill and dale on the noblest animal the earth contained, outstripping the wings of the wind. And a horse could teach a boy all manner of things.

Though there had been boys of ten in the stable, Lucas was barely eight. When he came into the parlour at my bidding, Holcroft took him between his knees, fingering the muscles of his arm under the thin stuff of his shirt and running his large, competent, gentle hands over the boy's head to feel the contour of his skull—for he is a believer in the science of phrenology, by which one can read character. Lucas stood straight, shoulders back, the way Godwin has taught him to stand. Holcroft was exceedingly tender with the boy, encouraging him to fall to chatting, one hand on Holcroft's knee, as he confided about the games he most likes to play. In the end it was decided he would be ready for the strenuous existence of exercising race-horses in another two or three years —and I am left with the problem of Lucas! I've been teaching him to draw to occupy his mind, giving him this morning my book of original stories for him to try to copy Blake's illustrations. At any rate, the effort has kept him from getting underfoot, and Mary can wholly attend to putting the house to order.

M W T O W G

April 8, 1797

I have just thought that it would be very pretty in you to call on Johnson to day—It would spare me some awkwardness, and please him; and I want you to visit often of a Tuesday—this is quite disinterested, as I shall never be of the party—Do go—you would oblige me—But when I press any thing it is always with the true wifish submission to your judgement and inclination.

Remember to leave the key with us of No 29—on account of the wine.
Saturday

Sunday, April 9, 1797

Since Godwin has only this morning written his mother of our marriage, he must keep up the fiction of an unaltered life, till she has had time to ingest her son's remarkable change of heart. He is dining to day in his quarters with his sister—whom I have yet to meet—and Mr. Marshal. It leaves me to my own devices, wondering whether I ought to sit down to write to Johnson, go immediately to speak to him, or wait till Wednesday when his nerves may be calmer. Godwin said that, in their altercation yesterday, there was more pain than anger. My concealment had hurt him. He could not understand why I had hesitated to confide in him. When Godwin brought up the subject of my debt and his own readiness to assume full responsibility for it, Johnson saw, in a flash, how he had been made to seem *villainously* to stand as an impediment. Such trenchant distrust of his feelings for my welfare made him dismiss Godwin with a bow of formality; fearing persistence might make matters only worse, he immediately left. The secrecy with which I tend to surround some thing yet fragile, which others may defy, is my usual mode of behaviour. I feared that Johnson would have considered my marriage dangerous to a stability which rested uneasily on the pretence of a legal union —confining me as a prisoner in my own tissue of lies.

MW TO WG

April 9, 1797

Pray don't set me any more tasks—I am the awkwardest creature in the world at manufacturing a letter—

April 10, 1797

I was pleasantly interrupted yesterday by the appearance of Amelia Alderson, surely sent by Providence to soothe away my cares. She hadn't heard a whisper of the news of our marriage—but how on earth had we managed to keep such a thing secret? was what she immediately wanted to know. I had to swear her to secrecy, saying that I wish our friends to be informed directly, rather than gathering the intelligence from stray gossip. Only to day Godwin is writing to Mary Hays—I having begged off from the task. I bade him remind her of the earnest way in which she pressed him to prevail upon me to change my name, which he had done on her behalf, becoming—it occurs to me with amusement— entrapped in his own toils; for we found there was no way so obvious for me to drop the name of Imlay, as to assume the name of Godwin.

Amelia Alderson, her hair dressed in a most becoming style, sat up in my blue arm-chair with a hectic, burning look of admiration—I am, she says in her hyperbolic manner of address, besides the lakes of Cumberland, the only other thing in all of life that has not disappointed her. Yet there was no impertinence in her curiosity, only irrepressible joy. I imagined in her eyes a twinkle of tears, when she said she thought our travails worthy of the finest narrative, its happy ending as perilously arrived at as in any novel that has ever disturbed her sleep. Although Dr. Alderson has been ill most of the winter, his health is greatly improved; only because of it has she felt free to make a visit to London. The claims of her father will always be, with her, she says, superior to any charms a lover can hold. I protested it would not be well for her to live in an unmarried state for ever. But she is averse to leaving her father for a husband. Only if Dr. Alderson would consent to live in her husband's house, can she imagine matrimony a happy state. Not every man, she admits, would accept such a condition. She has invited us, this evening, together with Holcroft, to sup.

Johnson appeared Sunday at Chalton Street, at the moment when Godwin, his sister and Mr. Marshal were about to sit down to dine, happy to join them at their simple fare, eager to make amends for his anger, the day before, when Godwin had gone to him to inform him of our marriage. Yet he had no occasion to express his feelings, since he rightly divined Miss Godwin's ignorance, Godwin not intending telling his sister of our marriage, till he has received a reply from Norfolk—though what objection his mother can have to a forty-year-old son marrying, I cannot imagine. Some thing in the way Godwin had presented matters rubbed Johnson the wrong way. I have not got the story quite straight, but assume Godwin's strained explanations lacked tact. When in the course of conversation my debts had come up, Johnson had drawn back with the abrupt remark that he was being treated less as a trusted friend than as a bondsman. Now, at dinner, he had no chance of expressing regret at his quickness of temper, other than by his conduct. It seems he entertained Miss Godwin by telling anecdotes about the poet Cowper, whom he has known for years, Miss Godwin, having certain pretensions to writing verse, admiring Cowper's poetry above all others. Accompanying Johnson to the door, Godwin was able to say how glad we shall be to see him at No. 29.

MW TO WG

April 11, 1797

I am not well to day. My spirits have been harassed. Mary will tell you about the state of the sink &c. do you know you plague me (a little) by not speaking more determinedly to the Landlord of whom I have a mean opinion. He tries one by his pitiful way of doing every thing—I like a man who will say yes or no at once.

MW TO WG

April 11, 1797

I wish you would desire Mr. Marshal to call on me. Mr. Johnson, or somebody, has always taken the disagreeable business of settling with tradespeople off my hands —I am, perhaps, as unfit as yourself to do it—and my time appears to me, as valuable as that of many other persons accustomed to employ themselves. Things of this kind

are easily settled with money, I know; but I am tormented by the want of money—and feel, to say the truth,
as if I was not treated with respect, owing to your desire
not to be disturbed—

April 11, 1797

What a charming, easy-going evening we passed at Amelia Alderson's—except for Godwin's long face, when my strictures on the
vanity of a certain lady raised a laugh. Mrs. Inchbald should get
as bad as she gives. News of our marriage has thoroughly shaken
her self-control. She wrote Godwin to day, saying, that, taking it
for granted that his joyfulness would obliterate from memory every
trifling engagement, she had entreated another person to perform
the office of securing a box at theatre on Frederick Reynolds'
night. And then adds: *"If I have done wrong, when you next
marry, I will act differently."* What nonsense! I have quickly written to Amelia Alderson, who was the person entreated to secure
the box, having prevented her from doing so, since Godwin already had provided us a place, for I thoroughly misunderstood
the business of Mrs. Inchbald's refusal to be seen with me. She
told Godwin as much, but he, playing for time to try to convince
her otherwise, led me into error. I would just as soon sit in the
pit as to sit with her. And Amelia Alderson may still get a box for
those Mrs. Inchbald will sit with. I can hardly say I shall be sorry
to resign her acquaintance; on the other hand, I very much regret
Mr. and Mrs. Twiss' decision to cast me henceforth beyond the
pale as one no longer to be acknowledged. I have heard my ban-
ishment extends to Mrs. Siddons, as well. Marriage to Godwin
is an admission, in their eyes, of my having formerly lived without
the benefit of a proper legal ceremony—an admission, I may add,
which has been far from secret these past six months. Yet now,
when I have resigned a name which disgraced me, when I might
have every reason to think my position in society secure, these
false friends hiss at previous errors suddenly declared iniquitous.

There will be more cause for gossip when they learn that Godwin and I do not entirely cohabit, but rather continue to live much
as we lived before. It is my wish that he should visit and dine out

as formerly, and that I shall do the same. In short, I still mean to be independent, even to the cultivating of these same sentiments and principles in my children's minds, for I hope to influence them to our views of personal liberty. I am proud perhaps, conscious as I am of my own purity and integrity, many circumstances having contributed to excite an indignant contempt for the forms of a world I should have bade a long good night to, had I not been a mother. Had fortune or splendour been my aim in life, they were within reach, for I have had it in my power, more than once, to marry very advantageously, would I have paid the price.

Holcroft raved last night that our marriage shall be a gaudy example to all the world, the brightest constellation of the heavens. He leaned back in one of Amelia Alderson's small chairs, a wineglass in hand, the lids of his eyes veiling their expression as he followed her languid movements when she arose and crossed the room. There was such intensity to his fixed regard that I wondered at its meaning, a look so full of interrogation that I fancied I heard it spoken. He had seemed to ask whether this warm and charming friend of ours, who drops into our lives like some returning harbinger of spring, to uplift our hearts with song, might become the wife he longs for. His eyes lingered when she spoke, and when she was no longer speaking. At the end of the evening he begged us all to have dinner at his house tomorrow night, where we plan to go, bringing Montagu.

April 15, 1797

Oh, dear! How can I get to my fiction, when life intrudes this way, thoughts to day of Mary Hays uppermost in my mind, as I struggle to think of some amelioration to her distress. It had been days without a word since Godwin's note, so that he decided yesterday to call. At the sight of him, it seems, her eyes flashed wide as though she beheld a ghost. She recovered sufficiently to ask him to be seated, staring, he said, with a woe-begone expression, as he spoke, speaking to a blankness that finally made him falter. I am not sure that he chose to tell me every thing said between them. It seems she criticised me with some bitterness. She had, poor creature, got into a state of fury against me, the colour completely drained from her face. He had tried to stop words which would only later be regretted and, finally, unable otherwise to interrupt her, he had risen to leave. Only then did it come to her how her aspersions against me were alienating the person in whom she hoped to evoke a spirit of agreement—and she had burst into tears. I have seen her weep and can well imagine the feelings her despair must have aroused in Godwin, standing in the middle of her parlour, hoping, he said, that no one should choose that moment to enter. The only advice I can give her is to conceal her wounded heart, her jealousy and spite, and come all smiling to me to assure herself of being part of our happiness. I can do nothing, since nothing is called for, on my part. One can only hope that time will heal &c.

WG TO MW

April 20, 1797

I am pained by the recollection of the conversation last night. The sole principle of conduct of which I am conscious in my behaviour to you, has been in every thing to study your happiness. I found a wounded heart, and, as that heart cast itself upon me, it was my ambition to heal it. Do not let me be wholly disappointed.

Let me have the relief of seeing you this morning. If I do not call on you before you go out, call on me.

April 20, 1797

Mrs. Inchbald may have, this morning, the satisfaction of knowing she has been the cause of a bitter dispute. It was obvious to every body last night at theatre that she was up to her tricks, insisting at her tardy entrance on a certain seat in our two boxes—the furthest from my presence—causing Amelia Alderson and Mr. Fenwick to have to move, even contriving Godwin's assistance, so that he seemed to dance attendance upon her. Not desiring to provoke open hostilities, as we were by then an object of curiosity from other boxes, I chatted with Mrs. Reveley as though nothing at all unusual were taking place. But when the house darkened, the curtain rose, and I found myself in the safety of darkness, I could scarcely keep my attention on the stage, so violent was my anger. It was not anger at Mrs. Inchbald that I felt—for she has merely dropped the mask of civility to show her true self—but at Godwin's refusal to choose between loyalties. I would have expected him to try to counteract such an arrogant display of rudeness. When I told him so, once we were alone, he played the innocent, unwilling to agree that Mrs. Inchbald's conduct had been insulting. How could he not have seen her determination to insult me and the small smile in the corners of her mouth which denoted a spirit of self-felicitation that her plan had been successful—to the unheard-of degree that Godwin, himself, was an accomplice?

He says he cannot drop her, as I may wish. He says he had been of particular assistance to her during the trying days of her "Wives"; he accompanied her to a performance of the play the day after we moved into the Polygon, it seems. They then dined together at Robinson's, the bookseller, some days later; seeing her home, he had confided that he had married, quick to assure her that he still retained his liberty. Then why marry? it seems she had asked. And was Mrs. Imlay not already married? He had to say I was not. She pretended outrage, pronouncing unequivocal distaste for my society. I extracted these admissions from him and endeavoured to lead him to the evident logical conclusion that such a dilemma demands an act of manly choice between the two of us. He insists on freedom—freedom to determine whom he will see and whom he will not see, which is a fundamental condition of our arrangement. But why had he so foolishly, when warned, brought me into Mrs. Inchbald's poisonous presence? Why had he not allowed her to obtain her own box and people it with those she wishes to see? Why had he *forced* us so unnaturally together, when that was neither her desire, nor mine? Had he not caused every one great embarrassment? And what was that nonsense about *when next you marry?* Had he communicated to her an impermanence to our relations, which such a remark implies? My questions received for answer a clenched set to the jaw and an injured look.

This morning things are no better. This talk of his of studying my happiness seems so hypocritical that it makes me laugh out loud. I have given him my terms in this business of his friendship with Mrs. Inchbald: he is to see her, if he wishes, but I shall not be obliged either to see nor to hear of her any longer. The tiresome part of it is that our various mutual friends will have to strain to keep us apart—but above all other consideration there is to be no repetition of last night's episode.

M W   T O   W G

April 20, 1797

Fanny is delighted with the thought of dining with you —But I wish you to eat your meat first, and let her come up with the pudding. I shall probably knock at your door in my way to Opie's; but, should I not find you, let me now request you not to be too late this evening. Do not give Fanny butter with her pudding.

April 26, 1797

Tomorrow shall be my thirty-eighth birthday. I am sitting here a moment, before setting to attack the last of love's labour to give Godwin on my birthday—an odd reversal, perhaps, yet like casting bread upon the waters, with expectations of reward—another revision of the beginning chapters of my M.S. which I hope to tie up and drop in a heap on his desk. The visit to Bedlam has proved to be an experience upon which I am constantly drawing. I have been looking again in the pages of "Caleb" for guidance, and in other books open on every side of me, among them "The Italian" and "Otranto."

There has been a constant, hectic round of visits. To all other occasions I prefer the informality I found at Holcroft's Sunday. He was in spirits, with a tide of tongue that flamdazzled the company—to use his phrasing. He did an imitation of the sort of person who has long been upon the town, an intimate of authors, actors and artists of every kind, knowing their private and public history. He acted as if he were accompanying a young man, just down from Oxford, about the playhouse on the first night of a new comedy, pointing out one and another among the crowd. We were like a sea-sick crew, heaving forwards and lurching backwards, holding our sides for laughter. He kept up a running commentary of gossip to his young companion, till the tinkling of an imaginary prompter's bell made him turn his satirical attention to the piece itself. In the midst of this recital, Amelia Alderson entered on the arm of Mr. Fenwick, an old friend of both Godwin's and Holcroft's, whom I do not know, though I have heard of the review that he edits. She seemed peculiarly tranquil in contrast to our dishevelment, going to sit off to one side, as Holcroft continued his performance. I have been waiting for a chance to speak to him on the subject of this young friend of ours, for I would have him understand that her inviolability is an enchantment that can be broken by one who has the key, if a key is what he desires, as I suspect he does. Our marriage makes our friends more seriously reflect upon their solitary situation and, envying us, wish also to enjoy a domestic scene. Opie is the saddest among them, his engagement cruelly broken by Miss Beetham's father; it puts him now in the restraint of sitting miserably in our reflected good fortune.

A week ago we supped at Opie's—Peter, Godwin and I. Opie showed us some paintings he was taking to hang next day at the Royal Academy, having much to say of a *horrible* new canvas on which Tom Lawrence expects to make a glorious reputation. It is, says Opie, of a boxer got up to look like Satan, his body oiled and sweating, feet apart as though to leap into a gulf that gapes before him; we, the spectators, standing in the gulf, look up at him as he looks down on us—all of this done in the undisguised grand manner of Fuseli. The entire hanging committee knows he has plagiarised Fuseli. Every one is thrilled with endeavouring to guess Fuseli's words when he sees it. It shall be the laughing-stock of the exhibition. And this is what Lawrence has been longing to give up his portraits for! Opie's new paintings are sober, studied, balanced, worthy of a Raphael, a painter to whom grandeur and sense seem to be one and the same thing, his figures totally absorbed in action, unconscious of any spectator, unlike Vandyke's in which the sitters always appear conscious of sitting for a picture, which is as bad as a player speaking a soliloquy to the audience. Handling several large canvases with care—he has not the army of young apprentices with which Lawrence is able to surround himself—he slid them away from the wall, lifting them to an easel. Engaged as he was, I did not notice the haggard, subdued expression upon his face, until he had rejoined us, sitting in that peculiar way of his upon the very edge of a chair, as though at any moment to dash up, grab a brush and set to work. There was still that buoyancy visible in his bodily attitude, but in the eyes a lost look, as if a shadow of ill health has marked him. Peter's jests had no effect. Even Godwin, who thinks those who suffer in silence often suffer the keenest, could not distract him. I left, feeling inquiet about his mode of life, particularly about the self-denial he practises with rigours I think hardly wholly necessary, doing every thing himself, never hiring a servant or apprentice, though his earnings certainly would allow it. He barely eats enough to keep himself alive, which Peter observes, whenever he invites him out, saying that it will be his first meal since last he'd invited him. But it is no laughing matter. He works relentlessly and, now that he is no longer permitted to see Miss Beetham, will work longer hours, eating less, becoming more solitary. What do I expect, Peter asked, when I mentioned my anxiety: what can one expect from a Cornish boy in tin-mines bred? I am exceedingly anxious over his state of mind—so is Godwin, who says that Opie's manner of suffering is one that does not relieve the inner grief.

The day before yesterday, to cheer him, Godwin went to call with Amelia Alderson, who chided Opie over a portrait he had started to paint of her some six years ago and never finished. Opie hunted it out from among those stacked against the wall. He has kept the portrait, hoping one day to finish it. She had been no more than twenty when she sat for it. When she saw it again, she cried with anguish, only half feigned, at how changed she is. Turning to study her full figure, Opie said in his blunt way that she ought not bother him to finish it, but rather should sit for him as she is now. She looked archly back and said he was the only man in her entire circle of friends who would not have rushed to save her by flattery from the recognition that she was now six years older and looked it. He said he was not in the business of flattery, but of painting people as they are. Her spirits had not crumpled at his honesty. Those of us who do not unduly worship fine phrasing value Opie's lack of artifice. I wonder if I should not engage to sit to him, in order to spend more time with him during a period so painful—it is some thing I must speak about to Godwin.

May 4, 1797

Although we sent the joint and pye to the baker's to relieve Mary, only slowly recovering from her illness, there is much to do to put the house in order, this morning, chairs all awry, cushions crest-fallen, the parlour with a look to it of having been a slipper in a terrier's jaws—though we were only last night a party of five. I had asked Dyson at the last moment to join the Southeys for dinner. Godwin would have preferred to have asked Montagu, I think, since young Robert Southey has recently entered himself at Gray's Inn to study law, after having cast his eye, he tells us, at various means of earning his livelihood: taking orders, which he determined not to do; studying medicine, to which he found himself ill suited, because of an invincible repugnance for cutting up corpses to learn anatomy; failing that, he hoped to find some sinecure in the office of the Exchequer, where he has some influence—though it could never have materialised, since he is known to be a Jacobin. He even quite seriously was considering emigrating. A volume of his verse has appeared, as well as a small book of travels. He makes a quite handsome appearance. He is perhaps twenty-two, slender, with dark curling hair, heavy dark brows and electric black eyes, a refined nose and well-shaped lips, whose impulse to smile provoked me, in the course of the evening, to become animated for the sheer pleasure of seeing his expression brighten.

He worships Godwin—the chapter on property in "Political Justice" having influenced Southey to hope to comprise all that was good in life by founding a utopian colony in the new world. He had imagined himself sawing down trees as he discussed metaphysics, criticising poetry while in the saddle hunting buffalo. Now he laughs at himself. But it was a dream that had the force to propel twelve young couples very nearly on shipboard from Bristol. He'd met Samuel Coleridge, two years his senior at Oxford, who shared the dilemma of wishing to be a poet and the necessity to devise a means of earning a livelihood. One evening when Coleridge had been drinking punch at the Salutation and Cat—where he can always be found, it seems, when in London—he met a man who had spent five years in America and had only lately returned as an agent to sell land, who convinced Coleridge that twelve men could clear three hundred acres in less than half a year's time. He'd said he knew where land could be had for six hundred dollars a thousand acres. Coleridge, asking where one might buy at such a price, was told of the Susquehanna, which is supposed to be of excessive beauty and quite serene from hostile Indians. The melodiousness of the name allured him; besides, he'd heard literary characters make money in America. Coleridge and Southey named their scheme pantisocracy—one's heard of it, of course.

> Join Pantisocracy's harmonious train;
> Haste, where young love still spreads his brooding wings,
> And freedom digs, and ploughs, and laughs, and sings.

My own former dream to raise my child on the banks of the Ohio revived at the recitation. It had been barely two years ago that the two of them had hastened to Bristol, where Coleridge earned money to pay his passage by lecturing, and where they married two young women who were sisters. I asked Mrs. Southey where Coleridge and her sister were presently living. She tells me they are with her mother and infant son and a disciple of Coleridge's at Nether Stowey, where he still dreams of maintaining himself and his family by raising corn and pigs on an acre and a half, though he occasionally also preaches in the Unitarian Chapel; unless he finds some means to devote himself entirely to philosophy and poetry, he will have the necessity of going into the ministry. I take Godwin's word that he is a man worth meeting —one of the few men, Godwin has said, who have made a profound intellectual impression on him. I am curious to meet him. I asked Southey to describe him. He was silent, a moment, explaining his hesitation by saying that those we know best are difficult to describe, and he cast his wife a glance full of meaning. I fancy the two men have suffered a recent falling out. Yet Southey extolled the brilliance of Coleridge's poetry and genius of his imagination; as to his person, he says he loves warm rooms, comfortable fires, food, natural scenery, music and books—though he does not care what kind of binding the books have, nor whether they are dusty or clean—and he actively dislikes fine furniture and handsome clothes, and the ordinary symbols and appendages of what's called gentility. He lives in a small village, where he might support a wife, an infant and a mother-in-law at 120*l.* a year, but it is all the same to him where he lives, since he seems to live wholly within himself.

Imagine my surprise to learn that the disciple who has been for months with the Coleridges is none other than Mary Hays' great passion, Charles Lloyd. I remember him sitting in my parlour—it was when Fanny and I were living in those small, close rooms in Pentonville, before removing to Judd Street, long ago, it seems to me now—with a look of contrition and helplessness on his features, as though suddenly struck by the magnitude of the cruel effect of his conduct. I had found him well spoken, knowledgeable, and regretted my involvement with that foolish business of the letters. The son of a banker at Birmingham, it appears he gave up the bank to follow Coleridge. Mary Hays will be curious to learn—for he had dropped out of sight like a stone into water—that he will publish some verses together with Coleridge and another young man by the name of Charles Lamb, who writes for Fenwick's little review.

The Southeys spoke of setting out to find a cottage by the sea, and settling there for the summer. At the mention of that invigorating coast extending from Southampton, the town itself decidedly too expensive for their purse, I seemed to smell brine in the air and hear the raucous cries of gulls, feeling a warmth of sun upon my face which I so loved in Norway, where I think I must have been, despite all reasons against being so, happy, alive, sentient, resigned to disappointment with a bitter-sweet peacefulness that being bereft often brings—despair, after all, the only cure to illusion. I seemed to hear the tide lapping on boulders and roots of trees, trees which shaded the water's edge, so that if one navigated the boat close to shore, one felt a delicious coolness and smelled the loamy richness of earth mingling with the salty sea-breeze. A wave of desire rose in me for the countryside, to walk freely with no destination in mind, aimless and unencumbered. Yet this cannot be; if no other duty bound me, being in the sixth month would be encumbrance enough.

It was a relief, that evening, to have Dyson, and have him without Dibbin, an extrication the one from the other which cost me a squabble with Godwin some days past. Finding the two young men at Godwin's, I had said to Dyson I hoped he would call on me soon. In my mind it was perfectly clear that I meant to involve him in my present work, for that I had asked him by himself, with no notion of excluding his friend, whom I shall always be glad to see. I conceded to Godwin's request to write saying as much—for he feared Dibbin had felt snubbed. I begged Dyson to set the matter right. I wish he would determine whether he shall be a writer or a painter or what, and set to the thing, for I sense a tendency in him to be too lackadaisical. It would be a pity if his very real talents came to nothing in the end, a mere scintillation rather than real gold. Other young men his age have made reputations for themselves, while he, with charming languor, converses on metaphysics, sipping wine. He sips wine, I may add, a bit more quickly than any one else, refilling his glass as soon as he empties it. I rebuked him in a playful manner, and caught a look from Southey, who, I fancied, did not think well of me for trying to distract Dyson from what is becoming an excessive habit and may contribute to the dissipation of those talents which I wish to see develop.

May 7, 1797

Godwin has had a reply from his mother. She will be glad to see us in Norfolk, though she says we must not expect great exactness there, as she has only a young servant, and is able herself to do nothing at all for the *cramp*, which has rendered her unable to put on her stockings by herself and obliges her to eat standing up—in the course of writing her letter she had got up forty times to walk about. Godwin says she is a tiny woman, brown, wrinkled, weak, her eyes dim and her hands unsteady, parsimonious in the extreme and utterly surrendered to the visionary hopes and tormenting fears of the methodistical sect. While his father yet lived, she was a teller of a good story and gay in appearance. She bore thirteen children, six now living. Her present delight in life seems exclusively to be to hear from them, especially of whatever might make them *an ornament to Religion,* which is what she supposes we are sent into this world for. Her son's broken resolution concerning matrimony has encouraged her to hope that ere long he will embrace the Gospel—his having been transformed in a moral sense making her hope a spiritual transformation possible as well.

These sermons of hers have contributed to making poor Hannah Godwin a queer, crabbed little creature with hectic enthusiasms and earnest endeavours. People, Mrs. Godwin says of her daughter, think her character injured by Marshal, a married man, who dines with her some times on Sundays—can William commend such a practice? Godwin and I together dined with her several Sundays past. She served a baked chicken from a bird that had been sent in a basket with sausages from Norfolk, all manner of things, it seems, sent in from the country. She showed me how she packs new-laid eggs, which come with friends or by carriage, in sawdust or bran and turns them so they will not spoil. She had delicious country butter from a seven-pound parcel, which we generously spread on muffins. She tells me William has been like a father to her, ever since she came to London a dozen years ago. He had told me he rebuffed any expectation to share his lodgings, when she came, for she had hoped to keep house for him, contributing her share of expenses by taking in millinery work, imagining being read to when at work by her dear brother, who would make her a clever girl. I am informed that she lost her first love— but then first loves, according at least to my beliefs, are meant to be lost, are they not? She chattered and laughed and saw that her brother had his plate filled and his wine-glass brimming. She spends the days of the week in a dress-making establishment which earns her a satisfactory living, when ladies of fashion do not too long delay in paying their bills. Sundays are the one day of the week which she might spend self-indulgently, either with friends or, every second week, dining with her brother, some times in the company of Marshal. In bright weather she makes excursions to the countryside, which she says refreshes her in a most extreme way and often gives her matter for occasional verse. *That* is a sorry business, for she can hardly spell—or spells the way they do in Norfolk, as she speaks in cant whose meaning often is obscure. Her ideas are unrelievedly banal—though she appears entranced by their originality. It is the case again of Sir Joshua Reynolds' sister! Godwin was tutored, schooled, prized for his intellect, nourished by good teachers, while poor little Miss Godwin hoped to become clever, as she sewed and listened to him read aloud, hoping for wisdom from mere scraps from his table.

I was curious about the others in the family: Hull, who stayed home, becoming a farmer; Jack, the unfortunate member of the family, who, when sent a heavy winter coat by his mother, laid it in pawn for drink; Joseph, a journeyman of some sort, who has abandoned wife and children; and Nathaniel, who is at sea.

We have been offered us a small feather-bed which would do for a servant and which will be sent by waggon, if we want it. Most of Godwin's neckcloths and pocket handkerchiefs have come from home. We shall surely receive that excellent butter and new-laid eggs from time to time. Mrs. Godwin's exhortation on the subject of marriage amuses me. "*Whatever you do,*" she says in her letter, "*do not make invitations and entertainments.*" How little she knows her son! There is some thing sad about how little one is known by those who have known one for ever. Too frail to make a trip to London, she will, fortunately, not see our unholy ways.

Miss Godwin says that if I buy seven yards of poplin, she will make me a morning dress for a wedding present.

Sunday, May 14, 1797

In the morning yesterday Godwin, receiving a visit from Thomas Wedgwood, who has just arrived in London, invited him and Mrs. Wedgwood to dine with us, so that I had to hasten to produce the entertainment about which Mrs. Godwin so darkly warned; sending Marguerite flying with letters to invite Opie and Montagu and Amelia Alderson, and Carlisle, a celebrated young surgeon at Westminster Hospital, while Mary prepared a couple of rabbits smothered in onions with some of her fine apple dumplings and a Blancmange for dessert.

Into the parlour entered a rather stout young man of florid complexion—into a parlour that has become the habitation of a host of young men, whose similitude consists of slenderness and willowy grace, characteristic perhaps of meagerly paid literary men. Amelia Alderson, excellent at winding others up, relieved any shyness the young couple might have felt in strange company. And Montagu spell-bindingly recounted a current case of his in criminal court, an aspect of the law he now seems to favour. Our conversation having taken a turn in the direction of legal occasions, Amelia Alderson was persuaded to tell how at Horne Tooke's trial he had feigned deafness in order to be allowed to sit close to the witnesses. Opie is at his best with a single companion or among a few friends; in strange company he is apt to wrap his jaw in his huge hand, remaining remorselessly, silently attentive.

I had but a moment to inquire after Everina's well-being. Mrs. Wedgwood says the children have formed a great affection for her, and that her company delights their mother. This Mrs. Wedgwood—how they keep straight *three* Mrs. Wedgwoods I cannot imagine—is country-bred, reserved if not actually timid, overwhelmed on this first visit to London by the blaze of lights along Oxford Street, that makes of midnight broad daylight, the traffic of carriages making the crossing of the street a frightening proposal. She will not venture out alone, but waits on her young husband. Her colour is as high as his, the pair of them appearing so feverish, that my first thought was to put them to bed with a potion of hot honeyed wine.

Carlisle is presently occupied in research on voltaic electricity and told us of his observations. In turn, we heard about Wedgwood's experiments; he has devised a method of copying paintings upon glass, or upon leather moistened by a solution of nitrate of silver, which undergoes a change on being exposed to light. Unable to fix the prints he has succeeded in producing, he is forced to store them in the dark. Carlisle asked to what single characteristic Thomas Wedgwood attributed his father's spectacular success. The young man ran his tongue over his lower lip, taking time to compose his thoughts, saying, after a moment, that he thought it might be his father's love of the practical. No detail was beneath his interest. He was, as some might know, a shrewd chemist, making trial of various elements, such as upon sulphate of baryta, which became the chief ingredient of his "jasper," a smooth paste resembling native jasper, for he dreamed of imitating the properties in clay of such precious substances as porphyry, agate and marble.

The Wedgwoods have asked Godwin and me to visit them,

which I shall probably be unable to do, though Godwin has expressed interest in making the trip, perhaps with Montagu, later this spring. It amused me to take young Wedgwood aside to probe him on his reaction to the news of our marriage, which his friend Montagu had to break to him by letter, since Godwin was too tongue-tied to express the change of heart he felt might be unacceptable to his young disciple—a vanity I do not encourage. If he imagined he stood as an example of celibacy, which is necessary to the purposes of philosophy, it was an example the others eschewed: Wedgwood has been married a year, and Montagu, recently widowed, now imagines himself in love with the youngest Wedgwood sister. Does it not serve a philosopher's purpose better to demonstrate an *ideal* married existence, in which two people thrive and cultivate their minds?

But I must break off. To day is Fanny's birthday—she is three. Godwin plans to hire a chaise in which we shall all go to a tea-garden where there are walks bordered with jonquils and pinks and carnations. It is a glorious spring day!

May 15, 1797

I shall have to answer George Dyson. Certainly he is correct when he writes that some of my incidents ought to be transposed and heightened by more harmonious shadings. I take kindly criticism that will help me form the story. Yet I am vext, to tell the truth, at his not thinking the situation of Maria sufficiently *important*. I can account for this by recollecting that he is a man—to whom a woman's distress seems trivial. For my part, I cannot suppose any situation more alarming than for a woman to be bound to such a man as I have described. I would despise any woman who could endure such a husband. Does he not see that this sort of matrimonial despotism degrades the mind? I am not convinced of the justness of his remarks respecting the style of Jemima's story; he confounds simplicity with vulgarity, while I have endeavoured to imitate a mixture of refined and common language, such as exists in the speech of persons who have received their education purely by chance. My peace is shattered by what Dyson has written, and I cannot leave it as it is, but must try to convince him, though perhaps I ought not persist, for he has demonstrated a curious incapacity for indignation, which appears to me to be, especially in some one young—for one grows coarser over the years—a sign of insufficient understanding. Yet I must try to get him to see what I am about in this book of mine. I shall ask him to drink tea with me, Wednesday or Thursday, since I am engaged to go tomorrow evening to Mrs. Reveley's, and Friday in the evening to Amelia Alderson's.

MW TO WG

May 20, 1797

I am sorry we entered on an altercation this morning, which probably has led us both to justify ourselves at the expence of the other. Perfect confidence, and sincerity of action is, I am persuaded, incompatible with the present state of reason. I am sorry for the bitterness of your expressions when you denominated, what I think a just contempt of the false principle of action, *savage resentment, and the worst of vices,* not because I winced under the lash, but as it led me to infer that the coquetish candour of vanity was a much less generous motive. I know that respect is the shadow of wealth, and commonly obtained, when that is wanted, by a criminal compliance with the prejudice of society. Those who comply can alone tell whether they do it from benevolence or a desire to secure their own ease. There is certainly an original defect in my mind—for the cruelest experience will not eradicate the foolish tendency I have to cherish, and expect to meet with, romantic tenderness.

I should not have obtruded these remarks on you had not Montagu called me this morning, that is breakfasted with me, and invited me to go with him and the Wedgwoods into the country tomorrow, and return the next day. As I love the country and think with a poor mad woman, I knew, that there is God, or something very consoliatory in the air, I should, without hesitation, have accepted of the invitation; but for my engagement with your Sister. To her even I should have made an apology, could I have seen her, or rather have stated that the circumstance would not occur again. As it is I am afraid of wounding her feelings, because an engagement often becomes important, in proportion as it has been anticipated. I began to write to ask your opinion respecting the propriety of sending to her, and feel, as I write, that I had better conquer my desire of contemplating unsophisticated nature, than give her a moment's pain.

Saturday morning   Mary

May 24, 1797

In the evening yesterday we went to Carlisle's with the Wedgwoods, Montagu and the Southeys, for Godwin supposes that Wedgwood is serious in his proposal to initiate putting a fund of money at the disposal of philosophers and artists, who might otherwise be unable to persist in their work. He thought it might benefit Southey, and Coleridge as well, on whose behalf he plans to speak. Learning of this altruistic intention, in which all three of the Wedgwood brothers share, I feel more comfortable in the knowledge that we have had to ask for *another fifty pounds*. I cannot seem to fix myself on any serious labour to earn money from my pen, and my debts mount; not only because there are days when I feel so feeble that I am unable to work, but because there are also days—and evenings—when friends are either visiting us here or we are elsewhere seeing them and, while I do not complain, for recreation is surely necessary to my spirit, the imagination exhausts itself over dramatic scenes from the evening, instead of being applied, each morning, to literary endeavours. I have made a note of reminder to myself—and have misplaced it, which is typical of the disorder which surrounds me—to put aside a day exclusively for visits, another for letters, and a third for projects. I must try to abide by some such schedule, perhaps the easier while Godwin is gone. At Carlisle's we were treated to a demonstration on electricity which was very entertaining, though at one burst of lightning, or what seemed such, Mrs. Southey gave an outcry and had to be revived by smelling-salts. She confessed privately that she has begun to suspect she is with child. I suppose it begins to be clear to all that I am expecting; yet every one is the soul of discretion—all save Opie, who looks at me hard, while I sit to him. He says he shall have to cast a shadow over my belly; then he puzzles the problem, saying that unless I hold both my arms overhead, as if abruptly frightened by a footpad, my arms shall be in shadow, and my hands, since he cannot exhibit the lap on which they might naturally rest, shall be lost to sight. He insists on painting me in morning dress with my worn-out green turban—such clothing, he says, not calling attention from the expression of my features. I made only a mild protestation about the turban; but he says its colour perfectly offsets the auburn of my hair and insisted on it.

At Amelia Alderson's, the other night, Fuseli offered me congratulations on marrying some one whose views of the odiousness of marriage so perfectly conform to my own. It was, I thought, a begrudging sort of well-wishing, spoken through a snarl. Yet, knowing him as I do, I imagined I discerned, through the scorn, genuine admiration. All would have been well on that evening except for Godwin's behaviour—but I do not wish to expatiate on a subject that has caused me pain, and about which we had such bitter words. In this day and age, no man seems to feel that conceit is a defect which must be eradicated from his character. I flinch at the unbecoming aspect of Godwin surrounded by worshipping young men and adoring women. It seems to me to be hardly a suitable attitude of his to fawn upon the well-born. For he dotes upon Wedgwood and Montagu, less, I feel, from pleasure in their company than from some sycophantic gratification. Tomorrow evening, at Holcroft's, we are to meet still another Wedgwood, an older brother who is engaged in supervising the showroom in St. Martin's Lane. I will have had a bit much of Wedgwoods this month—but nothing to do.

May 27, 1797

From a speech by Charles James Fox in Parliament:

> I hope gentlemen will not smile if I endeavour to illustrate my position by referring to the example of the other

sex. In all the theories and projects of the most absurd speculation, it has never been suggested that it would be advisable to extend the elective suffrage to the female sex, and yet, justly respecting, as we must do, the mental powers, the acquirements, the discrimination, and the talents of the women of England, in the present improved state of society—knowing the opportunities they have for acquiring knowledge and that they have interests as dear and as important as our own, it must be a genuine feeling of every gentleman who hears me, that all the superior classes of the female sex of England must be more capable of exercising the elective suffrage with deliberation and propriety than the uninformed individual of the lowest class of men to whom the advocates of universal suffrage would extend it; and yet why has it never been imagined that the right of election should be extended to women? Why, but because by the law of nations, and perhaps also by the laws of nature, that sex is dependent on ours; and because therefore their voices would be governed by the relation in which they stand in society?

May 31, 1797

Godwin has taken to going Tuesdays to Johnson's. We divide social territories like two military strategists. There is also a middle ground, which is generally *ours*. But Johnson's Tuesdays I wish to belong exclusively to him, for reasons which perhaps are sentimental: For I want the two persons, who are closest to me, to love one another. *Voilà tout!* Earlier this month, when Godwin went to dine, he found agreeable company; last night there was Fuseli; the Dr. Moore who was in France during the September massacre; and John Hewlett, a treasured old friend of mine, who was, last month, appointed Morning Preacher at the Foundling Hospital. It was through him that I met Johnson. Having published a "Speller," he tried to convince a very desperate and unhappy young schoolteacher, head over ears in debt, that she might earn some money writing books. In my first letter to his publisher, I asked to be sent to my address at Newington Green a copy of the

"Speller." He was pleased to hear of my marriage, and expressed respectful best wishes. I shall send him a note to come for tea, a meeting I look forward to, especially since I shall have plenty of time to myself.

MW TO WG

June 3, 1797

How glad I am that you did not go to day! I should have been very uneasy lest you should have pushed on in the teeth of the weather, laying up a store of rheumatism in your bones—and who knows what effect it might have had on future generations!!!

Have you seen, or heard any thing of Montagu?
Saturday morning

WG TO MW

June 3, 1797

I write on the back of Tarleton's address, which you may preserve.—Montagu called this morning. We talk of setting out in an hour or two. I shall appear at the Polygon shortly.

June 3, 1797

What a sight they were, Godwin and Montagu, crushed together in back of the whisky, with a Roxinante between its guide-poles. Godwin had been all strenuously engaged in tucking things here and there, strapping down the baggage, while Montagu made halfhearted attempts to help, but was useless, so discountenanced was he at the idea of riding through London in the contraption Godwin had hired. What would he look like coming through the broad gates of Etruria, where his true love, gazing from her window, might see him in a child's cart pulled by a little pony—that is, if it held up for the journey? Fanny was enchanted with the beast, patting its pink nose and lifting her arms to be upheld and embraced by the travellers. We older women must be more discreet, though we might *feel* as languorously affectionate. We stood back. Godwin smartly cracked his whip over the horse's flanks and off it went at a trot, as we waved and shouted—Marguerite, Fanny and I, and then Lucas, who had come out and was adding his own cries to ours—at which point the little horse stopped dead. Godwin looked back at us, chagrined. Again he snapped his wrist, the horse leapt forwards, Montagu grabbed his hat, and this time the whole machinery, looking as if it might come apart at each downward jolt, gathering speed, moved brightly off. At least it was not a tearful farewell.

WG TO MW

June 5, 1797

I write at this moment from Hampton Lucy in sight of the house and park of Sir Thomas Lucy, the great benefactor of mankind, who prosecuted William Shakespeare for deer stealing, & obliged him to take refuge in the metropolis. Montagu has just had a vomit, to carry off a certain quantity of punch, with the drinking of which he concluded the Sunday evening.

Is that the right style for a letter?

We are going to dine today at the house of Mr. Boot, a country farmer, with Dr. Parr & a set of jolly fellows, to commemorate the victory, or rather no-victory, gained last week by the High Sheriff of Warwickshire & the oppositionists, over the Lord Lieutenant & the ministerialists, in the matter of a petition for the dismission of Mr. Pitt and his coadjutors. We sleep tonight at Dr. Parr's, 60 miles from Etruria, at which place therefore we probably shall not arrive till Wednesday. Our horse has turned out admirably, & we were as gay as larks. We were almost drowned this morning in a brook, swelled by the rains. We are here at the house of a Mr. Morley, a clergyman with whom we breakfasted, after a ride of twenty two miles. He is an excellent classic, &, which is almost as good, a clever & amiable man. Here we met Catherine Parr, the youngest, as blooming as Hebe, & more interesting than all the goddesses in the Pantheon. Montagu is in love with her.

We slept the first night at Beaconsfield, the residence of Mr. Burke, 23 miles. The town was full of soldiers. We rose the next morning, as well as to-day, a little after four. We drove about twenty miles to breakfast, & arrived at Oxford, 53 miles from town, about twelve. Here we had a grand dinner prepared for us by letter, by a Mr Horseman, who says that you & I are the two greatest men in the world. He is very nervous, & thinks he never had a day's health in his life. He intends to return the visit, & eat a grand dinner in the Paragon, but he will find himself mistaken. We saw the buildings, an object that never impresses me with rapture, but we could not see the collection of pictures at Christ Church library because it was Sunday. We saw however an altar piece by Guido, Christ bearing the cross, a picture that I think of the highest excellence. Our escort, one of whom thinks himself an artist, were so ignorant as to tell us that a window to which we were introduced, painted by Jervas, (as they said) from Reynolds, was infinitely superior. We had also a Mr. Swan, & his two wives or sisters to dinner; but they were no better than geese.

And now, my dear love, what do you think of me? Do not you find solitude infinitely superior to the company of a husband? Will you give me leave to return to you again, when I have finished my pilgrimage, & discharged the penance of absence? Take care of yourself, my love, & take care of William. Do not you be drowned, whatever I am. I remember at every moment all the accidents to which your condition subjects you, & wish I knew of some sympathy that could inform me from moment to moment, how you do, & how you feel.

Tell Fanny something about me. Ask her where she thinks I am. Say I am a great way off, & going further & further, but that I shall turn round & come back again some day. Tell her I have not forgotten her little mug & that I shall chuse a very pretty one. Montagu said this morning about eight o'clock upon the road, Just now little Fanny is going to plungity plunge. Was he right? I love him very much. He is in such a hurry to see his *chère adorable*, that, I believe, after all, we shall set forward this evening, & get to Etruria to-morrow.

Farewel

Stratford-up, Monday

MW TO WG

June 6, 1797

It was so kind and considerate in you to write sooner than I expected that I cannot help hoping you would be disappointed at not receiving a greeting from me on your arrival at Etruria. If your heart was in your mouth, as I felt, just now, at the sight of your hand, you may kiss or shake hands with the letter and imagine with what affection it was written—If not—stand off, profane one!

I was not quite well the day after you left me; but it is past, and I am well and tranquil (excepting the disturbance produced by Master William's joy, who took it into his head to frisk a little at being informed of your remembrance). I begin to love this little creature, and to anticipate his birth as a fresh twist to a knot, which I do not wish to untie. Men are spoilt by frankness, I believe, yet I must tell you that I love you better than I supposed I did, when I promised to love you for ever—and I will add what will gratify your benevolence, if not your heart, that on the whole I may be termed happy. You are a tender, affectionate creature; and I feel it thrilling through my frame giving and promising pleasure.

Fanny wanted to know "what you are gone for," and endeavours to pronounce Etruria. Poor papa is her word of kindness—She has been turning your letter on all sides, and has promised to play with Bobby till I have finished my answer.

I find you can write the kind of letter a friend ought to write, and give an account of your movements. I hailed the sunshine, and moon-light and travelled with you scenting the fragrant gale—Enable me still to be your company, and I will allow you to peep over my shoulder, and see me under the shade of my green blind, thinking of you, and all I am to hear, and feel when you return—you may read my heart—if you will.

I have no information to give in return for yours. Holcroft is to dine with me on Saturday—So do not forget us when you drink your solitary glass; for nobody drinks wine at Etruria, I take for granted. (Tell me what you think of Everina's behaviour and situation; and treat her with as much kindness as you can—that is a little more than her manner, probably, will call forth—and I will repay you.)

I am not fatigued with solitude—yet I have not relished my solitary dinner. A husband is a convenient part of the furniture of a house, unless he be a clumsy fixture. I wish you, from my soul, to be rivetted in my heart; but I do not desire to have you always at my elbow—though at this moment I did not care if you were. Yours truly and tenderly,

Mary

Fanny forgets not the Mug—

Miss Pinkerton seems content—I was amused by a letter she wrote home. She has more in her than comes out of her mouth—My dinner is ready it is washing-day—I am putting every thing in order for your return. Adieu!

I did not think it necessary to forward T.W.'s letter to you—

June 6, 1797

It was Godwin's idea to have Miss Pinkerton help me. I thought I would find it intolerable to have her underfoot, since as it is I can hardly find a corner to call my own, and must fight for peace and quiet. But the arrangement does not seem as bad as I might have imagined. Miss Pinkerton is to copy corrected pages, and go to the bookseller's or whatever, while Godwin is away. Once he returns, we are to share her between us. She is willing to learn, having literary pretensions, and hoping by such menial servitude that some thing from our great experience will brush off. She is tiny waisted, pink and white, with huge china-blue eyes and a pert little mouth, her general emotional state one of perpetual wonder at the ways of the world; yet I find, on closer familiarity, that she is not nearly as empty-headed as she first appears, for she will come out with some startlingly pertinent remark, long after an event, as if she must carry an idea for a very long term before delivery. Her description of my household to her family was quite sharp and funny. I can only imagine that she showed me her letter to have me admire a style reminiscent of the young Miss Burney in "Evelina"—but I dare say she knows as much and forces the comparison to mind. When she says how terribly she would like to write books, I tell her not to moon about, since the future comes in its own good time—but I suspect the mooning and longing and languishing air of this young miss puts Godwin on his pedagogic mettle. Who knows—who knows about any one of that age, soft and shapeless and pink as they all are—if she shall some day write and think and make her fortune in the world? She has, after all, *two great men* to tutor her.

WG TO MW

June 7, 1797

More adventures. There are scenes, Sterne says, that only a sentimental traveller is born to be present at. I sealed my last letter at Hampton Lucy, & set off for Mr Boot's, farmer at Atherston, where I expected to meet Dr. Parr to dinner. Our way lay through Stratford upon Avon, where, after having paid our respects to the house, now inhabited by a butcher, in which Shakespear is said to have been born, I put your letter in the post.

But, before we entered Stratford, we overtook Dr. Parr. After a very cordial salutation, he told us that we saw him in the deepest affliction, & forbad our visit at present to his house, though he pressed us to wait upon him upon our return from Etruria. He however went on with us upon his trot to the dinner at Atherston. His affliction was for the elopement of his daughter with a Mr. Wynn, a young man of eighteen, a pupil of the

Doctor's, son to a member of parliament, & who will probably inherit a considerable fortune. They set off for Gretna Green on the night of Sunday the 4th. To do the Doctor justice; though in the deepest affliction, he was not inconsolable. He had said to the young man the Friday before, Sir, it is necessary we should come to an issue; you must either quit my house, or relinquish your addresses to Miss Parr: if, after having ceased to live with me, you chuse to continue your addresses, I shall have no objection to you; but I will have no Gretna-Green work: I allow you till Monday to give me your answer. I cannot help however believing that the Doctor is not very sorry for the match. What do you think of it? I certainly regard Miss Parr as a seducer, & have scarcely any doubt that the young man will repent, & that they will both be unhappy. It was her & her mother's maxim, that the wisest thing a young woman of sense could do, was to marry a fool; and they illustrated their maxim from their domestic scene. Miss Parr has now, it seems, got her fool, & will therefore learn by experiment the justice of her maxim.

I expected to have been rallied by the Doctor upon my marriage. He was in high spirits, but abstained from the subject. I at length reminded him of his message by the Wedgwoods. I mentioned it with the utmost good-humour, but desired an explanation, as I was really incapable of understanding it. He appeared confused, said he had been in high good-humour the evening he supped with the Wedgwoods, & had talked away at a great rate. He could not exactly say how he had expressed himself, but was sure he did not use the word mean. We had a good deal of raillery. I told him that he understood every thing, except my system of Political Justice; & he replied, that was exactly the case with me. Montagu afterwards told me, that Dr. Parr had formerly assured him, that I was more skilful in moral science than any man now living. I am not however absolutely sure of the accuracy of Montagu's comprehension.

We left the doctor at the farmer's house, & came on upon Monday evening to within ten miles of Birmingham & 50 miles of Etruria. (I forgot to say in its right place, that Miss Parr vowed, upon hearing of my expedition, that she would give me the most complete roasting she ever gave to any man in her life, upon my marriage. She however has got her husband, & I have probably lost my roasting. Though I think it not improbable that we shall find Mr and Mrs Wynn at Dr Parr's on our return.)

Every night we have ceased to travel at eleven; every morning we have risen at four; so that you see we have not been idle. We breakfasted on Tuesday at Birmingham, where we spent two hours, surveyed the town, & saw the ruins of two large houses, that had been demolished in the Birmingham riots. I amused myself with enquiring the meaning of a hand-bill respecting a wax-work exhibition, containing, among others, lively & accurate likenesses of the Prince & Princess of Wirtemberg, & poet Freeth. As I had never heard of poet Freeth, my curiosity was excited. We found that he was an ale-housekeeper of Birmingham, the author of a considerable number of democratical squibs. If we return by Birmingham, I promise myself to pay him a visit.

From Birmingham we passed through Walsall, a large and handsome town of this county, 8 miles. We went forward, however, & came at twelve o'clock to Cannoc, a pretty little town, 8 miles more. Here we proposed giving our horse some water & a mouthful of hay. Montagu had repeatedly regretted the hardship imposed upon the horse, of eating his hay with a large bit of iron in his mouth, & here therefore he thought proper to take off his bridle at the inn door. The horse finding himself at liberty, immediately pranced off, overturned the chaise, dashed it against a post, & broke it in twenty places. It was a formidable sight, & the horse was with great difficulty stopped. We however are philosophers; so, after having amused ourselves for some time with laughing at our misadventure, we went for a smith to splinter our carriage. By two we had eaten our dinner, the chaise was hammered together, we paid the smith his demand of two shillings, & bid adieu to Cannoc, the scene of this memorable adventure.

Our next town was Stafford, which I viewed with un-feigned complacence, as having had the honour of being represented in four successive parliaments by Richard Sheridan. We did not however stop here (8 miles), but proceeded to Stone, (7 more), & nine short of Etruria. Here we took tea, & here I wrote the first 18 lines of this letter. You cannot imagine the state of intoxication of poor Montagu, as we approached the place of our des-tination. It was little less than madness, but the most kind-hearted madness imaginable. He confessed to me that he had set out from London in extreme ill-humour, from preceding fatigue, & from doubts of the capacity of the horse to perform the journey, in which however he was agreeably disappointed. He added that it was infi-nitely the most delightful journey he had ever made.

We reached Etruria, without further accident, a little after eight. Our reception appears to be cordial. Tho. Wedgwood however wrote me a letter to prevent my coming which I wish you to forward to Gen. Tarleton for me. His address is No. 4, Little Rider Street, St. James's; is it not? You must not however, till further orders, send me any thing after Saturday, as we shall probably leave this place, before it could arrive. If you hear nothing fur-ther from me on that point, I request you to make Mr. Davis, the painter, 91, Chancery Lane, acquainted with this regulation some time on Monday morning, & not be-fore. Farewell, my love; I think of you with tenderness, & shall see you again with redoubled kindness (if you will let me) for this short absence. Kiss Fanny for me; re-member William; but (most of all) take care of yourself. Tell Fanny, I am safely arrived in the land of mugs.

Your sister would not come down to see me last night at supper, but we met at breakfast this morning. I have nothing to say about her.

MW TO WG

June 10, 1797

Your letter of Wednesday I did not receive till just now, and I have only a *half* an hour to express the kind emotions which are clustering about my heart, or my letter will have no chance of reaching Gen Tarlton to day, and tomorrow being Sunday, two posts would be lost. My last letter, of course you had not got, though I reckoned on its reaching you Wednesday evening.

I read T W's letter—I thought it would be affectation not to open it, as I knew the hand. It did not quite please me. He appears to me to be half spoilt by living with his inferiours in point of understanding, and to expect that homage to be paid to his abilities, which the world will readily pay to his fortune. I am afraid that all men are materially injured by inheriting wealth; and without knowing it, become important in their own eyes, in consequence of an advantage they contemn.

I am not much surprised at Miss Parr's conduct. You may remember that I did not give her credit for as much sensibility (at least the sensibility which is the mother of sentiment, and delicacy of mind) as you did, and her present conduct confirms my opinion. Could a woman of delicacy seduce and marry a fool? She will be unhappy, unless a situation in life, and a good table, to prattle at, are sufficient to fill up the void of affection. This ignoble mode of rising in the world is the consequence of the present system of female education.

I have little to tell you of myself. I am very well. Mrs. Reveley drank tea with me one evening and I spent a day with her, which would have been a very pleasant one, had I not been a little too much fatigued by a previous visit to Mr. Barry. Fanny often talks of you and made Mrs. Reveley laugh by telling her, when she could not find the monkey to shew it to Henry, "that it was gone into the country."

I supposed that Everina would assume some airs at seeing you—She has very mistaken notions of dignity of character.

Pray tell me the precise time, I mean when it is fixed —I do believe I shall be glad to see you!—of your return, and I will keep a good look out—William is all alive— and my appearance no longer doubtful—you, I dare say, will perceive the difference. What a fine thing it is to be a man!

You were very good to write such a long letter. Adieu! Take care of yourself—now I have ventured on you, I should not like to lose you.

Saturday, half after one o'clock   Mary

June 10, 1797

Holcroft has just left me. I had been telling him that, having a daughter, I wish for a son, yet shall treat him no better—nor love him more—than my Fanny. Never, as my mother used to do, shall I extend every privilege to a son which I withhold from a daughter. I would also hope to inculcate in his heart true sympathy and love for the female sex. Now is the time to begin to prepare Fanny for the changes in my body which have already aroused her curiosity. I want her to love her brother, not be jealous, as so many children seem to be on sharing their exclusive domain. I have thought, this evening, of using the example of the puppy. Peter and Opie brought to my door, one day, a small, bright-eyed, brown dog which, having followed them in the streets, stood wagging its tail in my doorway with the most expectant expression. I gave it a saucer of milk, which it lapped up as if it were a desert of dryness. Lucas was still crying about Puss having had to be drowned, so I let him keep the poor homeless animal, which he named George, only to discover weeks later that its belly was swelling. Now I have George—whom we have renamed Georgette— and one of her pups. Since Fanny is used to seeing it suckle, I might use it to teach her a lesson about human mothering, and teach her that once she, too, could not help herself any better than he. She could only open her mouth, and, as the puppy sucks now, be put to my breast, for there was milk enough for her.

I shall make a reader for Fanny—which will serve other children —Johnson shall print it and we shall make a fortune of money!! It will start with such simple words as *House. Wall. Field. Street. Grass.*—becoming more and more difficult, with longer and more complex sentences, and always of such matter as a child is likely to be most curious about . . .

Have you seen the baby? Look at him. How helpless he is. Three years ago you were as feeble as this. When you were hungry, you began to cry, because you could not speak. You were without teeth. At ten months you had four pretty white teeth, and you used to bite me. Poor mama! Still I did not cry, because I am not a child, but you hurt me. So I said to papa, it is time the little girl should eat. She is not naughty, yet she hurts me. I have given her a crust of bread, and I must look for some other milk. The cow has got plenty, and her jumping calf eats grass very well. He has got more teeth than my little girl. Yes, says papa, and he tapped you on the cheek, you are old enough to learn to eat. Come to me, and I will teach you, my little dear, for you must not hurt poor mama, who has given you her milk, when you could not take any thing else. You were then on the carpet, for you could not walk. When you were in a hurry, you used to run *quick, quick, quick, quick,* on hands and feet, like the dog. Away you ran to papa, and putting both arms round his leg, for your hands were not big enough, you looked up and laughed. What did this laugh say, when you could not speak? Can you guess by what you now say to papa? —Ah, it was, *Play with me, papa!—play with me!* Papa laughed louder than the little girl, and rolled the ball.

Then he put the ball on a chair, and you were forced to take hold of the back, and stand up to reach it. At last you reached too far, and down you fell: not, indeed, on your face, because you put out your hands. You were not much hurt; but the palms of your hands smarted with the pain, and you began to cry, like a little child.

It is only very little children who cry when they are hurt; and it is to tell their mama, that some thing is the matter with them. Now you can come to me, and say, *Mama, I have hurt myself. Pray, rub my hand; it smarts. Put some thing on it, to make it well.*

My mama took care of me, when I was a little girl, like you. She bade me never put any thing in my mouth, without asking her what it was. When you were a baby, with no more sense than William you put every thing in your mouth to gnaw, to help your teeth to cut through the skin. Look at the puppy, how he bites that piece of wood. And William presses his gums against my finger. Poor boy! he is so young, he does not know what he is doing. When *you* bite any thing, it is because you are hungry.

See how much taller you are than William. In four years you have learned to eat, to walk, to talk. You can wash your hands and face? Very well. I should never kiss a dirty face. And you can comb your head with the pretty comb you always put by in your own drawer? To be sure, you do all this to be ready to take a walk with me. You would be obliged to stay at home, if you could not comb your own hair. You can trundle a hoop, you say. And jump over a stick. Oh, I forgot!—and march like the men in the red coats, when papa plays a pretty tune on the fiddle.

You know much more than William, now you walk alone, and talk; but you do not know as much as the boys and girls you see playing yonder, who are half as tall again as you; and they do not know half as much as their fathers and mothers, who are men and women grown. Papa and I were children, like you; and men and women took care of us. I have more sense than you; therefore I take care not to eat unripe fruit, or any thing else that would make my stomach ache; or bring out ugly red spots on my face. When I was a child, my mama chose the fruit for me, to prevent my making myself sick. I was just like you; I used to ask for what I saw, without knowing whether it was good or bad. Now I have lived a long time, I know what is good; I do not want any body to tell me.

My hand aches, I can write no more to night, in the morning I shall go on with it. It is a useful occupation. In less than a year I shall be able to start to teach Fanny to read and to reason. I would not want my darling to turn out like Miss Parr or, for that matter, Miss Pinkerton, whose lisping good manners are meant to ingratiate, which is the usual manner of females rising in this world. I mean Fanny to be independent and proud, with a sense of her own superiority *through accomplishment*, so that she need fawn on no one, using not artifice, but reason.

Among the satires that were written to make a mockery of my

philosophy, the one written by some supposed Launcelot Light and Laetitia Lookabout, that was meant to be a droll exaggeration of my "Rights of Woman," entitled "The Rights of Boys and Girls," moved me to observe the truth of remarks meant to be taken facetiously. When Laetitia writes—the conceit being that she is a schoolgirl—thanking Mrs. Mary with the hard German name for having provided her with some original ideas of the importance, dignity and privileges of the sex, and saying it seems clear to her that girls have a natural, unalienable, and perfect right to do what they like, I thoroughly agree with her, wishing only to add that girls have the perfect right to do what they like *within reason*. Such new liberties shall be general, as the writer indicates when she says that she doubts not but that she shall make her part good; and not her own part alone, but that of all the sisterhood. With great good sense she goes on to say that there ought to be no sexual character of distinction in work. She would even do away with distinction in dress. Rather than laughing at such a notion, I take quite seriously the principle of equality extended to dress, and agree with her good judgement when she chooses a kind of middle way for girls, betwixt loose petticoats and men's tight breeches, namely, the Highland dress. My only cause for laughter is when she adds that she should like it vastly *for she has good legs*.

I did not even think it beyond reason to take seriously another satire at my expense, "A Vindication on the Rights of Brutes," defending poor, dumb animals from slaughter, trapping and hunting—though blood-sport and red meat be the very soul of our British character. Reason tells me even brutes have natural rights—but reason is held in low esteem at this point of progress of society.

WG TO MW

Etruria, June 10, 1797

You cannot imagine how happy your letter made me. No creature expresses, because no creature feels, the tender affections, so perfectly as you do: &, after all one's philosophy, it must be confessed that the knowledge, that there is some one that takes an interest in our happiness something like that which each man feels in his own, is extremely gratifying. We love, as it were, to multiply our consciousness, even at the hazard of what Montagu described so pathetically one night upon the New Road, of opening new avenues for pain & misery to attack us.

We arrived, as you are already informed, at Etruria on Tuesday afternoon. Wednesday I finished my second letter to you, which was exchanged that evening for your letter written the preceding day. This is the mode of carrying on correspondence at Etruria: the messenger who brings the letters from Newcastle under Line, 2 miles, carries away the letters you have already written. In case of emergency however, you can answer letters by return of post, & send them an hour after the messenger, time enough for the mail.

To the letter I now write, I cannot, if we prosecute our plans, receive any answer. Indeed I begin to apprehend, as I write, that it cannot be sent to-day. I wrote last on Wednesday, a letter, which of course you were to receive this morning. It is probable that you are now reading it: it is between twelve & one. I hope it finds you in health & spirits. I hope you hail the hand-writing on the direction, though not probably with the surprise that, it seems, the arrival of my first letter produced. You are now reading my adventures: the elopement of Mrs Wynn; the little, good-humoured sparring between me & Doctor Parr; and the tremendous accident of Cannock. These circumstances are presenting themselves with all the grace of novelty. I am, at the same time reading your letter, I believe, for the fourth time, which loses not one grace by the repetition. Well; fold it up, give Fanny the kiss I sent her, & tell her, as I desired you, that I am in the land of mugs. You wish, it may be, that my message had been better adapted to her capacity; but I think it better as it is; I hope you do not disdain the task of being its commentator.

One of the pleasures I promised myself in my excursion, was to increase my value in your estimation, & I am not disappointed. What we possess without intermission, we inevitably hold light; it is a refinement in voluptuousness, to submit to voluntary privations. Separation is the image of death; but it is Death stripped of all that is most tremendous, & his dart purged of its deadly venom. I always thought St Paul's rule, that we should die daily, an exquisite Epicurean maxim. The practice of it, would give to life a double relish.

My sentence towards the close of the preceding page is scarcely finished "I wrote last on Wednesday" Thursday I ventured to intermit. To-day is Friday, so, I fear, no post day; since no mail is delivered in London on a Sunday.

Yesterday we dined at Mrs. Wedgwood's the elder; Everina was not of the party. They sat incessantly from 3 o'clock to eleven. This does not suit my propensities; I was obliged to have a ride in the whisky at five, & a walk at half after eight.

Montagu's flame is the youngest of the family. She is certainly the best of the two unmarried daughters; but, I am afraid, not good enough for him. She is considerably fat, with a countenance rather animated, & a glimpse of Mrs Robinson. Perhaps you know that I am a little sheepish, particularly with stranger ladies. Our party is numerous, & I have had no conversation with her. I look upon any of my friends going to be married with something of the same feeling as I should do if they were sentenced for life to hard labour in the Spielberg. The despot may die, & the new despot grace his accession with a general jail delivery: that is almost the only hope for the unfortunate captive.

To-day we went over Mr. Wedgwood's manufactory: Everina accompanied us, & Mr Baugh Allen; no other lady. For Everina, she was in high spirits. She had never seen the manufactory before. The object of my attention was rather the countenances of the workpeople, than the wares they produced. I explained to her the affairs of the letters, & of the £20 from Mr. Johnson. She says, there was a parcel to have been sent by you, the arrival of which, as she imagined, would have been the proper signal for her to have written again. I found no item of this in my instructions.

Tell Fanny we have chosen a mug for her, & another for Lucas. There is a F on hers, & an L on his, shaped in a garland of flowers, of green & orange-tawny alternately. With respect to their beauty, you will set it forth with such eloquence as your imagination will supply.

We are going this evening, the whole family in a party, to see the School for Scandal represented by a company of strollers at Newcastle under Line.

The reason I desired you not to stop Mr. Davis's communications till Monday next, was that I am desirous to give the painting as little interruption as possible. I shall certainly write again on Sunday or Monday, before we leave Etruria.

It is now Saturday, June 10, 1797. I shall probably write again, before I leave Etruria, which we propose to be on Tuesday. I see I had said that before. Your William (do you know me by that name?) affectionately salutes the trio M, F, & last & least (in stature at least) little W.

WG TO MW

Etruria (finished), June 12, 1797

Having dispatched one letter, I now begin another. You have encouraged me to believe that some pleasure results to you, merely from thus obtaining the power of accompanying my motions, and that what would be uninteresting to another may, by this circumstance, be rendered agreeable to you. I am the less capable of altering my method, if it ought to be altered, as you have not dealt fairly by me this post. I delivered a letter of mine to the messenger, but I received none from him in return. I am beginning a fourth letter, but of yours I have as yet, only one.

The theatre, which was at Stoke-upon-Trent, two miles from Etruria, was inexpressibly miserable. The scene was new to me, & I should have been sorry to have missed it; but it was extremely tedious. Our own company, consisting of nine persons, contributed one half of the audience, exclusive of the galleries. The illusion, the fascination of the drama, was, as you may well suppose, altogether out of the question. It was the counterpart of a puppet-show at a country-fair, except that, from the circumstance of these persons having to deliver the sentiments of Sheridan & Shakespear (the School for Scandal, & Catherine & Petruchio) their own coarseness and ribaldry were rendered fifty fold more glaring & intolerable. Lady Teazle was by many degrees the ugliest woman I ever saw. One man took the two parts of Crabtree & Moses. Another, without giving himself the trouble to change his dress, played Careless & sir Benjamin Backbite. The father of Catherine had three servants; &, when he came to the country-house of Petruchio, he had precisely the same three servants to attend him. The gentleman who personated Charles in the play, was the Woman's taylor in the farce, & volunteered a boxing match with sir Oliver Surface in the character of Grumio. Snake, who was also footman-general to every person in the play, had by some means contracted the habit of never appearing when he was wanted, & the universal expedient for filling up the intervals, was for the persons on the stage to commence over again their two or three last speeches till he appeared. But enough of these mummers. Peace be to their memory! They did not leave us in our debt: they paid the world in talent, to the full as well as they were paid in coin.

Which is best, to pass one's life in the natural vegetative state of the potters we saw in the morning, turning a wheel, or treading a lay; or to pass it like these players, in an occupation to which skill and approbation can alone give a zest, without a rational hope of ever rising to either?

Saturday morning our amusement was to go to a place called the Tunnel, a portion of under-ground navigation, about a mile & a half, at the distance of three miles from Etruria. We went in a small boat, which was drawn along by a horse. As we approached the Tunnel, we saw a smoke proceeding from the mouth, which gave it no inadequate resemblance of what the ancients feigned to be the en-

trance to the infernal regions. We proceeded to about the
middle of the subterranean, the light that marked the
place of our entrance gradually diminishing, till, when
we had made two-thirds of our way, it wholly disappeared. The inclosure of the Tunnel was by an arch of
brick, which distilled upon us, as we passed, drops of water impregnated with iron. We discerned our way by
means of candles, that we brought along with us, &
pushed ourselves along with boat-staves, applied to the
walls on either side as we passed. Our voyage terminated,
as to its extent, in a coal-pit, of which there are several in
the subterranean. We had the two elder children with us,
who exhibited no signs of terror. I remarked, in coming
out, that the light from the entrance was much longer
visible in going than returning; &, indeed, in the latter
instance, was scarcely perceived till it, in a manner, burst
upon us at once.

The only ladies who accompanied us in this voyage,
was Mrs Josiah Wedgwood & Mrs Montagu elect. Here,
and at the play, where I contrived to sit next her, I saw
more of this latter, than I had yet done. I am sorry to
observe that she does not improve upon me.

Another evening, & no letter. This is scarcely kind. I
reminded you in time that it would be impossible to write
to me after Saturday, though it is not improbable that
you may not see me before the Saturday following. What
am I to think? How many possible accidents will the anxiety of affection present to one's thoughts? Not serious
ones I hope: in that case, I trust I should have heard.
But headaches; but sickness of the heart, a general loath-
ing of life & of me. Do not give place to this worst
of diseases! The least I can think is, that you recollect
me with less tenderness & impatience than I reflect on
you. There is a general sadness in the sky: the clouds are
shutting round me, & seem depressed with moisture:
every thing tunes the soul to melancholy. Guess what my
feelings are, when the most soothing & consolatory
thought that occurs, is a temporary remission & oblivion
in your affections!

I had scarcely finished the above, when I received your letter, accompanying T W's, which was delayed by an accident, till after the regular arrival of the post. I am not sorry to have put down my feelings as they were.

We propose leaving Etruria at four o'clock to-morrow morning (Tuesday). Our journey cannot take less than three days, viz., Tuesday, Wednesday, and Thursday. We propose however a visit to Dr Darwin, & a visit to Dr Parr. With these data from which to reason, you may judge as easily as I, respecting the time of our arrival in London. It will probably be either Friday or Saturday. Do not however count upon anything as certain respecting it, and so torment yourself with expectation.

Tell Fanny the green monkey has not come to Etruria. Bid her explain to Lucas the mug he is to receive. I hope it will not be broken upon the journey.

WG TO MW

June 15, 1797

We are now at The George in the Tree, 10 miles north from Warwick. We set out from Etruria, as we purposed, at five in the morning, Tuesday, June 13. We bent our course for Derby, being furnished with a letter of introduction to Dr Darwin, & purposing to obtain from him a further letter of introduction to Mr Bage, of Tamworth, author of Man as he is, & Hermsprong. Did we not well? Are not such men as much worth visiting, as palaces, towns, & cathedrals? Our first stage was Uttoxeter, commonly called Utchester, 19 miles. Here we breakfasted. Our next stage was Derby, where we arrived at two o'clock. At this place, though sentimental travellers, we were, for once, unfortunate. Dr Darwin was gone to Shrewsbury, & not expected back till Wednesday night. At this moment I feel mortified at the recollection. We concluded that this was longer than we could with propriety wait for him. I believe we were wrong. So extraordinary a man, so truly a phenomenon as we should probably have found him, I think we ought not to have scrupled the sacrifice of 36 hours. He is sixty seven years of age, though as young as Ganymed, & I am so little of a traveller, that I fear I shall not again have the opportunity I have parted with. We paid our respects, however, to his wife, who is still a fine woman, & cannot be more than fifty. She is perfectly unembarrassed, & tolerably well-bred. She seemed however to me to put an improper construction on our visit, said she supposed we were come to see the lions, and that Dr Darwin was the great lion of Derbyshire. We asked of her a letter to Mr Bage; but she said that she could not do that with propriety, as she did not know whether she had ever seen him, though he was the Doctor's very particular friend.

Thus baffled in our object, we plucked up our courage, & determined to introduce ourselves to the author of Hermsprong. We were able to cite our introduction to Dr Darwin by the Wedgwoods, & our intention of having procured a letter from the doctor. Accordingly we proceeded from Derby to Burton upon Trent, 16 miles. This is a very handsome town, with a wide & long street, a beautiful river, & a bridge which Montagu said was the longest he ever saw in the world. Here we slept, & drank Burton ale at the spring, after a journey of 48 miles. The next morning, between six & seven, we set out for Tamworth, 15 miles. At Elford, eleven miles, we saw Mr Bage's mills, & a house in which he lived for forty years. His mills are for paper & flour. Here we enquired respecting him, & found that he had removed to Tamworth five years ago, upon the death of his younger son, by which event he found his life rendered solitary & melancholy. The people at the mill told us, that he came three times a week walking from Tamworth to the mill, four miles, that they expected him at eleven (it was now nine); & that, if we proceeded, we should meet him upon the road. They told us, as a guide, that he was a short man, with white hair, snuff-coloured clothes, & a walking-stick. (He is 67 years old, exactly the same age as Dr Darwin.) Accordingly, about a mile & a half from Tamworth, we met the man of whom we were in quest, with a book in his hand. We introduced ourselves, &, after a little conversation, I got out of the chaise, & walked back with him to the mill. This six or seven miles was very fortunate, & contributed greatly to our acquaintance. I found him uncommonly cheerful & placid, simple in his manners, & youthful in all his carriage. His house at the mill was floored, every room below-stairs, with brick, & like that of a common farmer in every respect. There was however the river at the bottom of the garden, skirted with a quickset hedge, & a broad green walk. He told me his history.

His father was a miller, as well as himself, & he was born at Derby. At twenty two he removed to Elford. He had been acquainted forty years with Dr Darwin. The other acquaintances of his youth, were Whitehurst, author of the Theory of the Earth, & some other eminent man whose name I forget. He taught himself French & Latin, in both of which languages he is a considerable proficient. In his youth he was fond of poetry; but, having some motive for the study of mathematics, he devoted his three hours an afternoon (the portion of time he allotted for reading) to this subject for twelve years, and this employment destroyed the eagerness of his attachment to poetry. In the middle of life, he engaged in a joint undertaking with Dr Darwin & another person respecting some iron works. This failed, & he returned once more to his village & his mill. The result filled him with melancholy thoughts, & to dissipate them he formed the project of a novel, which he endeavoured to fill with gay & cheerful ideas. At first he had no purpose of publishing what he wrote. Since that time he has been accustomed to produce a novel every two years, & Hermsprong is his sixth. He believes he should not have written novels, but for want of books to assist him in any other literary undertaking. Living at Tamworth, he still retains his house at the mill, as the means of independence. It is his own, & he considers it as his security against the caprice or despotism of a landlord, who might expel him from Tamworth. He has thought much, & like most of those persons I have met with who have conquered many prejudices, & read little metaphysics, is a materialist. His favourite book in this point is the *Systême de la Nature*. We spent a most delightful day in his company. When we met him, I had taken no breakfast, &, though we had set off from Burton that morning at six, & I spent the whole morning in riding & walking, I felt no inconvenience in waiting for food till our dinner-time, at two; I was so much amused & interested with Mr Bage's conversation.

I am obliged to finish this letter somewhat abruptly, at the house of Dr Parr, where we arrived Thursday (yesterday) about noon, & found Mr. & Mrs. Wynn, but not the doctor, he having thought proper to withdraw himself on their arrival. It is most probable we shall be in town tomorrow evening, but may possibly not arrive till Sunday.

I should have added to the account of Mr Bage, that he never was in London for more than a week at a time, & very seldom more than fifty miles from his home. A very memorable instance in my opinion, of great intellectual refinement, attained in the bosom of rusticity.

Farewel. Salute William in my name. Perhaps you know how. Take care of yourself!—Tell Fanny that her mug & Lucas's are hitherto quite safe. I hope I shall find that the green monkey has resumed his old station by the time of my return.

June 17, 1797

You cannot imagine any thing like Mr Wynn & his wife. He is a raw, country booby of eighteen, his hair about his ears, & a beard that has never deigned to submit to the stroke of the razor. His voice is loud, broad & unmodulated, the mind of the possessor having never yet felt a sentiment that should give it flexibleness or variety. He has at present a brother with him, a lad, as I guess, of fifteen, who has come to Dr. Parr's house at Hatton, with a high generosity of sentiment, & a tone of mind declaring that, if his brother be disinherited, he who is the next brother, will not reap the benefit. His name is Julius, and John Wynn, the husband, is also a lad of very good dispositions. They both stammer: Julius extremely, John less; but with the stuttering of Julius, there is both an ingenuousness & warmth, that have considerable charms. John, on the contrary, has all the drawling, both of voice & thinking, that usually characterise a clown. His air is *gauche*, his gait negligent & slouching, his whole figure boorish. Both the lads are as ignorant, & as destitute of adventure & ambition, as any children that artistocracy has to boast. Poor Sarah, the bride, is the victim of her mother, as the bridegroom is her victim in turn. The mother taught her that the height of female wisdom, was to marry a rich man & a fool, & she has religiously complied. Her mother is an admirable woman, & the daughter mistook, & fancied that she was worthy of love. Never was girl more attached to her mother, than Sarah Wynn (Parr.) You do not know, but I do, that Sarah has an uncommon understanding, & an exquisite sensibility, which glows in her complexion, & flashes from her eyes. Yet she is silly enough to imagine that she shall be happy in love & a cottage, with John Wynn. She is excessively angry with the fathers on both sides, who, as she says, after having promised the contrary, attempted clandestinely to separate them. They have each, beyond question, laid up a magazine of unhappiness; yet, I am persuaded, Dr. Parr is silly enough to imagine the match a desirable one.

We slept, as I told you, at Tamworth, on Wednesday evening. Thursday morning, we proceeded through Coleshill (where I found a permanent pillory established, in lieu of the stock), & where we passed through a very deep & rather formidable ford, the bridge being under repair, & breakfasted at the George in the Tree, 16 miles. From thence the road by Warwick would have been 14 miles, and by a cross-country road, only six. By this therefore we proceeded, & a very deep & rough road we found it. We arrived at Hatton about one, &, after dinner, thinking it too much to sit all day in the company I have described, I proposed to Montagu, a walk to Kennelworth Castle, the seat, originally of Simon de Mountfort, earl of Leicester, who, in the reign of Henry the third, to whom he was an implacable enemy, was the author of the institution of the house of commons, &, more recently, the seat of Robert Dudly, earl of Leicester, the favourite, & as he hoped & designed the husband, of queen Elizabeth, to whom he gave a most magnificent & memorable entertainment at this place. The ruins are, beyond comparison, the finest in England. I found Montagu by no means a desirable companion in this expedition. He could not be persuaded to indulge the divine enthusiasm I felt coming over my soul, which I felt revived, &, as it were, embodied, the image of ancient times; but, on the contrary, expressed nothing but indignation against the aristocracy displayed, & joy that it was destroyed. From Dr Parr's to Kennelworth across the fields is only four miles. By the road, round by Warwick it is nine. We, of course, took the field way, but derived but little benefit from it, as we were on foot, from half after four, till half after ten, exclusive of a rest of about ten minutes. One hour out of the six we spent at Kennelworth, & two hours & a half in going & returning respectively, so utterly incapable were we of finding the path prescribed us.

To day, Friday, as fortune determined, was Coventry fair, with a procession of all the trades, with a female, representative of lady Godiva at their head, dressed in a close dress, to represent nakedness. As fortune had thus disposed of us, we deemed it our duty not to miss the opportunity. We accordingly set out after Breakfast, for Montagu proved lazy, & we did not get off till half after eleven. From Dr Parr's to Warwick is four miles, from Warwick to Coventry ten miles. One mile on the Coventry side of Warwick is Guy's Cliff, Mr Greatheed's. My description of his garden was an irresistible motive with Montagu to desire to visit it, though I by no means desired it. We accordingly went, & walked round the garden. Mr Greatheed was in his grounds, & I left a card, signifying I had done myself the pleasure of paying my respects to him, & taken the liberty of leading my friend over his garden. This delay of half an hour precisely answered the purpose of making us too late for lady Godiva. We saw the crowd which was not yet dispersed, & the booths in the fair, but the lady, the singularity of the scene, was retired.

It is now Sunday evening: we are at Cambridge. Montagu says we shall certainly be in town to morrow (Monday) night. The distance is 53 miles: we shall therefore probably be late, & he requests that, if we be not at home before ten, you will retain somebody to take the whiskey from Somers Town to Lincoln's Inn. If Mary be at a loss on the subject, perhaps the people of Montagu's lodging can assist her.

Farewel. Be happy; be in health & spirits. Keep a lookout, but not an anxious one. Delays are not necessarily tragical: I believe there will be none.

M W T O W G

June 19, 1797

One of the pleasures you tell me, that you promised yourself from your journey was the effect your absence might produce on me—Certainly at first my affection was increased; or rather was more alive—But now it is just the contrary. Your latter letters might have been addressed to any body—and will serve to remind you where you have been, though they resemble nothing less than mementos of affection.

I wrote to you to Dr Parr's you take no notice of my letter—Previous to your departure I requested you not to torment me by leaving the day of your return undecided. But whatever tenderness you took away with you seems to have evaporated in the journey, and new objects —and the homage of vulgar minds, restored you to your icy Philosophy.

You told me that your journey could not take up less than three days, therefore as you were to visit Dr. D and

P—Saturday was the probable day—you saw neither—yet
you have been a week on the road—I did not wonder,
but approved of your visit to Mr. Bage—But a *shew*
which you waited to see & did not see, appears to have
been equally attractive. I am at a loss to guess how you
could have been from Saturday to Sunday night travelling
from C to C—In short—your being so late to night, and
the chance of your not coming, shews so little consideration, that unless you suppose me a stick or a stone, you
must have forgot to think—as well as to feel, since you
have been on the wing. I am afraid to add what I feel—
Good-night.—

Monday, almost twelve

June 20, 1797, Tuesday evening—

Having breakfasted this morning in Epping Forest, Godwin arrived home as the sun reached its zenith. I was not glad to see him,
when he entered, but he soothed my feelings, was ladened with
gifts for all, and so genuinely delighted, full of embraces and shining looks, like a soldier back from his exploits, that it was hard to
resist. He has brought me a handsome tea-caddy of jasper from
Etruria, on all four sides white medallions representing angels
at such industries as weaving, metal-work and printing; for Fanny
and Lucas mugs which have them still crowing with pleasure, and
he did not forget a remembrance for Marguerite, nor for poor
Mary. And so I spent all my anger *on Montagu,* whom I prayed
to leave us *en famille,* as he was about to lift his dirty boots upon
the rungs of a chair and settle comfortably in for a chat. I overheard Godwin in the hall excuse my sharpness, putting the blame
on my physical uneasiness, which may be true, but is all the same
not why I wished Montagu to be gone. It's true my belly has swollen horribly, a network of blue veins visible under taut, almost
transparent, skin which feels stretched to bursting; and my back
is broken with fatigue, no matter how many hours I spend reclining, which I hate. It was hardly the time for Godwin to go away
and enjoy the country, when I needed him about to divert me. Yet
I was glad to see him go, for his sake, to tell the truth. And now

he is back, so no matter! At the moment, he is at his apartments with Miss Pinkerton. Having finished revisions for a new edition of "Political Justice" before he left on tour, he has given up the idea of next writing a life of his favourite Robespierre, since Robinson and Johnson have advised it is decidedly too dangerous for the writer, publisher and printer, while Pitt is in power; now he has in mind a tragedy. In the balm of country air and sunshine and sweet-smelling fields and woods, his mind grew clear as they rode in their little chaise, the regular beat of hooves some times the only sound beside bird-song. The play is to be called "Alonzo," or perhaps "Antonio," he has not yet decided which, and from what I can gather from his excitable account of it, it has to do with Alonzo-Antonio and his sister Helena—to be played, *il va sans dire*, by Mrs. Siddons—who gladly dies under her brother's sword to vindicate the glory of the race and expiate her fault, which behaviour, not understanding Spaniards, I'm afraid, I could not discern the motive of. But he has never been more sure of success than he is at the moment. As soon as he can read through his post, he hopes to resume his quiet, regular, blissful mornings which he says he yearned for, while away.

M W T O W G

June 25, 1797

I know that you do not like me to go to Holcroft's. I think you right in the principle; but a little wrong in the present application.

When I lived alone I always dined on a Sunday, with company in the evening, if not at dinner, at St. P's. Generally also of a Tuesday, and some other day at Fuseli's.

I like to see new faces, as a study—and since my return from Norway, or rather since I have accepted of invitations, I have dined every third Sunday at Twiss's, nay oftener, for they sent for me, when they had any extraordinary company. I was glad to go because my lodging was noisy of a Sunday, and Mr. J's house and spirits were so altered, that my visiting him depressed instead of exhilarated my mind.

I am then, you perceive, thrown out of my track, and

have not traced another—But so far from wishing to obtrude on yours, I had written to Mrs. Jackson and mentioned Sunday—and am now sorry that I did not fix on to day—as one of the days for sitting for my picture.

To Mr. Johnson—I would go without ceremony—but it is not convenient for me, at present to make haphazard visits.

Should Carlisle chance to call you this morning send him to me—But, by himself, for he often has a companion with him, which would defeat my purpose—

Sunday, June 25, 1797

Because this child of mine seems to be so restless, I wondered if I ought to change diet, or be more or perhaps less active, as the case may be. It was not this way, as I remember, when I carried Fanny; and I was in less robust a state of health, with constant anxieties at the time. Carlisle was here. He looked at my colour, pinching my cheek to see how long a time it took for the colour to rise again, and plucked up both eyelids; then he gave me a brisk slap on the cheek, saying I was only imagining things, smiling with a bonhomie I found patronising. What, after all, does he know of how I feel? It is my body that bears a child; no man can imagine the burden. Yet if being stoical is all that is wanted, I can be as manly as any woman before me has had to be, till she comes to term. I wished he were less bluff over my discomfort. *Think of other things*, he said. Well, I shall try.

When asked his opinion of midwives, he gave me to understand that birth rarely demands any other aid than experienced mothers can safely give, that it might even be mischievous to tamper with pregnant women under the pretence of hastening, easing or retarding delivery; for, according to the most eminent members of the medical profession, the womb naturally expels her contents like the bowels, assistance as absurd in the former case, as it would be in the latter. I do not much care for the analogy, though I agree that nature is dependably instructive. It was time to decide on the midwife whom I shall employ, to stand by in readiness to clean and clothe the infant, for I will want no other assistance for my-

self, having sufficient experience. Carlisle said my wishing a midwife somewhat surprised him, he would have supposed me above
such modesty. Once I gathered his meaning, I said in a cold voice
that my decision to be attended by a midwife, rather than by a
physician, had little to do with false modesty. I do not hold with
the view of decorum currently common in England, that says no
man should be allowed to enter the chamber of a woman in labour, as if giving birth were an act of indecency, or such exposure
a lack of chastity. He said I must have misunderstood his meaning. I blushed and hastened to apologise. He gave me his frozen
smile, as if to say I had jumped to conclusions quite excessive. He
then leaned forwards in a confiding manner to ask if I had heard
how the ladies of America not only prefer midwives of their own
sex, but actually employ female physicians. He, personally, ascribed
to the practice, believing that diseases of women should be attended to solely by women, but some of his colleagues, holding
less advanced views, were using the old saw which goes:

Where does America get her fashions?
From England.
Where does England get them from?
From France.
And where does France get them from?
From the devil.

I believe in women studying medicine, and said as much in my
"Rights of Woman," not because we ought to be shamed and insulted by being touched by a male physician, nor that it is pollu-
tion, loss of honour, an affront to nature—all those terribly base
notions favoured here in England, which Mrs. Reveley says surely
denotes a society that has lost its perspective on common human functions, which ought never be considered shameful. I
choose to have beside me a woman experienced in caring for an
infant, lest I be too weak myself to do so. I again recall the wisdom
of the North American Indians, who have not been vitiated by
false standards: they, I remember from my readings, especially
from Charlevoix, make child-birth a tribal occasion, the women
accompanying each other in labour, so that the experience is made
less solitary, all heaving and groaning each time the child in the

womb causes a spasm of pain; thus the child becomes the child of every woman, the mother solaced by one and all. Am I stupid to imagine myself desiring to be the centre of a circle of friends, who have had the experience of having felt within their own bodies the rhythms of those considerable contractions which seem some times to break one's very bones?

Godwin has gone to dine at Holcroft's to day. He wishes Holcroft's Sundays to belong to him. This does not seem to me quite fair, especially since I yielded my rights to Johnson's Tuesdays, and Johnson is a friend of mine. But I concede the point—for the time being. For I must admit my performance last Sunday at Holcroft's may have proved embarrassing, or at least distracting. My waist-band being too tight, after the meal—of pork pye which I find quite indigestible—it was impossible to catch my breath as I sat at table, and I went to lie down. Godwin grew quite pale, thinking I was taken ill. I was not ill, merely uncomfortable. Sophy Harwood, Holcroft's daughter, saw to me. Tooke was scarcely agreeable at the interruption, annoyed, I wager, because my spell caused Peter, who was also there, to come sit with me, our light banter becoming more of an attraction than Tooke's diatribe. In fact, even Holcroft left the table to join us so that there was set up a sort of contest to see who would stay or go, I am sorry to say. Godwin said I had interrupted the course of conversation, and he would prefer hereafter to go to Holcroft's by himself, which I think rather selfish of him, but to which I yield without a murmur, since *hereafter* I define not in any theological sense of infinite punishment, but only to a point when I shall find myself less physically hampered.

I have promised to take Fanny to visit little Henry Reveley to day, and shall stay there to dine.

MW TO WG

June 26, 1797

The weather, I believe, will not permit me to go out to day, and I am not very sorry for I feel a little the worse for my yesterday's walk—or rather confinement at dinner—I have not been able to employ myself this morning, and have ordered my dinner early hoping to make it up in the evening—I send for the paper—and I should ask you for some novel, or tale, to while away the time 'till dinner, did I suppose you had one.

June 29, 1797

Imagine my astonishment, on Monday, when I sorted through the post, and slit open a letter that was some gibberish which made me turn the letter over to see it was addressed to Godwin, not to me. I fanned it in the air a moment, wondering whether I ought to continue reading it. One cannot put out of mind what is already half perceived. One cannot say some thing does not exist when it has manifested itself. A distasteful sensation, one not unfamiliar, had stolen over me, a prickly apprehension of secrets unwittingly prised open. There was nothing really to do but have full knowledge of what already had been partly divined. The letter, which I then read in full, was a girlish confession from Miss Pinkerton. As much as I could gather, through ellipses and fancy phrasing, an ardour for learning is making her burgeon like a bud in spring, and only to Godwin can she divulge her ineffable feelings, to him alone find words for her considerable intellectual distress. Why, in heaven and earth, should she send such a letter? What was I to do with this itching amorousness, for it strikes me as such, despite all circumlocution? Should I have handed the letter to him, as though it were a banking transaction I had mistakenly opened? If I were a disciple of perfect sincerity, I dare say I would have given it to Marguerite to run to the Evesham Buildings. But I am not a disciple of perfect sincerity. I lay on the sofa, holding the letter which had the power to destroy the smooth, even course of my domesticity. I thought it over for perhaps a quarter of an hour, then reached for some paper and a pen.

I wrote first to Holcroft to come and dine with his daughter and son-in-law in two days' time, then at greater length to Maria Reveley. In writing her I said Godwin desired me to excuse him for not having called the previous Wednesday, but that he had only returned on Tuesday. He'd been in despair at not having been able to come—*en déséspoir* rather, for he turns inevitably to French to express strong feelings, as if we are not to have any in English—and I asked if she would dine with the same friends whom she had dined with before, with the addition this time of Godwin. Her coming with this party, however, was not to prevent her from paying me a haphazard visit, alone, when I promised to show her one of Mr. Godwin's epistles from a Fair One, this, of course, entirely *entre nous*. Then to Miss Pinkerton I wrote a polite note asking her to dine with us on Wednesday. And I put her epistle between the pages of the book I was reading, where it will remain for a while *misplaced*.

Mrs. Reveley, this morning, has brought little Henry. Marguerite led the two children, with their tiny rakes and pitchforks, to the fields opposite where they might make hay, while we talked. I admired Mrs. Reveley's turban, whose ends were loosely tied about her neck, and a long simple muslin morning dress I have come to like so well, with a Greek key pattern. Her comment on our present style of dress is that soon we shall be carrying about a thyrsus, since every thing seems to come from the ancients these days. I'd laughed at that: I could see us as bacchantes rushing up Oxford Street. She says she must show me her Turkish dresses, which she no longer wears, truly ideal garments, to her way of thinking, loose, flowing and graceful, giving both warmth and liberty of movement. She did not mind that I lay back on several pillows, for I had been feeling ill all morning. She sat in my open-armed chair, the ends of her turban untied, baring her fine long neck. She is small and holds herself erect with a self-containment that is very attractive. It makes one look at her and keep on looking to try to read her thoughts. Some say she has a cold expression. It is merely so in repose, for a smile melts her features into the warmest glow, and her laugh—I love her laugh—is low and vibrant and shakes her dark curls about her face. I had been seeing her often, while Godwin was away, for Fanny is a little in love with Henry.

I had wanted her to see the letter. There is no dismissing such a letter; there is about it too much of an odour of closeted conversations, of which this one on paper is merely one more in an habitual long line. These interviews between Godwin and his little pupil have been taking place, I can only suppose, for some time; I have no idea how long. I can only surmise from certain meaningful signals that passed between them yesterday evening that there has been time for them to create one of those vocabularies of reference so personal that it excludes the rest of the world. If it were a one-sided attachment of a young innocent for an older man, it would be easy enough to convince Godwin that we must give her a physic to get her over her idyll, for only concerted action will make her understand we are as one mind, and that she must take us together or not at all. But Godwin, I can see, is flattered. He would undoubtedly have concealed his friendship with this young miss, had not his tour into the country demanded some stringent measure: he actually, I see now, had me watch over her.

Mrs. Reveley is confident that the relationship has not evolved; for if it were a guilty union, Godwin would have been more secretive, she thinks. It is this freedom of his to bring her any where, it seems to me, which presents the danger; she is introduced as our literary assistant—what Marshal is to Godwin, Miss Pinkerton is supposed to be to me. And so she mingles among our friends and makes herself at home here at No. 29 and comes and goes in Godwin's rooms. I threw up my hands in a kind of panic, as it came to me how intrusive she has become. Maria Reveley, patting my hand, said that I was to leave the matter to her. She will pass by Godwin's, at which point she will simply say how *forward* she had thought Miss Pinkerton; how uncommonly *rude* she had been to have extricated Holcroft for so long from the rest of the company, merely to bore him with a recitation of her literary ambitions; that she had made young Major Harwood bristle at her *boldness*—that such a common flirt must be cautioned—which Godwin will do, if he thinks Miss P's flirtatiousness generally condemned. I smiled at the stratagem. Mrs. Reveley smiled back. We were in one of those moments of complicity between women, when a world of understanding is silently shared.

I was told Mr. Reveley does not go out in society, but that turns out not to be entirely true. He does not like Godwin and detests Holcroft. The incident which led to his refusal ever to be in any company where Holcroft was to appear took place at the time of the trials. Maria Reveley had been willing to give public evidence for Holcroft, in readiness to face every odium to save him; but she was not prepared to ruin herself and her family, should her exposure have scarcely a possibility of advantage to him, and the evidence she was able to give have nothing singular or particular to it—that is, she would not be sacrificed from mere puerile conceit. Holcroft had asserted that, whatever her reluctance, he would force her to do her duty—an asseveration that had infuriated Mr. Reveley. He had thereafter considered Holcroft a man devoid of moderation or moral scruple; yet he did not object to his wife, if she found such philosophical low-life stimulating, occasionally calling on him. Maria Reveley has put behind her any feelings of resentment against Holcroft, who apologised with tears in his eyes, blaming himself for having lost his composure. Holcroft puts doctrine first—once at terrible personal cost, when he hunted down his own son as if he were a common criminal: the boy then, in fear, or shame, we shall never know the reason, firing his father's pistol into his brains.

One day, while she was sewing, and I idly stretched out, Maria Reveley told me how her father had refused to give her a dowery, when she had decided to marry Mr. Reveley, as he might well have refused to give her a dowery, had she had designs to marry any one else; for he neither wished her to leave him, nor did he choose to part with his money. Used to personal liberty, brought up as she had been in the casual household of a society of foreigners living in Turkey, she has not habituated herself to the restraints of English life, which has led to misunderstandings with her husband, who at times displays an explosive temper that terrifies her. It astonished me to learn that a man so seemingly mild should have fits of rage, during which the blood rushes into his face, suffusing his features with a raw, red look, as he shouts things which make her stop up her ears. He has even once flung at her from his drawing-table the knife with which he sharpens his nibs. The least small thing may set him off. Yet she has refused to live obedient to his frivolous commands. How different it is, she said, as she held her head averted, bending over a shirt that seemed wholly to occupy her attention, from what she had imagined marriage to be. Mr. Reveley had been nearing the end of five years' touring through Greece, Egypt and Italy, when she'd met him, his skin as brown as an African's from being out in the sun sketching antiquities; he had been making drawings of the pyramids from measurements calculated according to mathematical principles. As she was then a pupil of Angelica Kauffmann's, she had imagined that they might help one another, for though she was not trained in architecture, she had a very facile hand, accompanying him on sketching trips in Rome, producing drawings which he some times preferred to his own. They had once hired a donkey to carry their equipment, and were walking hand in hand, so blissfully forgetful that the donkey had taken a turn, while they sauntered straight ahead—only later remembering their companion and having to return along dusty roads to search till dusk. Now she no longer touches pen to paper. It is not that there is no time; it is that what is expected of her is so burdensome that she has lost the sense of aimlessness such work requires. And how could her notion of beauty ever contribute any thing to Mr. Reveley's commissions for plans for an infirmary at Canterbury or for wet docks on the Thames? His established habits and hers are as different, due to the difference in sex, as a Hottentot's from a Hindoo's.

MW TO WG

July 3, 1797

Mrs. Reveley can have no doubt about to day, so we are to stay at home. I have a design on you this evening to keep you quite to myself. (I hope then nobody will call!) and make you read the play—

I was thinking of a favourite song of my poor poor friend Fanny's—"In a vacant rainy day you shall be wholly mine"—&c

Unless the weather prevents you from taking your accustomed walk, call on me this morning for I have something to say to you—

Monday morning

July 3, 1797

It rains so mournfully. The trees beyond the window drip, a steady drumming of rain that sets my nerves on edge. I cannot seem to put from mind Fanny Blood's sad song. It has been a long time since I have let my imagination settle into a train of thought that brings her alive again. Small things instantly call her to mind: whenever I am gathering mulberries, or see children gathering them by shaking the branches, I recall the scrupulous way Fanny would nibble them to avoid staining her fingers or blotting the juice upon her frock; a certain way the early sun slants through a window on a table reminds me of how she would hastily remove from direct sunlight her father's portrait in its blue velvet frame, pale blue being *fugitive,* as she explained to me; whenever I hold a wooden egg under a sock to darn a hole, I think of Fanny holding my hands in hers to show me how to do it—so many things did she teach me when I was sixteen, and she two years older and so much the wiser. I think I loved her then with all the passion of my uninstructed heart. She was the one person whose expressions I unendingly studied to learn to read her soul, a practice which gave me for ever an understanding of human nature, since our first love is the school that serves us always. I have changed so much in these last dozen years, since her death, that I some times wonder if she would recognise the Mary whose welfare she so desired to promote. I find it difficult to imagine her coming and going from the Polygon, so much a part of the past does she seem, dressed in clothing no longer worn. Death which wrenched her away from the continuity of life has now a kind of terrible inevitability to it. After she died, I abandoned the school, so utterly dispirited and broken-hearted was I that I could not conceive of fighting against ever-increasing debt and the loss of boarders which greeted my return from Portugal. It was to pay for the Bloods to go to Ireland that I then wrote the little book which Johnson gave me ten guineas for—and my life took on a new impulse. Perhaps my having gone to Portugal to be with Fanny, when she gave birth, already determined the loss of the school, for I might have foreseen that my sisters would quarrel and mismanage things. Perhaps a premonition that it would be the last time I should hold Fanny in my arms made me go to the lengths I had to go, accompanying an old sick Portuguese gentleman on his trip home to die to pay my passage, those thirteen days upon seas which raised the ship to the very heavens and dashed it down between mountainous waves, in those gales of wind, which the captain was afraid would dismast the ship, none of us being able either to stand or walk, my poor invalid coughing, gasping for breath, never expecting to live to see land. It was from this terrifying dream into another that I went. For Fanny was already in labour, prematurely, when I arrived, four hours later delivered of a boy. Though she tried to smile to welcome me, she was worn out and, I think, knew from the moment I clasped her that her recovery would be almost a resurrection. Yet on the third day some of the most alarming symptoms abated—and, half afraid to indulge my hopes, I began to look forward to days that, alas!, never came to be. She was too weak to receive the slightest nourishment. Her constitution had been enfeebled by working for the improvement of her family; her lungs had been infected. When I was with my first child—whom I determined to name after my dearest friend, were she to be a girl —my teeth some times chattered with fear connected with that confinement in Lisbon, where the contractions of labour had made my dear friend arch upon the bed in spasms of agony, which periodically released her only to let her lie half dead, barely breathing, hardly recognising who it was who hovered over her and wiped the dampness from her brow. So many women, constitutionally weakened, die in child-birth, that it is not an idle thought that keeps intruding. I had imagined that those fears had long since departed from memory, but on a grey day with an onslaught of sullen rain, being left alone to brood . . .

MW TO WG

July 3, 1797

I have been very well till just now—and hope to get rid of the present pain before I see you. I have ordered some boiled mutton as the best thing for me, and as the weather will probably prevent you from walking out, you will, perhaps, have no objection to dining at four. Send some more of the letters, and, if you bring *more* with you, we might read them after dinner, and rescue my favourite *act* till we are sure of not being interrupted.

You are to send me yesterday's as well as today's paper.

Yours truly and kindly—

MW TO WG

July 4, 1797

I am not well—no matter. The weather is such, I believe, as to permit us to keep our appointment—and it may as well be over.

What will you do about Addington? Let me have the remainder of Mrs. V's letters, when you have finished them, that I may not prevent your returning them, when Addington calls.

To be frank with you, your behaviour yesterday brought on my troublesome pain. But I lay no great stress on that circumstance, because were not my health in a more delicate state than usual, it could not be so easily affected. I am absurd to look for the affection which I have only found in my own tormented heart; and how can you blame one for taking refuge in the idea of a God, when I despair of finding sincerity on earth? I think you wrong—yes, with the most decided conviction I dare say it, having still in my mind the *unswervable* principles of justice and humanity. You judge not in your own case as in that of another. You give a softer name to folly and immorality when it flatters—yes, I must say it—your vanity, than to mistaken passion when it was extended to another—you termed Miss Hays' conduct insanity when only her own happiness was involved—I cannot forget the strength of your expressions—and you treat with a mildness calculated to foster it, a romantic selfishness, and pass for conceit, which will even lead the object to— I was going to say misery—but I believe her incapable of feeling it. Her want of sensibility with respect to her family first disgusted me—Then to obtrude herself on me, to see affection, and instead of feeling sympathy, to endeavour to undermine it, certainly resembles the conduct of the fictitious being, to whose dignity she aspires. Yet you, at the very moment, commenced a correspondence with her whom you had previously almost neglected— you brought me a letter without a conclusion—and you changed countenance at the reply—My old wounds bleed afresh—What did not blind confidence, and unsuspecting truth, lead me to—my very soul trembles sooner than endure the hundredth part of what I have suffered, I could wish my poor Fanny and self asleep at the bottom of the sea.

One word more—I never blamed the woman for whom

I was abandoned. I offered to see, nay, even to live with her, and I should have tried to improve her. But even she was deceived with respect to my character, and had her scruples when she heard the truth—But enough of the effusions of a sick heart—I only intended to write a line or two—

The weather looks cloudy; but it is not necessary immediately to decide.

July 4, 1797

I can do nothing useful, prey to echoes of the argument of yesterday, from whose savagery I have not been able to recover. I found what I hoped to be the right moment to give the letter to Godwin. That was on Friday—to day is Tuesday. Godwin admitted Miss Pinkerton is a little in love with him, and that *therefore* he had started a correspondence—would ordinary logic not have impelled him to conclude, at signs of amorousness, *therefore not* to have started a correspondence? His judgement is flustered when his vanity is stirred. I am told—I am told very little, certainly, and not always the entirety of things—that he went to her and informed her that her letter had been intercepted—the word he used, though immediately retracted, when I repeated it incredulously. I do not *intercept* letters sent to my home. Of course not, he hastened to say, but in perfect clarity had been illuminated the scene at Miss Pinkerton's: her downcast looks, his efforts at consoling her and their agreement to be in future more careful. I sat in glum concentration at this vision of their faction against me. I have become, then, the wifely shrew.

Next day, I suggested calmly that what may be difficult to say in the presence of some one whose feelings one would like to spare, might be better said on paper; that since there has started some sort of frequent correspondence between them, would it not be wise to write how inappropriate it is for one whose affections are bound to arouse exclusive feelings in one not similarly circumstanced. I don't know now quite how I put it, not in my own words, but in the style of what I imagine Godwin's didactic epistles to Miss Pinkerton to be. He admitted to having difficulties in suggesting a hindrance to spontaneity to a young woman who wished there to be no disguises between them. This annoyed me, but I held my tongue. I only said if it were a question any where of being without disguise, it ought to be between the two of us. He agreed. He brought me his effort at writing the letter which intended to clarify the limitations of their friendship—but, oddly, he did not express what he'd meant to say, which was that visits and letters must cease. I suggested a phrase which struck him as relatively innocuous, which said precisely that, and he began to add it to the bottom of his letter, hesitated, and stopped altogether, saying he would rather *say* such a thing than write it—the written word, when being read and reread, having the disadvantage of assuming a tone of harshness, whereas in declaring it, he might see to it that he was purposefully light and friendly. I did not object, or rather I did not say I objected, though I saw through the subterfuge: it meant another call at her lodgings. He carried with him the letter. And a reply came back which I handed him— by this time it was a point of honour between them to exchange their letters openly. He tore open the reply and visibly changed countenance. It let me know he felt physical sensations which friendship does not precipitate. I could not help the stab of jealousy that went through me. Was it to be the same old story that I suffered with Imlay? After recovering composure, he handed the letter to me to read. She had understood not one word of the implications of his address. Fool that she was, she was more self-deceived than had been Mary Hays. I said as much. He bristled at the comparison. Miss Hays' past conduct with Mr. Lloyd had been *insanity*. He could barely speak for anger: why, Miss Pinkerton's conduct was all mere innocence and folly. He sees it so, since the beacon of love is turned towards him. He faced me and said I might comprehend how innocent an admiration it was, had I not been jilted by Imlay, that in Miss Pinkerton I see that woman of Imlay's for whom I was abandoned. He said it with venom. Am I as unreasonable as he makes me out to be? I do not think I am, not even with Imlay's mistress, whom I offered to live with, since we three seemed inextricably united. Is this a similar circumstance? Must I prepare myself for more of Miss Pinkerton?

July 4, 1797

I have not finished the news papers. I do not mean to return the letters to Addington to day. I am much hurt at your note; but Mr. Fell is with me, & I cannot answer it.

July 6, 1797

I have just returned from Opie's, his bitterness quite the tonic needed. I had fallen silent in my pose, gazing at the ochre wall against which leaned several large canvases, showing only their blank backs, the whole having taken on a resemblance, by diverse angles and pitched shadows, of a building under construction, or one that has half caved in. I dreamed awhile on this fabric and felt a start of slow tears—for no reason I could discern. Opie laid aside brush and palette and came up peering at me from below, so wrinkled with anxious interrogation that I burst out laughing, at which agitation the tears spilled over. He led me to the couch, from which he had to remove several sketching pads before we could sit. And out came my misery! I asked if he remembered our conversation on Arnolphe's maxims in "School for Wives"? With china-blue eyes that are all vacuity, yet sparkling with deceit, Miss Pinkerton plays at such submission which has *captivated* Godwin, for beneath his egalitarian doctrines, he retains the conviction that feminine perfection comes in the shape of a porcelain doll devoid of demonstrable will. If this is what men idealise, how can love last—since ultimately every woman slips free from that inhibiting chrysalis to become a woman with a will of her own?

If Opie had tried to reason with me, I should have become more than ever determined in my misery. But he largely agreed, giving full vent to his own pessimism. Divorce, a broken engagement and the habit of solitary work have made him lately misanthropic. He so greatly exaggerates the impossibility of any true understanding between men and women that I positively brightened at his caricature of rampant faithlessness. Perhaps he had meant to work me around to contradiction. I do not know. He seemed most melancholy, actually. He blames Miss Beetham for being distracted by her father, whom he considers a tyrant. But young women, I hasten to point out, are always tyrannised; and fathers are either villainous tyrants or benevolent ones. It is the nature of our society to give unexamined power to them—I forget the Latin for it, but it was law to the Romans. Opie says he shall scour the doorways of the Polygon to find an *émigré* foundling free of family bonds. I'm glad to learn he is still searching for a wife. It is safe *now* for him to say he wishes to have a wife with half my brains. Mary Bunn was silly, Miss Beetham inconstant. To take him out of himself, I recount Mrs. Reveley's complaints. Dining at her house the other night had some thing decidedly unpleasant to it—I prefer to see her on her own—for Mr. Reveley makes cutting remarks. It was not a pleasant evening, yet I was glad we had planned to go out, since Godwin had come home in a rage. I do not know the best course: to make clear what one is angry about, or, in order to spare the other, restrain oneself till anger makes a hole in one's abdomen and the other is left at sea about one's true feelings. Clearly I am of the school that believes in a heart that scorns disguise and dissemblement. There Godwin and I disagree. For he would be flattered and soothed. I told him he has Miss Pinkerton for that. Opie, who came last night to sup with us, says he noticed no estrangement. That is what is so tedious in these unresolved differences: they flare up, then die down, but do not entirely go out. I asked Opie if he agreed that intermittent unhappiness was the best one could expect in an enduring relationship. He picked pigment from the back of his hand, reflecting. Intermittent happiness was one's safest expectation. I laughed at his cynicism—laughing helped. And so *pace*, for a little while.

M W T O W G

July 7, 1797

Opie has just been here to put me off till Sunday, papa. Should the morning prove favourable have you any objection to calling with me, by way of sparing my blushes, on Mrs. Carr—and Nicholson.

Remember that I have no particular desire to interfere with your convenience—only say the word.

I have just recollected that Sir. R. Smith is to set out to day—Had you not better forward your letter, for Miss W.—under cover to him immediately—

July 7, 1797

I obey, with a pious & chearful obedience, & will be ready to squire you to Thornhaugh & Newman Street at any hour you shall appoint. Sir Rob. Smyth told me he should set out on Tuesday: if you will tell me how you come to know of his having delayed his journey, I should eagerly make use of his conveyance. Send me an answer to these two questions. Send me also the Fair Syrian, & as many of Mrs. V's letters as you have entirely done with.

July 7, 1797

Don't laugh at me—I saw the letter and thought today Tuesday—

I shall be ready at half past two—Between then and three I shall expect you—Have you now sent me all Mrs. V's letters? You forgot that I wished to see the one addressed to you—I have been very much affected by her account of one scene with her husband—

July 12, 1797

To day I go with Godwin to take tea at Johnson's. I no longer attend to the business of the *Analytical*, a relief to have turned the care of it over to others. I thought so yesterday when Elizabeth Fenwick brought her little Eliza to play with Fanny. We went into the fields opposite and sat together in the shade, while the two children gathered loose hay into a haystack, to resemble the ones which appear with regularity on every side. We then took a little walk along the far side of the wall, the children delighted by a herd of sheep led home by several barking dogs. Elizabeth Fenwick tells me cocoa-butter relieves the stretched skin across the abdomen—I had been using a mixture of tincture of camphor and eucalyptus, which has given little relief. I am very heavy. If I drop some thing on the floor, I have to stand by helplessly, calling Mary or Marguerite, or even Fanny, to pick it up for me. Does any man know the humiliation of such incapacity?

M W TO W G

July 13, 1797

Send me The Fair Syrian—that is, the first volume, if you have not finished it. I still feel a little fatigue from my walk—

W G TO M W

July 15, 1797

I thought you expressed yourself unkindly to me in the beginning last night. I am not conscious of having deserved it. But you amply made up your injustice, in what followed; so I was tranquil and easy. Today you have called on me, and said two or three grating things. I entreat you not to give me pain of this sort, without a determined purpose, and not to suppose that I am a philosopher enough not to feel it. I would on no account willingly do any thing to make you unhappy.
Saturday

M W TO W G

July 15, 1797

Mr. Johnson goes to Dorking to day, of course will not dine with us tomorrow. I wanted the Fenwicks to take tea with us tomorrow—they had mentioned to you an intention of coming to day and I wished to put it off. But you may be free notwithstanding.

I do not quite understand your note—I shall make no comments on the *kindness* of it, because I ought not to expect it according to my ideal—you say *without* a determined purpose!! Do you wish me to have one?

M W T O W G

July 18, 1797

I have thought more of it, and think that I ought to write on the subject which gave me some pain at first. I should only wish you so far to allude to it, as to convince her that we coincide in opinion. I am very well—and will walk to Kearsley's—say when?

July 19, 1797

A subject which gave me some pain—I put it in the past tense, when I speak of it to Godwin, although it *still does* give me pain, kindling arguments between us—is perhaps coming to some conclusion. On our walk yesterday to call on the painter Kearsley, Godwin agreed to seek an opportunity to day to prepare Miss Pinkerton for the note I have decided to write her, which I wish him to do, since I do not want it to appear that I am of one mind, and he of another. I have thought it only proper that he should inform her that her behaviour is causing an inconvenience to both of us. We were in a spirit of agreement as we set out, my arm through his, on a day gloriously clear, the sky the colour of lapis, so cloudless and dazzlingly bright that it caused even the birds to sing more joyously. There were many fine things in the studio, among them the head of a boy with angelic fair drifts of golden curls. Kearsley has some thing a bit vague in his brushstroke that lacks determination and virility, but his portraits have a certain charm—and modesty. He himself reminds me of a sleek, little brown rabbit that will make a dash for the shadows as soon as it hears a footfall, his intelligent, whiskery face all apprehension and sadness. But Godwin seems to wind him up, and, I am sure, left him happier in his leafy lair than when we entered.

Since we were in the neighbourhood, across from Hatton Gardens, I bade Godwin pay a call with me on Mary Hays. Even were she to be out, I wished to saunter through the gardens which are now exploding with the scent of strawberries, which one can see carried on the heads of the young women who come to London from Wales expressly for strawberry picking. It is unparalleled slavery to pay them the wages of no more than eight or nine shillings a day for carrying as much as fifty pounds of fruit upon their heads—the sight of them, however, calling to mind antique friezes of Arcadian maidens, the straightness of their carriage and the healthy beauty of their complexion making it seem that there has appeared among us a race of goddesses, who will suddenly vanish till next midsummer.

There has been an estrangement between us and Mary Hays, since we announced our marriage. She has not the rudeness of Mrs. Inchbald with her *when next you marry* song; but, after a single formal call, she has not come round. And, largely from the press of so many social obligations, as well as my not having felt well, I have called on her only once, and never included her in our more intimate evenings, when Holcroft and his daughters come to the house, or Amelia Alderson, or Opie, or Montagu. Also, it seems, she made unfortunate remarks to Godwin, just those very comments he had braced himself against, which he did not relish hearing from the lips of Mary Hays, who took him to task for the contradiction between his doctrines and his own actions. It was neither necessary nor tactful to put him on the defence in the way she did; I cannot blame Godwin, who is sensitive to criticism on the best of occasions. There is still another reason for the estrangement, which I almost hesitate to allude to. While all the world has turned several hundred revolutions, while all of us have married and conceived children and raised them and nursed them through their illnesses, and lost in the process the fiery romantic illusions of youth, growing in time more acceptant of the ways of the world—Mary Hays remains seventeen in spirit, only her sagging flesh an indication that time has touched her. I do not mean to be brutal in my allusion to this reluctance of hers to grow older, but it is what most disturbs me in her character. I find her often sour with Fanny, which annoys me. She has the same scolding manner that so irritates me with my sister. I distrust—especially these days—women who do not have the right touch with children; I prefer, if truth were told, the company of those who do, such as Mrs. Reveley and Mrs. Fenwick, who indulge their own children and treat my Fanny with the same loving indulgence. Mary Hays, I have noticed, has always considered Fanny, when she enters the room in the midst of our conversation, an unwelcome intrusion, whereas Elizabeth Fenwick will simply lift the child to her lap and go on talking, while she strokes her hair or examines a cut on her knee.

Our visit was not a great success. I sensed that Mary Hays blames the estrangement largely on Godwin. I cannot quite make it out; she does not now seem resentful of me, although I am the other half of the marrying. In fact, she has promised to come to call in a few days. I cannot follow her reasoning. She lives in the imagination in a way that confounds me: as she once imagined Mr. Lloyd in love with her, so now, it seems, she sees Godwin as an enemy. It is, as I say, far from easy to make sense of her reasoning.

MW TO WG

July 23, 1797

If it interferes with no previous plan will you accompany me, before dinner, the later the better, to see those stupid Carrs?

Do not suppose it necessary to go with me for I only want to go, because I ought—and such a motive will not spoil by keeping. Some morality!

WG TO MW

July 23, 1797

I think it not right, Mama, that you should walk alone in the middle of the day. Will you indulge me in the pleasure of walking with you?

I had written the above, before you sent. I will call on you presently.

July 29, 1797

I was resting this morning when Fanny burst into the room. When she saw that I was ill, she came to me and whispered that she would take her ball into the gardens to play, for she did not want to make any noise. She had the sense, dear angel, to know that noise would only make my head worse. It is a lesson she learned the other day, when Godwin was tired and, after dinner, had fallen asleep on the sofa. The noise of her romping woke him, and I had to scold her. She had stood penitently by watching him drink a cup of camomile tea, impressed that he drank it without making a face, then gone into the gardens. To day she understood at once that her playing would disturb me. She crept away, shutting the door as softly as ever I could have done myself, which proves my point that when a child at first does wrong, she does not know any better; but, after she has been told, she understands the principle.

Godwin has received a letter from Holcroft, who has gone to the country with Fanny, Sophy and his son-in-law. He writes amusingly of a visit they paid Godwin's mother. Their arrival occasioned some little alarm, it seems, for when they were seen from the window of the farm as they approached the gate, Holcroft having on spectacles, he was taken for Godwin, and one of his daughters was taken for me. Once it was known who they were, they were treated very kindly, given all the good things that could administer to their pleasure. Having quitted her farming business, Mrs. Godwin's faculties seem to be weakening much faster than they would have done had she continued to exert them. He then goes on to describe the county of Norfolk as containing more flint, more turkies, more turnips—and, though there are said to be more illiterates there than in other parts, more famous men. We must, as he has asked, look into his house and his library to make sure there has been no mischief done.

It is well to think of Holcroft to day, when my head beats so unmercifully, for he believes diseases of the body produced by the mind. I've heard him say that as one man laughing shall make a whole audience laugh, the mind of one person in health shall cure a whole nation of sickness. The mind, he believes, will even cure a cancer. Why, it will even do away with the necessity to die, for death, in his estimation, is error and error cannot exist. This sort of heady reasoning proves inspirational to a point. Death is surely an ill that shall remain in the world, not to be eradicated by a dose of *mind*. This shrugging off of death makes him contemptuous of those comforts which most of us accept; I mean, of course, a belief in the divinity. He prides himself on being an atheist. One can say whatever one likes, but all the same there is a certain *spirit* that informs the world, felt more acutely in the countryside, for as the mad woman said, there is God in nature. Certainly there is a feeling of union with a force which persists and renews itself with each roll of the seasons. In Holcroft's and Godwin's presence, I remain mute about my feelings, fearing ridicule.

WG TO MW

August 1, 1797

I forgot to tell you that I intend, if the weather favour me, to dine at Johnsons to-day. Do you know any reason why I should not?

MW TO WG

No—But you will remember that you have an engagement with a *Dame ce soir*.—

August 1, 1797

How easy it is to forgive one's enemies when they have fallen on evil days. I ought to bite my tongue for saying such a thing, yet why shall I deny myself one good victorious crow at the sight of Mrs. Inchbald? An alteration which she has lately had upon her teeth—exchanging her real ones for wooden ones—has set her mouth into a pout, the entire assemblage of features utterly devastated. A blow of fate fell six weeks ago, when her secret love, Dr. Warren, died. She has made a public point of her adoration by having written an obituary for the *Morning Chronicle*, praising him as the best of men. I do believe, poor creature, that she cared for him—though I had thought she cared for no one but herself. Godwin made her grief the basis of a plea to beg me to let him invite her to join us in our box at theatre last night. I have never once, these months, inquired whether he continued seeing her, nor made it possible for him as much as to mention her name. He began, the other night, about her teeth; went on to her scorbutic complaint, for which she pops into her mouth, every few hours, a Ward's White Drop; then he showed me the obituary of Dr. Warren, whose death, he says, has made her feel frightfully alone. It seemed a moment to be charitable.

I greeted her with a warm handshake which, I could see, a little shook her equanimity. Mine was such a smiling, effulgent, warm welcome that I could then, without giving offence, continue chatting and laughing with two of the young men, neither of whom I had met before—for Godwin's old lot all seem to have disappeared in various directions into the country or the sea-side, leaving us to make do with a whole new strange assortment who ring us round in some sort of midsummer ritual. I did not wish to rise during the intermission—I appear so awkward standing—so the two young men stayed with me, while Godwin and Mrs. Inchbald went to see who was about. As she rose and was about to turn to go, our eyes met on a level, hers coldly, calculative, like an opponent who has only for the moment laid aside her weapon. If I had imagined that grief might have changed her, that icy look from the depths of her grey eyes told me otherwise.

I much prefer, these days, the company of such unguarded friends as the Fenwicks. Fenwick turns out to be an incredible fellow, as tall and oddly co-ordinated as a giraffe—though I admit, never having seen one, half-believing them to be mythological creatures, like the griffon or many-headed Cerebus. He has spent a fortune of money upon his review, throwing away his family's future independence as if there is always more money to be secured, of which he seems to have convinced himself and his wife, who looks into his exalted face in the sweetest, most trustful manner; so that I, too, have somewhat begun to fall under a spell of belief that money for their necessities will always be produced by magic. Godwin adds to the illusion by engaging to take steps to speak on Fenwick's behalf to the Wedgwoods. Johnson does not think the *Albion* has the look of a review with a long life; he distrusts its ephemeral pallor. But if it fails, what on earth shall the Fenwicks do? Godwin says Fenwick will always find literary work. He judges him a man of considerable intellectual purity. I sense in him, however, a scattering of intention; I fear he might have to run after the small business of literary hack-work, such as Marshal must find, in order to keep leather upon his feet and a cloak about his shoulders, content to have some index to collate or a quick translation. Attending to the wants of a husband and child, and expecting another child, has taken precedence over Elizabeth Fenwick's literary labours. She says she does not mind that her time is not her own. In the way that Mrs. Reveley is prevented from painting by not having sufficient unscheduled time, so Mrs. Fenwick appears to be kept from her writing by all those domestic tasks which, once accomplished, might give her liberty then to begin. But it never seems to occur. Once all is done, she is so fatigued that all she wishes to do is to lie down and stare out the window at the stirring leaves of the chestnut trees which line the street, some times reading a few pages of a book, which she bangs closed as soon as she hears footsteps on the stairs. I fear it is for the Mary Hayses of the world to persist in literary endeavours. I fear it, I say, for I refuse to be one of those women who *once* wrote books and finds no more time to do so. Many a time have I had to jump up from my table at a cry from Lucas, when he spilled a kettle of boiling soup upon himself, or from Fanny who has had a mishap. I have not only my own cares, but those of the children, the servants, Godwin and the many friends he invites to the house; yet, by Heaven, I shall persevere, and set an example to other women. To both Maria Reveley and Elizabeth Fenwick I can speak freely of ordinary domestic concerns—and I have begun to speak as well of our common dilemma *as women with minds.*

The other evening we all three supped at the Reveleys'. I studied Mr. Reveley to try to discern how one might make him understand his wife's distress. An intelligent man such as he would be quick to argue against the divine right of kings—yet not against the divine right of *husbands.* It is useless to try to reason with him, as useless as it would be to have reasoned with the aristocrats in France, who stood to lose their vast properties and powers; did ever mere justice seem sufficient blessing to acquiesce in the loss of personal prestige? It is the same with husbands such as Mr.

Reveley. Elizabeth Fenwick has chosen another sort of man. She herself is robust, red-cheeked, with masses of thick, coal-black hair on the nape of her neck, a full bosom and stout arms, having almost the appearance of one of Fuseli's Amazons. They are a conspicuously eccentric couple—he with his tall limbs and spiritual daze, and she beside him as ruddy as a milkwoman. She tells of early years growing up on a farm in Cork, on the property of a gentleman who decided to see to her education, making a kind of experiment of it, for he educated her as well as a young boy, to see if, their opportunities being equal, they might yet display distinctions occasioned by the difference in sex. She was taught Greek and Latin, and still to day peruses classical authors, unlike any of the women in our circle of friends. Her considerable learning gives her a certain self-assurance. I enjoy her company, and have encouraged her to come mornings with her little girl, an agreeable companion for Fanny, the two of them cooing and conversing with one another with a sensible air, very like their mothers.

August 3, 1797

We were sitting quietly together in the parlour last night, reading, when Godwin began rubbing his eyes without removing his spectacles, which clattered to the floor. I took off my own and folded them on the table. We sit reading like two old owls. For more than an hour we had been engrossed, each in our separate books, when our glances met. I could tell that he had some thing in mind that he wished to impart. Having finished revisions for the third edition of "Political Justice," which Robinson intends to issue next month, he has begun working on a play, which goes steadily but slowly, some days being added to by no more than ten lines, which though discouraging, has not dampened his enthusiasm. But now he has begun a separate work which he intends to write alternately with the play. In two days he has managed to write eight pages which he had brought home to read. I asked him first to go upstairs for my shawl. I recognised a kind of boyish haste in his footsteps on the stairs, as he hurried down, clasped round my shoulders the thick, warm wool and drew the lamp

closer to his chair, turning up the wick. He held pages covered
with his small even handwriting, as he announced he was about
to read the story of his life.

It opened with a description of his great-great-grandfather, one
William, born in 1661. He had been the Mayor of Newbury. After
him there came Edward, a dissenting minister; and another Edward destined for the profession of the ministry; then John, Godwin's father, often aloof, whose flock lay variously dispersed, and
who would compose in swift shorthand his Sunday sermon Saturday evening after tea. Then comes the birth of our hero, seventh
child among thirteen. Godwin remembers very little from his earliest years, except that he would preach sermons in imitation of his
father's in the kitchen *in his high chair*. By eight he had read
through the whole of both the Old and New Testaments. He wondered whatever he should do when he had read through all the
books there were in the world. Once he managed to get possession
of the key of the meeting-house, that he might preach from his
father's pulpit to a friend from school who, he remembers, soon
began shaking on the hard wooden bench in mortal fear of damna-
tion. Then comes a curious account, which I shall copy, for Godwin has left me these pages that I might read them over to myself
and comment in detail on their style. This is Godwin at the age
of twelve:

> All my amusements were sedentary; I had scarcely any
> pleasure but in reading; by my own consent, I should
> sometimes not so much have gone into the streets for
> weeks together. It may well be supposed that my voca-
> tion to literature was decisive, when not even the treat-
> ment I now received could alter it. Add to this principle
> of curiosity a trembling sensibility and an insatiable ambi-
> tion, a sentiment that panted with indescribable anxiety
> for the stimulus of approbation. The love of approbation
> and esteem, indeed, that pervaded my mind was a nice
> and delicate feeling, that found no gratification in coarse
> applause, and that proudly enveloped itself in the con-
> sciousness of its worth, when treated with injustice.

Why, at present, should Godwin choose to write his life? He

has spoken of writing a life of Robespierre, but never of writing his own. I wonder what impels him now to think in autobiographical terms. I imagine he may perceive his destiny rounded in a way unlikely to have occurred to him before our marriage, the past now seeming a series of stepping-stones to the present, and the future a continuum almost predictable. I myself feel for the first time in my life no longer free to every sort of possibility under the sun, but only to a few limited variations. It had always seemed in the past that, until I could form some idea of the whole of my existence, I must dance on a string, pulled here and there with barely a will of my own. I know finally who I am. I wonder, sitting here, if Godwin has not undergone the same sort of transformation, as if one's outline is in bolder, blacker ink; while a stronger light illuminates the long sweep of the past.

I asked Godwin to take down the first volume of the "Confessions," for I wished to find the exact place where Rousseau says he may transpose facts, make mistakes in dates, but cannot go wrong about what he felt and about what those feelings led him to do. Though it is a favourite passage of mine, I was unable to put my finger on it; instead I read aloud, smiling with fond memory, where he boasts of being unlike any one he has ever met, and ventures to say he is like no one in the whole world. He may be no better, he says, but at least he is different. The path into which I would like to lead Godwin—and this has been my greatest complaint from the time he wrote me poems which described my graces rather than *his own feelings*—is to say simply what he felt and what those feelings led him to do! Every thing is in that admonition. There is no other requirement, as far as I can see; omissions, transpositions, forgetting dates, all small peccadilloes surely. I have always been intrigued at how much Rousseau remembered—or invented—of his early life, when at the age of fifty-four he began to write of childhood scenes, those things experienced in our earliest years imprinting themselves most profoundly upon our sensibilities. Godwin has promised, whenever we shall have an evening without an engagement, to read Rousseau aloud. He has spent the last several days in his study rereading "Werter," and I almost envied him a pleasure which he did not share with me. The finest tribute ever paid me was when he called "Mary" a female "Werter."

Two nights ago I asked Amelia Alderson to see what Opie has made of me. A painter always hates to part with his painting, Lawrence known to request his portraits back and to keep them for years. Aware as I am of the habits of artists, I had given Opie till the first of August to hang the portrait above my chimney-piece. I held him to his promise and threw his supper into the bargain. And now it stares at me, or rather gazes off in one of those private reflective regards which he says are quite characteristic. It is less a portrait of me as I see myself, than it is what others must see. For I perceive myself to be a creature who has come through infernos of experience to an unexpected place of rest, marked in mind and mien, while up there I am all smooth cheeks and youthful glow. Do I really radiate such calm? And look ahead so confidently? Godwin says I do. Well, it will be fine when I am a little bent old woman, cold to the bone, and see myself as once I was. I shall mutter: "Ah, yes, Mary Wollstonecraft, femme Godwin. I knew her once." I am reminded of Mrs. Robinson upon her sofa raising her glance to Romney's young woman with the muff. I still find it very odd to share my parlour with a looking-glass self, one with not a lock of hair out of place, while down here I daub my neck with my cambric handkerchief in an oppressive heat that augurs rain.

I caught Amelia Alderson sending the portrait sidelong glances, as we drank the excellent India tea I had bought in a new shop near the Reveleys'. (When alone I now take an infusion of red clover blossoms to improve my milk.) She was elegantly dressed in a loose, pale gown with one of those hanging pockets that are worn *outside* the skirt, rather than inside, a new fashion from France, beaded and braided and rather heavy, I observed. Opie thought it alluring, especially to footpads. Where Opie's humour leaves some people in perplexity, Amelia Alderson simply smiles, unaffected by the sting. I have not had a chance to ask her, *tête-à-tête*, what she thinks of him. He says he will paint her now, if she will sit to him, but she declined, due shortly to return to Norwich, wishing not to leave her father unattended for too long a period of time. Next visit, Opie persisted. I would wish these two to know one another better than they do. Who can tell what affinities they may find. The common element which makes me choose them both for friends might make them befriend one another. A year ago, overtaking them in the street, Godwin had seen them laughing, as they walked arm in arm, taking such obvious delight in each other's company that he, who had only some weeks before asked her father for her hand in marriage, had been subject to the keenest anguish. It occurs to me that, given time, such as the long days during which one poses for a painting, they might discover each other's essential qualities and feel some mutual attraction—if Opie is not too blinded by bitterness from his recent infatuation, and Amelia Alderson not too completely bound by assumed obligations to her father.

Godwin has a strange theory which he put to me yesterday. He has been trying to recollect, from a time when he had been studying for the ministry, the refined distinctions between such sects as the Sandmanians, the Arians and the Trinitarians, when into his room, looking remarkably like his own older brother, had come young William Hazlitt. He, too, has studied at the Dissenting Academy at Hoxton. He had at his fingertips the very information Godwin needed—to prove his theory that intellectual concentration will often almost magically bring forth those things that contribute to the application of one's work, as if contemplation is a sort of magnet. He has often been on the point of writing what he did not yet quite comprehend, when some one would appear before him in the street who easily clarified the question; he cannot say *how* this occurs, but only that it *does*. Thus Hazlitt, who looks barely older than Lucas, with his sharp, small, white face, was not as much an interruption as a providential visitation. He came here for a moment, looking very tense and ill at ease. I took him for a boy from the printer's; when Marshal does not run back and forth with Godwin's corrected proofs, there is some boy who does so. The way Hazlitt hung back, standing on one foot, gave me the impression that he was waiting for some thing. But when I understood that he was a young man just arrived from the country, who intends to make his fortune as a painter, I bade him sit and talk to me. He has a loose, weak, unsteady gait like a colt unsure of standing on its own legs. There was, despite awkwardness, some thing appealing about this youth with the white face and black ringlets and restless eyes. I think I might take him around to Lawrence's just as soon as I am out of confinement. Lawrence might take him on as a pupil. Godwin speaks of bringing him to

Northcote, but I would regret seeing him spend time in company with such a cranky old man, who will not improve manners already tending towards unsociability.

August 5, 1797

Another hot breathless day. I ask Marguerite if she feels the heat as intensely as I do, while I eat a bowl of gooseberries. Their tender, transparent plump sweetness seems to give me the strength to dress, with Marguerite's assistance. I can do nothing by myself. I feel her fingers glide against my upper arm. When I have struggled through the neck-piece of my undergarment, our eyes meet, as if we have accomplished some supernatural feat. She admires the shine of my skin, which glows with a rosy phosphorescence, and says it feels like the smoothest of satins. So there is some compensation for this eternal tiredness and breathlessness and mortal heaviness. I had dreamed during the night that I was running in the fields of the fjords near Gothenburg, as I once did, when my young friend who rowed the boat pulled into one of the small coves where she unwrapped some pears from a linen napkin. We lay down in the sun a long while; when the sun was low and we were preparing to leave, I felt impelled to run to a small copse of trees on the far side of the field, racing as fast as my feet would carry me, the way I used to do when a child playing in the meadows above my village. In my dream I had run, jumped, kicked my heels in the air from sheer exuberance of spirits and physical strength. I realised, with Marguerite holding out my skirt, that what I most longed for was relief from the heaviness of my body, yearning for that buoyancy one feels when one lets oneself sink into deliciously cool salty water that gives an immediate sense of physical lightness. I would have liked to float weightlessly upon the tide, gently rocked as I lay under the wide expanse of a clear blue summer sky.

This last month of confinement is the hardest—that it coincides with an intense August heat, which has brought on an infestation of horse-flies, does not make it easier. When I stand too long, I feel sharp pains in my lower back; when I sit too long, the full womb presses up against my rib cage, crushing my breath. I recline most of the morning in the parlour, the shades drawn against the early sun, so that the room might remain cool and free of insects; but my imperious infant reprimands me for my laziness by a good sharp kick. I remember from past experience with Fanny that those times, when the unborn child is most commonly awake, turn out to be the precise hours it will later want to nurse, for it seems to have a presentiment of its future life. Marguerite is dubious of such precocious talents; to show her how much the lively animal is very nearly human, I placed her hand on my stomach, the other day, so that she might feel him hiccuping. At first her expression was blank with disbelief, then a smile dawned, and she gave a shout of laughter at each regular little spasm that pulsated against her hand. I have observed that he is much distressed by noise and will jump when the dogs begin to fight—Bobby, already the equal of Georgette, pounces upon her to try to wrest away her bone.

Whenever asked when I expect to give birth, I ordinarily answer that I shall be delivered just as soon as the hop-picking begins. Godwin is amused by my reply and has taken to repeating it. He very kindly interrupts writing his "Life" to come and accompany me on my walks, when he can. Yesterday he appeared most unexpectedly. I had not seen him earlier in the morning, since he had gone to his study while I was still sleeping; some nights he sleeps in his own apartments in order to avoid disturbing my rest, when he rises early. I was lying about, somewhat lackadaisical, when he entered with a brisk step, insisting I come out and watch the men in the fields making hayricks. He had Marguerite bring him a pillow that he might carry under one arm for me to sit upon. I felt suddenly, almost shamefully, indulged. There was a little breeze stirring. It was still early so that the sun spared us her severest rays.

Godwin sauntered slowly at my side, holding my hand in the crook of his arm. He found us a grassy mound in the cool shade of an oak tree that must be centuries old, its spiky leaves making us a comfortable, cool bower. I had brought on my wrist a tiny painted paper fan of ivories. Godwin teased me that I had not also tucked away some where in the voluminous folds of my skirt the tiny pair of *cloisonné* opera-glasses from the days when I was obliged to see plays from the topmost balcony. Men in loose shirts were moving over the golden carpet of cut wheat. Some meadow saffron, known also by the name of autumn crocus, has begun to blow. Godwin would have picked me a nosegay, but I stopped him, for I wished them to be free to grow where they were, rather than to wilt and die. We spied the stooped figure of the truffle-hunter, his sack flung over one shoulder, coming home from the woods. I have never been partial to truffled dishes, a gustatory delight hardly worth their dearness in the market. But I will send Marguerite out the instant the woman with apricots raises her voice; they have just now appeared, with a fine soft gossamer on them, scented so strongly that from my blue-and-white bowl in the bookshelves their fragrance permeates the entire house. Strawberries are done, pears and apples not yet in season, nor peaches which are still hard and flavourless. Godwin comes home these days either with a book, a bright nosegay or a bunch of early grapes from a fruit shop, where he has gone specially to see if he might find some thing to tempt my appetite. He had, last night, brought me a little horn of macaroons.

As we were returning from the hayfields, a chorus of birds reached our ears. We looked up to see martins and swallows by the hundreds over the church tower. Godwin says they never cluster thus but on sunny days. It is too early, I think, for them to have gathered with the intention of flying south; I have watched such gatherings in September at St. Paul's, when thousands of birds skim and hover above the great dome, or sit chattering all in a row. This group of ours, surprised in agitated conversation, must be the first broods, rejected by dams busy with their second. I have lain still in the early dawn at the first sound of bird-song. There was a nightingale this morning; I listened with all my attention and a secret prayer that he would not fly away, for I felt much less lonely in my sleepless vigil. I have heard young nightingales try to imitate the virtuosity of those swelling melodies. That the adult nightingale still sings is a sign they will build another nest— as do we all.

August 7, 1797—Monday

Godwin has left me some more pages of his "Life." A woman who loves a man loves also the boy he once was, and sees, in miniature, the man he will become. Thus this incident delights me, recognisable as it is of the larger William, who gives me a cold look, when I ask him to speak to the Landlord about the state of the sink:

> When I was about thirteen or fourteen years of age I went by myself one day at the period of the assizes to the Sessions House. Having gone early, I had my choice of a seat, and placed myself immediately next the bench. The judge was Lord Chief-Justice De Grey, afterwards Baron Walsingham. As I stayed some hours, I at one time relieved my posture by leaning my elbow on the corner of the cushion placed before his lordship. On some occasion, probably when he was going to address the jury, he laid his hand gently on my elbow and removed it. On this action I recollect having silently remarked, if his lordship knew what the lad beside him will perhaps one day become I am not sure that he would have removed my elbow.

Not having wished to leave me alone yesterday, it being Sunday, Godwin stayed home to dine. In the morning he wrote a page and a half of his play, read several acts of a tragedy from which he hoped to learn some stage-effects, and came home with "The Confessions" under one arm. We agree that the merit of Rousseau's life lies in its being so resoundingly explicit. I value speaking from the heart, a harder thing for women than for men, given the conventions which bind us and the obloquy that is general should we fail to adhere to a prescribed code of conduct. I owe a large debt to Rousseau, but owe equally a debt to experience in life which taught me that, however much we resist the vision of ourselves as we are, it is impossible to deny one's true self, without being turned into some ludicrous, mincing stick-figure of a human being, pulled here and there by the approval of others like a puppet dangling upon string. My "Letters Written in Sweden" came as close as I have ever come to writing my life; should I again sit down to my memoirs, writing this time as a woman more secure, older, wiser, beyond the ravages of circumstances which impelled her to want to do away with her very life, why then perhaps I shall be able to say things that I have not yet found the words for, free to try to express feelings which in a younger self had to be silenced for fear . . . fear of what, in truth? We are led a pretty dance by those fears of ours which, in the end, prove to be as much an illusion as so many other things that set us into agitation.

Godwin says the trouble he foresees in writing his "Life" is an inveterate fear of ridicule. At times he has been inarticulate, vacillating, cowardly, even stupid. If he should draw such a portrait, who would take seriously his philosophy? Then he wonders if Rousseau does not make himself out to be worse than he is. If he cannot be the best of men, he will appear to be the worst. Godwin has been reading, this morning, a passage which concerns the death of some one Rousseau called the staunchest friend he ever had. Speaking, next day, in the deepest and sincerest of grief, the vile and unworthy thought came to him that he should inherit his clothes, particularly a fine black coat which had caught his fancy. No sooner did the thought occur to Rousseau than he gave it utterance; for in the presence of Mme. de Warens—whom he called *Maman,* as she called him *mon petit*—thought and speech were as one. These, apparently, were the words Godwin had wished to read me: that *thought and speech should be to him as one,* was a notion both elusive and alien, containing a wealth of mystery. Yet to whom could he have expressed his heart if not to Mme. de Warens who loved him? I dared suggest a parallel: that Godwin, free to unburden his heart, might freely express to me humiliating feelings he could not yet bring himself to write of. We are made in such a way that contradictory feelings, such as grief together with avidity for one's dead friend's coat, live side by side. If we cannot understand our own natures, how are we to understand our children, who have not yet learned to conceal those of their thoughts which society scorns? Godwin smiles with a soft look of love upon Fanny, when she bounces upon his knee to report with a glow of pride, first thing in the morning, that she has just plungity plunged; he nods his head as though the news is every bit as significant as the parliamentary intelligence. We are fortunate in life if we find some one to whom we can confide our thoughts without reserve. But how shall I, who did not know the small William, so severely ruled, ever teach him that, under no circumstance, will he be ridiculed by me? We are, as Rousseau believes, the product of our early years, much of his oddity having come from his mother's dying in child-birth, so that he would call his birth the first of his misfortunes. I felt before I thought, he writes, I had grasped nothing, I had sensed every thing, giving me the strangest, most romantic notions about human life, which neither experience nor reflexion has ever succeeded in curing me of.

M W T O W G

August 9, 1797

If you find nothing *objectionable* in the enclosed note put a wafer in it, and send it by Mary. I do not now feel the least resentment, and I merely write, because I expect to see her to day or to morrow, and truth demands that I should not seem ignorant of the steps she takes to extort visits from you.

If you have the slightest wish to prevent my writing at all—say so—I shall think you activated by humanity, although I may not coincide in opinion, with respect to the measures you take to effect your purpose.

Wednesday morning

August 9, 1797

I have just enclosed to Godwin a note which reads:

Miss Pinkerton, I forbear to make any comments on your strange behaviour; but, unless you can determine to behave with propriety, you must excuse me for expressing a wish not to see you at our house.

Mary Godwin

The last time the creature was here to tea, she simpered and whined a long, pointless tale. I cannot listen. I cannot see why any one should want to. Yet Godwin says that, conscious as she is of her failings, she extorts visits from him by an urgent need to unburden her heart and salve it with resolutions to mend her ways. It almost makes it seem that he ministers to her. Be that as it may, she must observe the ordinary courtesies of life; if not, she must learn that they are expected of her, despite fulsome emotions from an exquisite sensibility.

WG TO MW

August 9, 1797

I am fully sensible of your attention in this matter, & believe you are right. Will you comply one step further, & defer sending your note till one or two o'clock? The delay can be of no consequence, & I like to have a thing lay a little time on my mind before I judge.

August 10, 1797

The Pinkerton affair is concluded. Godwin kept my note several hours, finally substituting for the words *strange behaviour* "incomprehensible conduct." I have this morning the young woman's reply:

At length I am sensible of the impropriety of my conduct. Tears and communication afford me relief.

N. Pinkerton

August 14, 1797—Monday

On Saturday Mary Hays called on Godwin in his study. They spoke, he tells me, of those things they once habitually conversed about, the present state of society, etc. Learning from him that her sister—who wrote that ill-fated novel I read last autumn in M.S.—was visiting, I sent around to ask them to dine with us on Sunday, for I had the feeling that Mary Hays had meant Godwin to pass on to me the fact that her sister had come down to London for one of her rare visits, and what a pity it was that it should coincide with my confinement. Not that I remain as confined as most women in my condition! Friday I sallied forth to sit conspicuously in a theatre box, enjoying an outing, if not the spectacle itself. Tomorrow night we plan to go to theatre once again, since I am fit for nothing more than distractions. "The Italian Monk" is being presented, which should be of far greater interest than the indifferent play we attended last night, leaving even before the musical interlude began. I welcome company at home these days. Many of our friends have gone off to the country. Amelia Alderson has taken leave with a kiss upon both my cheeks and a long look at me from arm's length, making me promise to send her news as soon as I can take pen in hand after the delivery of my child. Wanting her to have a keepsake, not having had the foresight to have provided one, when I went out for my walk past shops and barrows and bookstalls, I reached up into the bookshelves, and brought down to place in her hand and clasp tight inside her fingers the moonshell I picked up in Norway two summers past. The shell had housed a sea-snail which grew large and perhaps careless in concealing itself from the long inquisitive beak of a gull. I had found it emptied of life, whole, without a chip, on its side a thick brown spiral whorl edged with white, the remainder of the shell a delicate, palest pink and mauve. I had held it in my hand and found its heaviness and smoothness consoling, hence had popped it into the pocket between my skirt and petticoat, and had it still to recall the sweet and open face of heaven from a shore redolent of pine that made underfoot the softest brown carpet. The gift was accepted in the spirit in which it was given, with a face averted to hide a quick sting of tears at parting. Another squeeze of the hand and she was gone. Holcroft, too, is away from London with his Fanny and Sophy, whom I would love to have about me these days, with their bright chatter and witty discourse. In fact, every one I could think of was in the country. And so I welcomed the notion of asking Mary Hays and her sister to come to dine with us. We were having that eccentric old fellow Ritson and, rather than have him alone, I had been wondering who else to ask.

Mary Hays' sister speaks well, though at first spoke not at all. When she did, however, it was to the point: It is her notion that this is an age in which women are beginning to write about all manner of things, and that even men might learn from them. She said we cannot despair of the rights of woman when there are so many brilliant women alive. Why, she even thought it might be useful for there to be a biographical dictionary of women writers, in order to encourage, by example, more women whose first stumbling steps might be aided by knowledge of their predecessors; it was a notion she had recently suggested to her sister, for she felt sure some London publisher would consider it a profitable venture. How might I have been inspirited, should I have had on my writing-table a book of biographies of women who had persevered in some hard, long task, when my own hand grew cramped with fatigue and discouragement? I thought of myself on George Street, when those of my family who were dependent on me had fallen into their luxurious slumber, leaving me wrapped in my great-coat, the fire having died, and I too poor to have lighted another, the globe surrounding my stingy light so charred it seemed to be a dying flame at the bottom of a coal shaft, while I was too phrenzied writing to exchange its glass for a clean one; too phrenzied and so enfeebled from persistent lack of sleep that I feared dropping it, were I to pick it up in my handkerchief, so as not to scorch my fingers. How comforted I might have been had my glance fallen on a thick volume devoted to the lives and achievements of other women, who had burned the midnight oil in pursuit of elusive fame. It was then that Mary Hays voiced her objections. She turned, I noticed, towards Godwin; she prefers to think of herself as an exception among females. I can understand the preference, since once I, too, felt myself above the common run; that was in the days of working for Johnson, when often I would be the only woman at his table, arguing with such as Fuseli, Blake, Bonny-castle or Paine. But I see how false was my position, my accept-ance among them tolerable only as long as they did not generalise about the fair sex. I had internalised their scorn of women, scorn-ing my very self, which I dare say is the case with Mary Hays. When I began to write my "Vindication of the Rights of Woman," reading all of Catharine Macauley's work on education, that woman who thought the amusements and instruction of boys and girls should be the same, I was raised furlongs from a misappre-hension of singularity, by the recognition that there existed in the world a woman who thought and spoke and reasoned very much as I did. I tried to say as much to Mary Hays, not persuading her in the least. Such an endeavour of making a collection of women's lives must then not be for her, but I hope some woman of a discerning mind will eventually gather together between boards such enlightening information.

Ritson is a threadbare, little literary man who went over to France in the early part of the Revolution, returning with extreme admiration for the republican form of government. He must have left France at the time I arrived—consequently his democratic sentiments remain more idealistic than mine. Godwin, Holcroft and Ritson would rid themselves of any religious views in favour of the French form of atheism. I cannot seem to join them in what they feel is the proper reverence for the Revolution—that is, by ridding oneself of any authority placed above man, whether royal or divine. I follow their reasoning, but am unable to scour from my heart its devotional tinge of thankfulness to some force which seems to lie outside the visible world. Perhaps I would say with Tooke, in this particular, that on the way to Slough, I get off at Honnslow. On the subject of Ritson's refusal to eat meat, I once tried to lead him to an admission that such a belief ensues from love of God's creatures, but he irascibly inquired *Whose creatures?* Mandeville's "Fable of the Bees," it seems, gave him a profound sense of the existence of a reasoning society among bees, and an illumination that all living things must have as intense a will to live as we. I had asked Mary to prepare her dish of turnips and carrots in cream—for he subsists largely on milk and vegetables— and, for the rest of us, a dish of pike prepared with slivers of preserved ginger.

Mary Hays began to speak of the working conditions of a young woman, with whom she had conversed at a haberdasher's several days ago, and said I might wish to use this story for my tale of Jemima: the young woman, in the shop by eight in the morning, was kept busy some times till ten-thirty at night, after which she had to put the place in order, which often was not finished till two in the morning. Mary Hays' indignation was so fiery, so full of threats of what she publicly would do to expose such an outrageous state of things, that it brought swiftly to mind what I have always loved in this friend of mine, who is some times so difficult. It is that she is not lukewarm; she has sufficient imagination to feel the mortal tiredness of the young woman of the haberdashery in every fibre of her body, the swollen feet, the aching head, the wretchedness of that poor young woman, who must have been at her wit's end. I knew then why I continued to cherish her, though she be often less agreeable company than those of my new friends, whom I choose these days to see. Can one imagine Elizabeth Fenwick in the sort of embroilment from a fevered imagination that created the incident with Mr. Lloyd? Or imagine it happening to Mrs. Reveley, who puts a constraint on all her impulses? These two face life with a practicality I admire. I had grown tired of Mary Hays' sulks and imaginary slights; one could never be sure what new Gothic plot had been hatched in her mind since last one had met—yet what made her always dear to me is just this advocacy of those mute and miserable creatures of our society whom society crushes under, the way a carriage with a swift, savage team of brutes will run down a poor child.

The *other* Miss Hays, who continues to live in a village which is the size of Beverly, or yet even smaller, and as provincial in character, is stouter and generally more optimistic about the world than her sister; there is yet a physical resemblance between them. The miscellaneity of her education makes her susceptible to all sorts of received opinions and cant, one of the defects of her unpublished novel. I am saddened by the wasted effort of those who write and never see their works in print. I shudder at the thought of how narrowly I missed such a fate. With lesser courage I might have stayed in my little room in the castle at Mitchelstown, bringing up the girls, of whom I had begun to be most fond, resigning myself to a life of dependency, and, writing in my room without the benefit of any intellectual exchange, writing from feelings, rather than from that necessary distillation of emotion and reason brought together; where reason is absent, the best one can create is a broth of vague fancies. Such I found, if memory serves me, in the novel I read last autumn, when Mary Hays asked for my opinion of her sister's work. I have read for Johnson a hundred, nay, a thousand of that sort. And what is one to say? Should one encourage an effusion from a soul that might be eased by such a practice? Or be a severe schoolmistress who cautions against the waste of time involved? I have never come to any conclusion on this matter. There is a gulf, however—of this I am convinced—that separates that poor little inexperienced governess at Mitchelstown who hankered for a better role in life, and that of one who makes a livelihood from the trade of books.

It was not for an account of yesterday, however, that I opened these pages and used my knife on my nib. Rather had I meant to report a scene that occurred this morning, when Marguerite was in my bedchamber. I need her by me a great deal of the time. And she has become as gentle and able as I had hoped she might become. She had put over my head one of my loose, light-coloured poplin morning dresses—in which I spend most of my time at home—and had finished dressing my hair, when I stood up and looked about me for my shawl of malachite green that I thought I had perhaps left in the parlour the night before, and was just about to pose the question whether or not Marguerite had seen it, when I noticed a slack look about her lips and an interrogation in the light grey eyes. I continued moving about to see if the shawl was mixed up in the bed-clothes, when her apparent dismay made me turn once again. I found it curious she had not replied to my question, and was about to put the question again, this time somewhat irritably, when I saw that some thing intensely troubling had hold of her spirit. When I found out what it was, I had to smile. Having noticed the change in the shape of my body, once I was standing, she had thought, poor child, that some thing had gone wrong. I begged for a looking-glass. The child in my womb has dropped, its head now engaged at the opening of the uterus, which is a natural occurrence some two weeks before being delivered. I had not felt the change, however. Marguerite remained speechless. I had to sit on the side of the bed, and draw her alongside, to explain the physiological process of birth. It was then that she said she wished to attend me during my delivery. She wishes to see the act of birth for herself, not to be spared the way I intend sparing Godwin from the necessary pain of the process, for she is a woman and wishes to have preparation for hardships she hopes some day to undergo. I put my arm around her shoulders and gave my word that she should assist Mrs. Blenkinsop.

It is very odd, this having determined upon a midwife. Dr. Fordyce, that dear and understanding friend, followed my reasoning, but I have found, with others, that it is necessary to say things I do not believe in order to gain any degree of acceptance. I chose a midwife, a woman, because the process of birth calls for no interference. I fear physician-accoucheurs and their instruments, especially the forceps which countless times are the cause of mangling the new-born, if not actually fatally dismembering them. Barbers, surgeons and physicians are permitted by law to use such brutalising means of *assisting* a woman in the delivery of her child: midwives, however—being mere females—are prohibited by law from using surgical tools. Hence, I feel ever so much safer in the hands of Mrs. Blenkinsop, a woman of some fifty years of age, who has given birth to several children, all now full grown, one an excellent bookbinder, who would be pleased to charge me a little less than usual. I was, of course, flattered, and will call on him when I can again walk about town. But I was saying that my choice of a midwife, rather than a lying-in hospital, or having a male physician attend me at home, is some thing Godwin has not been able to comprehend; thus, to end a long discussion, one night, I pretended to agree with him that I am motivated by a sense of decorum—which, in all truth, I am not.

August 17, 1797

Yesterday we had to dine with us Godwin's old, unalterable friend Marshal, so dependably a friend of one I love that my love extends quite naturally to him. It is curious, I think, that he has never brought his wife to meet me. I am told she is simple and uneducated and therefore does not go out into society. When I point out that many men I know, desiring their young wives' companionship, have educated them, I was answered that Dr. Johnson, however, did not. Well, no matter. I cannot be expected to raise understanding every where. But it rankles me. Would she bore us, does he think, or does he perhaps like to let her rusticate far away from worldly ways? And yet I have never once heard him criticise the freedoms we females assert among ourselves in our circle of friends, we women who will not be *Arnolphed*. Marshal rushes among us, providing all sorts of services to ingratiate himself, going to great lengths to turn up an antique book or to write down the address of a chemist where one might find a new pomade, always very methodical in his dealings, though somewhat ill at ease, having the nervous habit of running one hand over his head, which resembles nothing so much as the tonsure of a monk. Just as we were rising from the table, Mrs. Reveley paid a call, and sat with us awhile. She took out a canvas which she is embroidering and began to recount a story she has heard about Tom Lawrence. Having declared his love to one Miss Siddons, he has become smitten with the other, putting that lovely forlorn older daughter, whose graceful figure I so well remember, in a fever of despair. There are whispered conferences in the household, the scene of an Italian drama, but no one can say what is to be done. Godwin tells us Coleridge was in similar circumstances, having proposed marriage to one young woman, and then having fallen in love with another; but Southey would not hear of his friend's committing an unprincipled action and shamed him into adhering to his original intention to marry, a marriage which, by all reports, is unhappy. To avoid such a dilemma as Lawrence's and Coleridge's, Godwin had originally written that it is absurd to expect that the inclinations of two human beings should coincide through any long period of time, or to assume that one must have a companion for life. He assures me that he has revised his much-disputed, much-quoted passage about marriage as the worst of all laws. Marriage, as now understood, he calls a monopoly, and the worst of monopolies. But he has softened his condemnation, adding that friendship may be expected to come to the aid of sexual intercourse to increase its delight; and he concludes in favour of marriage—in which there is room for repentance, and to which liberty and hope are not strangers—as a salutary and respectable institution.

Into our midst came Elizabeth Fenwick, *barefoot*, looking more than ever like one of the healthy, young milkmaids in the park, unable to explain the reason for her plight for the sallies we made to accompanying laughter. It was a matter of having stepped in some fresh dung at the cross-roads, and leaving her shoes to be scrubbed by Marguerite downstairs and having the *sans gêne* to enter rather than wait all alone. I poured the tea, and Marshal, steady and faithful in the exercise of such services, carried the tea-cups. Elizabeth Fenwick and Maria Reveley, knowing first hand the boredom of waiting to be brought to term to rid oneself of this restless animal within one's body, have, both of them, the nicety to call almost every day—to brighten my idle hours with chit-chat.

Basil Montagu is another who also appears quite faithfully. I begin to forgive him the glory of his name. He was able to speak lately of his young wife, who died in child-birth—the child to be raised by the Wordsworths—but he says the wild grief he felt at his wife's death seems now to have been enacted by another. It worries him how inconstant our hearts are; I soothed him by saying it is well our nature is so, otherwise we might languish from grief. Until the assizes begin, he is free to go where he wishes, but has no desire to leave London, quoting Dr. Johnson's *When a man is tired of London, he is tired of life.* He is as inveterate a walker as Godwin—the two of them often perambulating for miles, speaking their high-minded thoughts, while a flock of sheep flows unheeded past them at their knees. Montagu says, were he able to write, he would Boswellise his friend's conversation.

Dyson often comes to sit. He tells me what they are saying at Debrett's or at Booth's, for he makes a daily round of the booksellers, never, he says, putting down a farthing for a news paper, but reading them instead at the bookseller's or in coffee-houses, where his outrage at the latest political intrigue will often get him into a long, amusing contest. He spends most of his day walking about the streets, cheerful and merry, keeping his eyes open, so that he may later entertain one with a report of what is in the shop windows on Piccadilly, or who was wearing what and, like his friend Cooper, will play out several parts in recounting a conversation, all in high spirits, very ingeniously. If any one is fit to Boswellise Godwin, it would, I think, be Dyson. Holcroft once told me he used to see Boswell in the streets, walking with a grave strut and elevated head, a peculiar self-important set to his face, and that he disliked the look of the man whom others, who had talked with him at coffee-houses, where he'd drink hard and sit late, saw as servile, selfish and cunning. His name excites indignation every where. Peter thinks him a man who full twenty years sat *mousing* before Sam's mouth like a watchful cat by a hole. When, now engaged as Godwin is, I suggested to him he might look into Boswell's book, he called it a miscellany of facts from which one can learn nothing. Dyson has the roving eye for detail which I admire in Boswell's life, which perhaps will be, as Holcroft is convinced it will be, one of those books that fades from view, mere ephemera, unworthy to be considered art. I do not know. But if drinking hard and sitting late be a requisite for that form of writing, Dyson is perfectly equipped. What may seem to be a waste of time and talent in his playing billiards half the day and chess the other half is perhaps, by the widest definition of terms, a sort of preparation for literary labour he shall one day undertake. And if conversation is any sign of literary style, his books shall be lively beyond belief.

M W T O W G

August 19, 1797

I send you Addington's Letters. I find the melancholy ones the most interesting—there is a grossness in the raptures, from which I turn—they excite no sympathy— Have no voluptuousness for me. Fanny promises to return at your *bidding*—and would not be with Mary—

August 22, 1797

Godwin has gone to dine at St. Paul's Church-yard—for it is Tuesday—and I have been trying to amuse myself in the pages of a novel which is the same gruel, somewhat more watery, that is in Lewis' "Monk." Enough of gloomy castles, tormented lovers! I have been dreaming of the sort of book which would fulfill my desires at the moment, the sort of domestic scenes we have here at the Polygon, with Fanny dashing in to sit upon the lap of her darling Basil Montagu, while Mrs. Reveley and I discuss marrying and giving in marriage and such heart-felt damages as those that Lawrence has shot from his quiver—to read of life as we live it, our entertainments and our languors all described. I long for some one to transcribe such of our conversations as may amuse and inform and enlighten others. It seems to be life I want, its teeming, manifold variousness. I let slide in a heap upon the floor all the terrific tales that I had hoped would help me pass the afternoon, and welcome Fanny, who comes back on Marguerite's hand from a walk in the gardens. She has recently grown quite conversational. Her manner of recounting how she spoke to a man on horseback, who must have seemed from her diminutive height a giant shouldering the clouds, had accuracy and vivacity in the telling

that held my interest. I had also to hear of an argument with little
Eliza Fenwick, who had wanted to carry home with her Fanny's
shovel and pail, which provoked a tug of war that ended in tears.
Fanny sat upon the arm of the sofa in stocking feet. My darling
grows into a fair-haired slender child, with great intelligent blue
orbs that take in the world and interpret its meanings unfailingly.
She put her hand gently on my belly, asking if her brother has
been kicking. She asks me questions which make me smile—will
he have fair hair like hers? Will he play ball? I make up a tale, as
she nestles close, telling her that the little one—it may be a girl,
not a boy, which I ought to prepare her for—will have to learn all
the hard things she has learned, and will not be able to do them
half so well for ever so long. I make her smile sleepily, when I say
the little one will not be able to talk, but only to cry. Fanny announces she will teach him draughts. I must tell Godwin. It is the
kind of remark he enjoys repeating to Montagu, who closes both
eyes, holds his breath, opens his mouth and lets out a whinny of a
laugh one can scarcely resist joining.

Saturday, August 26, 1797

Yesterday, at two in the afternoon, I began to feel violent contractions. I did not at once send for Mrs. Blenkinsop, but tried
to sit tranquilly with an eye on the little clock on my commode.
I was in my bedchamber, having come upstairs with the intention
of lying down, which I then did not wish to do. Instead I sat staring at the paper, unable to make sense of what I read. I had a kind
of waking dream which I cannot recollect, except for that part
which concerned Fanny in Lisbon. The next contraction so
doubled me over in pain that, when it abated, I cried for Marguerite and sent her immediately to fetch Godwin. He hurried
into the room, looking alarmed. His presence quieted me, and I
was able to try to make some sense out of what was happening, the
very irregularity of the contractions having confused me. It was
then, his reasonable questions calming my fears, that it first occurred to me that I might not be in labour. Mrs. Blenkinsop had
warned me, should I find myself having contractions which should
seem to have a random meaningless pattern, that it was but the

uterus preparing itself, but not yet ready for the expulsion of the infant. Walking would halt it, were it only false labour. Hence, I went into the circular gardens inside the Polygon, leaning on Godwin's arm, and walked up and down the flagged paths with their borders of heartsease. Godwin spoke in a low tone, very soothingly. When I tired, we sat for a while on a circular bench around the trunk of the mulberry, which threw a dappled light over my skirt, making it appear some exotic Indian weaving in whites and greys. We spoke then of future journeys to the country, perhaps the following summer making a walking trip in the Swiss Alps, leaving the children with Marguerite in one of the rustic inns which Rousseau has described, where they might have their fill of fresh milk and good country bread and butter, with an egg which Fanny herself might fetch from the roost, if she would promise not to go in a rush and frighten the hens into a flurry of feathers, but on tiptoe. In the midst of our imaginary travels, Godwin asked me how I felt, when, to my delight, I was aware that my pains had vanished and that we were sitting, hand in hand, under the mulberry trees. I am very glad I did not, in panic, send for Mrs. Blenkinsop.

August 28, 1797

This evening, because he has been too much underfoot, beginning to look as burdened and afflicted as I, I sent Godwin out. Nothing will happen this evening, I assured him. And yet I fancy he looked over his shoulder with an anxious air as he went. He will resent these days of dalliance. I fear he has done no work for a fortnight. He says his mind is scattered. That makes a pair of us —I have no mind and only hope it shall be reborn in September with the birth of my animal. Thus Godwin has gone off into the ordinary world to call on Fuseli, who should be just the one to give him a good shaking up, if any one will, and perhaps even to pay a call on his once literary muse, Mrs. Inchbald, neither of the two of them very viviparous in their concerns, which should take his mind off the subject. He asked if I would like to attend a performance of "The Merchant of Venice," but I cannot sit for any length of time and said he should go by himself. It is a danger even in our irregular domesticity to stay too much together and thus be bored, whereas, if one of us goes out, he may revivify the other. So, in a sense, I send my William into the world for the two of us. A little patience and all will soon be over.

August 29, 1797—6 in the morning

I wonder where the hop-pickers are. I am by myself, William having gone to his quarters. To walk all the way to Booth's to browse among the books yesterday was too much for me. I found nothing new to tempt me, and the walk much too tiring. Seeing how useless I was, Godwin, immediately after dinner, took down my old worn copy of "Werter" in a half-roan binding with pink marbled sides that are coming loose. Borne upon wings of time, my thoughts flew to Waldheim to wish with Werter for a single glance from Charlotte—wondering what a child is man that for a look of love he should suffer such longing. Shortly, from some thing not yet conscious, I was jolted into the present and, turning my gaze, let it rest across the room on Godwin reading in a faltering voice, his eyes brimming with tears. In my own eyes was drawn a swift sting from those wretched sorrows of Werter. But there was some thing else, some thing more, some thing slowly coming clear: The many occasions which might have separated Godwin and me had not done so, for here we were in the summery dusk, having made the passage from one August to the next, which is not a little accomplishment, it seems to me, given the hazards of love.

MW TO WG

August 30, 1797

I have no doubt of seeing the animal to day; but must wait for Mrs. Blenkinsop to pass at the hour—I have sent for her—Pray send me the news paper—I wish I had a novel, or some book of sheer amusement to excite curiosity, and while away the time—Have you anything of the kind?

MW TO WG

August 30, 1797

Mrs. Blenkinsop tells me that Every thing is in a fair way, and that there is no fear of the event being put off till another day—Still, *at present*, she thinks, I shall not immediately be freed from my load—I am very well—Call before dinner time, unless you receive another message from me—

MW TO WG

August 30, 1797
Three o'clock

Mrs. Blenkinsop tells me that I am in the most natural state, and can promise me a safe delivery—But I must have a little patience.